Building the Ivory Tower

POLITICS AND CULTURE IN MODERN AMERICA

Series Editors: Margot Canaday, Glenda Gilmore, Michael Kazin, Stephen Pitti, Thomas J. Sugrue

Volumes in the series narrate and analyze political and social change in the broadest dimensions from 1865 to the present, including ideas about the ways people have sought and wielded power in the public sphere and the language and institutions of politics at all levels—local, national, and transnational. The series is motivated by a desire to reverse the fragmentation of modern U.S. history and to encourage synthetic perspectives on social movements and the state; on gender, race, and labor; and on intellectual history and popular culture.

Building the Ivory Tower

Universities and Metropolitan Development in the Twentieth Century

LaDale C. Winling

PENN

University of Pennsylvania Press

Philadelphia

ART HISTORY
PUBLICATION INITIATIVE

This book is made possible by a collaborative grant from the Andrew W. Mellon Foundation.

Published by
University of Pennsylvania Press
Philadelphia, Pennsylvania 19104-4112
www.upenn.edu/pennpress

Printed in the United States of America on acid-free paper
10 9 8 7 6 5 4 3 2 1

Library of Congress Cataloging-in-Publication Data
    Names: Winling, LaDale C., author.
    Title: Building the ivory tower : universities and metropolitan development in the twentieth century / LaDale C. Winling.
    Other titles: Politics and culture in modern America.
    Description: 1st edition. | Philadelphia : University of Pennsylvania Press, [2018] | Series: Politics and culture in modern America | Includes bibliographical references and index.
    Identifiers: LCCN 2017013306 | ISBN 978-0-8122-4968-2 (hardcover : alk. paper)
    Subjects: LCSH: Community and college—United States—History—20th century—Case studies. | University towns—Economic aspects—20th century—Case studies | Cities and towns—United States—Growth—History—20th century—Case studies. | Cities and towns—Effects of technological innovations on—United States—History—20th century—Case studies. | Land use—United States—History—20th century—Case studies.
    Classification: LCC LC238 .W56 2018 | DDC 378.1/03—dc23
    LC record available at https://lccn.loc.gov/2017013306

For Kate, Ernest, and Sammy

Contents

Introduction
The Landscape of Knowledge

Harvard University was on top of the educational world. In January 2007, administrators announced the plan for expanding their campus in the Allston neighborhood of Boston.[1] The nation's oldest institution of higher education had the largest endowment in the country and was financing a bold move to build scientific laboratories and an art museum across the Charles River from its traditional Cambridge campus. At that time, Boston was one of the centers of the new economy, with researchers, graduates, and entrepreneurs from Harvard and the Massachusetts Institute of Technology (MIT) composing much of its creative class. The *New York Times* pointed out that Harvard amenities would replace nothing more than "a gas station and a Dunkin' Donuts" at Barry's Corner, an industrial site and working-class neighborhood in Allston.[2] Mayor Thomas Menino hailed the 2007 announcement for the Allston campus as the first step in making Harvard "the future of Boston."[3] Harvard's ambition was central to the growth of the region. Contractors began clearing the site at the end of 2007.[4]

The fall was steep. Two years later, Harvard president Drew Gilpin Faust sent a letter out to the university's deans in the midst of the economic crisis, announcing that the endowment, once $36 billion, had lost nearly a third of its value. There would be budget cuts. The university instituted a faculty hiring freeze and halted construction on the new campus, leaving a hole in the Boston landscape. The nation's wealthiest and most prestigious university had been laid low, its signature efforts to lead the nation in biological research were in embarrassing disarray, and a three-decade-long expansion initiative had stalled.

The proposed science and art complex in Allston represented the volatile potential of this new direction for growth in higher education. The increasing reliance on philanthropy to compensate for shrinking public support had paid off handsomely in boom times. Harvard and universities across the country could buy more land, conduct more research, enroll more students, and provide more financial aid than ever.[5] Residents of Allston, upset by the halt to construction, felt the promise had been empty. Harvard had bought their property, forced their businesses out of the neighborhood, promised them jobs and entry into the tech economy, razed their community, and then parked bulldozers and stacked leftover materials on a nearly vacant site. A casual observer might have thought that the federal government had authorized a new wave of urban renewal: the results looked strikingly similar to slum clearance and redevelopment efforts in Boston a half-century before.

The Harvard case reflects an important moment in a transformation more than a century in the making, as universities of all types became central to American economic growth and key drivers of urban development. They made the creation of knowledge a foundation of economic growth—through education, research, and cultural production. This production of knowledge required the production of space: laboratories, libraries, and offices for research; classrooms and lecture halls for teaching; buildings for administration, recreation, and retail services. Across the country, higher-education institutions catalyzed changes in land development in rural or suburban areas, and brought people together in dense settlements—nodes of communication, recreation, and inquiry—to create new knowledge.[6] The economic vision for higher education required a complementary spatial vision for universities and their campuses.

Despite a long and intimate relationship between universities and cities, scholars have largely written universities out of urban history.[7] Higher-education historians emphasize the impact of the Morrill Land Grant Acts, which often provided land outside of urban centers and promoted agricultural education.[8] This emphasis has maintained the image of university campuses as bucolic, rural places more like farms than cities. Urban historians typically break the twentieth century into a pre-Depression era of industrial vitality and immigrant influx and an era of suburbanization and urban crisis that starts, at earliest, in World War II.[9] In neither of these eras do universities figure in scholarship on urban life.

In this book, I put universities at the center of metropolitan transformation and cities at the center of university transformations. Turn-of-the-century industrial magnates plowed their profits into higher education institutions and helped create the postwar economy that sacrificed manufacturing might in favor of knowledge work, often in suburbs. The crisis of the Great Depression prompted an active federal investment in higher education that was carried forward and intensified during World War II and the Cold War. Simply put, the "meds and eds" economy has roots far earlier in the century than historians have acknowledged and was closely linked even then to metropolitan growth.

To fully appreciate the economic value and power of universities, we must retrace that relationship back to its origins in the nineteenth century. American industrialization and the Civil War changed the stature of colleges and universities when policy leaders identified them as instruments to fulfill state ambitions. The Morrill Land Grant Acts of 1862 and 1890 reflected this bargain, providing federal resources to support the creation of engineering and agricultural colleges, where scientific knowledge could be made practical and applied to promote economic growth and improved health and welfare for the growing nation.[10]

Civic boosters in the nineteenth century hardly distinguished colleges and universities from factories or other state institutions that could help attract new residents and new customers to their cities, and colleges were small ones at that.[11] From their founding, however, universities introduced class differences to cities in ways that only intensified as the institutions became key platforms for social and economic mobility—for those who were allowed to enter. Progressive Era reformers at universities emphasized expertise, education, and the use of scientific knowledge to tame the city and manage American life. They created settlement houses to minister to immigrant masses and government institutes to improve urban political administration.[12] The philanthropic origins of the University of Chicago and Stanford University in the era are well documented, but many other colleges and universities were born of founding alliances with business interests.[13] In Southern California, for example, two real-estate developers, brothers Harold and Edwin Janss, helped turn a teacher training school into the University of California, Los Angeles, which became a major research university. The wealthy Duke tobacco family transformed Trinity College, a small private institution in Durham, North Carolina, into Duke University, beginning in the 1890s. By the 1930s, it was among the nation's top schools.[14] What these relationships demonstrate, in part, is that regional leaders in the early part of the century were essential to the creation and expansion of universities. Moreover, this regional support helped incorporate and expand higher education into the realm of statecraft by promoting local economic growth and putting universities to work solving issues of interest to the state.

The Great Depression ironically brought about significant opportunities for universities to grow.[15] The New Deal expanded the federal commitment to higher education, and the Roosevelt administration fundamentally transformed the relationship among universities, the government, and cities. The National Youth Administration employed students, the Works Progress Administration funded faculty research, and the Public Works Administration (PWA) paid for new construction. These expenditures fulfilled short-term work relief goals and long-term economic development ambitions, transforming the American economy and workforce. Franklin Roosevelt's administration did not invent the state commitment to higher education, but it provided unprecedented resources for its growth, fundamentally changing the character of college life. In the process, they made universities central parts of the project of building the liberal state.

Investments in spatial political economy constitute some of the most enduring effects of New Deal education aid. Federal programs such as the Home Owners' Loan Corporation, the Federal Housing Administration and Veterans Administration mortgage guarantee programs, and the Interstate Highway System subsidized suburban development and privileged outlying areas at the expense of central cities, creating new forms of racial segregation and economic inequality.[16] But the PWA provided funds for 1,286 buildings on college campuses across the country, granting $83 million and lending another $29 million for new construction, renovation, and expansion of existing facilities. These investments catalyzed nearly $750 million of construction at colleges and universities—one-sixth of the nation's total construction spending at the Depression's low point in 1933.[17] More than just "priming the pump," as in Roosevelt's famous phrase, this construction was an investment in the future of the nation's economy. Using what Roosevelt called "bricks and mortar and labor and loans," these projects built new laboratories, classrooms, and dormitories that served millions of students over the subsequent decades, increasing professional knowledge while expanding university capacity and student access to higher education.[18] This growing access meant rising enrollments, necessitated the expansion of existing campuses, and led to establishment of new ones. These campuses grew increasingly urban, became busier places that anchored growing parts of their cities, and made the institutions more prominent political forces.

PWA investments also helped strengthen racial segregation. Southern states usually had two (or more) land grant institutions, one for black students and one for whites, and the PWA lent more to Southern institutions that could not provide a local match than it did to Northern institutions.[19] Thus, these investments relayered segregation on the new urban investments, meaning the new American city was not so different from the old one—but with larger colleges and universities and a more productive economy.

When World War II reached American shores, universities were already proven allies for federal action. They had accepted aid and fought economic Depression, and were ready and willing to help fight a global war as well. Through efforts such as the U.S. Navy V programs and the Manhattan Project, universities took on national goals and gratefully accepted federal resources. By 1944, when Congress passed the G.I. Bill, perhaps the best-known example of aid for higher education, universities were already indispensable tools for enacting federal policy.

At the end of World War II, universities and cities faced linked crises. Higher education had taken on massive new responsibilities and struggled to adjust to the increasingly democratic promise of education. Millions of new students and scores of new programs meant jam-packed campuses and classrooms, while global research imperatives put teaching and scholarship in tension. These were the problems of a surplus of resources and vitality. Cities, meanwhile, had suffered from fifteen years of neglect and disinvestment. Industrial cities, especially, saw overcrowding and overuse of real estate and infrastructure—too many people packed into a single house, too many conversions of apartments to small kitchenette studios. Suburban growth began to solve a number of issues for political and economic leaders, but began to drain population and economic activity from central cities. For universities located in the arsenals of democracy—the industrial cities that had led the productive efforts in World War II—urban problems became university problems. They turned to the federal government for aid and became what one historian has called a "parastate."[20] Universities could meet federal goals and allow the actual state to deliver services to the public indirectly. Channeling federal expenditures through universities had the benefit of realizing political objectives while helping neutralize conservative fears of government expansion.

Tangled in the web of federal relationships, universities increasingly faced criticism from within and without, beginning in the transformative middle decades of the twentieth century. Mid-century urban policy—urban renewal, suburban development subsidies, and unequal community investments—maintained racial segregation even after the *Brown v. Board of Education* ruling, providing opportunity and security to whites at the expense of blacks.

Political dissent over race emerged from and found homes in universities, from chapters of the Congress of Racial Equality (CORE) to Students for a Democratic Society (SDS). This dissent and fragmentation eventually undermined the fragile foundation of the New Deal coalition. When this political chaos combined with economic stagnation in the 1970s, the liberal policy edifice also crumbled, including the commitment for affordable, democratic access to higher education. Urban crises wrought university crises in a long feedback loop between policy and politics.

Urban leaders, education administrators, and economic thinkers responded to the crisis by embracing the logic and rhetoric of the marketplace and, with it, neoliberalism. Universities became laboratories for developing and adapting this market rhetoric in economics seminar rooms and administrative offices. According to this market logic, academic research had to be made profitable. University investment returns had to be maximized in the increasingly complicated and diffuse financial marketplace to take over for dwindling public support. Nonprofit universities had to compete with private enterprise for employees and, by the end of the century, students. Similarly, cities had to unfetter real-estate markets and entrepreneurs from regulations and tax burdens to regain urban vitality.

The market era of neoliberal policy meant fundamental changes for universities and cities.[21] Two key changes in higher education characterized this era, one external and one internal. First, the equalizing potential and redistributive nature of higher education was on the wane. The emphasis on markets, deregulation, and low taxes meant less economic redistribution from the wealthy to provide affordable higher education to the poor and working classes. Thus, universities increasingly relied on philanthropy and their endowments, as well as tuition, to meet their goals. Second, this shift meant that universities changed their structure and curricula to become more vocational, to serve job markets more directly, and to emphasize discoveries with commercial potential and industry support.

This policy transformation did invigorate a number of cities, especially those home to major universities, by making them more attractive to an affluent generation popularly dubbed the "creative class."[22] The children and grandchildren of postwar suburban knowledge workers sought residence, employment, and entertainment back in cities at the end of the twentieth century. In some cases, they preferred the decrepit signs of central city disinvestment over the new, verdant infrastructure of the metropolitan periphery. But just as their parents had enjoyed suburban subsidies, the new creative class rode a wave of tax breaks and federal policy that starved the state and scavenged the postindustrial urban landscape. The promise of the California Master Plan for Higher Education, for example, was funded by defense contracting and suburban expansion. Market-oriented tax incentives, such as historic preservation tax credits and enterprise zones, and tax policy including Proposition 13 starved California cities of traditional lines of revenue and channeled development in new directions. They facilitated the back-to-the city movement by whites in the 1980s and 1990s, helping to reinvigorate and gentrify neighborhoods in San Francisco and Oakland.

By the end of the twentieth century, the importance of universities in U.S. society was incontrovertible. No city could be great without a great university, and a college degree now vies with home ownership among the key symbols of class status and means of solidifying upward mobility across generations. Education and community politics intersect at universities; at this intersection, we find powerful battles over the nature of urban life and the future of metropolitan America.

This book lays out several periods in the twentieth century and the varied settings for higher education that prevailed over each period. Each chapter presents a case illustrating a moment or period of transformation that rendered changes in American society and political ideology spatial. University administrators extended the spatial ideology of their institutions in order to translate that economic and political logic into new educational spaces. My intent is to give a sense of the diversity of U.S. institutions and their relationship to urban development as well as to illustrate commonality among universities or continuity across eras. Each institution described here faced issues and transformations that affected a wide range of institutions.

In Chapter 1, we witness regional leaders favoring white-collar jobs, workers, and neighborhoods over their industrial and working-class counterparts in reorganization of regional political economy. Over the course of the twentieth century, higher education expanded to serve the growing needs of a developing industrial society by defining and providing the training of skilled professionals.[23] This shifting mission led to a building boom. A growing middle class sent their children to college in increasing numbers, philanthropists gave to colleges and universities, and city boosters incorporated universities in their development plans. What they chose to build gave physical form to an institutional ideology of aspiration and the bourgeois values of civic leaders.

In Muncie, Indiana, the Ball brothers, makers of glass jars for fruit and vegetable canning, scavenged a four-times-failed for-profit teacher training school and donated it to the state. Thus they turned a private enterprise into a public endeavor and fused philanthropic and entrepreneurial efforts in the Indiana State Normal School (later Ball State University). The Balls leveraged their economic and political power to promote the development of Muncie, including a hospital, a museum, and an airport, in addition to the college. At the same time, sociologists Robert and Helen Lynd, with their best-selling book *Middletown* and follow-up study *Middletown in Transition*, made Muncie's name and helped it stand in for industrial cities around the country. Muncie *was* America, from its industrial history to the economic transformation accelerated by investments in higher education.

The establishment of the normal school helped create a new racial, class, and economic geography in the burgeoning industrial city. The school was part of a speculative real-estate gambit. The Ball brothers' initial investment and subsequent influence illustrate what I call the gravity of capital—investment drawing additional investment toward itself. The Balls led the Muncie business class to build a new city that would have been almost unrecognizable to nineteenth-century eyes, with white business families at the northwestern edge, intense industrial development to the south, and a new economy on the rise.

By the middle decades of the century, as detailed in Chapter 2, local boosters found in the New Deal and wartime programs a new partner for supporting higher education—the federal government. Through its resources came the ability for dramatic reconfiguration of education communities and their surrounding cities. The New Deal provided stimulus and structured new markets for agricultural products, housing, and the circulation of capital. At the same time, the federal government invested in colleges and universities through student aid and investments in physical plants, remaking higher education. In the process, Roosevelt gave priority to investments in the South above all other regions. Political leaders built on these successes, which the federal government continued and amplified during World War II and through the 1950s, to make higher education central to the midcentury liberal agenda.

No university or American city flourished without federal backing, and no university or city eclipsed the growth of either the University of Texas or Austin in this period. Early in the twentieth century, Austin had been a small, racially segregated southwestern city: through the 1920s, it was smaller than Muncie.[24] Prominent politicians in the city, including a young Lyndon Johnson, lobbied for PWA grants, wartime research, and training funds that enabled the university to expand its physical and intellectual capacity and leap to national stature. When wartime mobilization and postwar prosperity reached the once-impoverished state, enthusiasm for the New Deal waned. Resurgent conservatives forced liberal retrenchment and abandonment of re-distributionist policies that aided the poor and began to address racial and ethnic inequality.[25] Co-opted by this postwar realignment, figures such as Johnson forged a martial compromise on domestic policy, physically and fiscally expanding government institutions and the state by redirecting them in service of Cold War defense.[26]

These development efforts created spatially decentralized institutions in Austin. A university research campus and military infrastructure, including an airbase that would become Austin's international airport, topped the list of new projects on the metropolitan periphery.[27] Postwar growth was not eq-uitably distributed, in part because the University of Texas did not admit African Americans. While civil-rights activists successfully challenged ra-cial exclusion at the university, in the late 1940s, federal support of subur-banization—a new mode of metropolitan segregation—took the place of Jim Crow in Austin.[28] With the development of the research campus that moved job growth, knowledge creation, and economic opportunity far from the city's center, the University of Texas was part and parcel to creation of the new, decentralized Austin.

As I show in Chapter 3, after World War II, cities and universities scram-bled to manage unprecedented federal largesse and the restructured politi-cal economy. The Cold War and the growing perception that cities were in crisis were intertwined issues in these decades. Federal highway and mort-gage subsidies facilitated suburban expansion and led to disinvestment in the urban core. Slum clearance and urban renewal brought real-estate capital to central cities but disrupted settled boundaries and exacerbated internal ten-sions within cities. At the same time, political leaders struggling to hold together a fragile global coalition against Communism sought economic dominance and military superiority. The federal government conscripted higher-education institutions to provide domestic economic growth and develop new weapons for fighting a global war.

Here I focus on the University of Chicago on Chicago's South Side, where administrators panicked when they faced racial transition from the Great Migration's influx of rural, Southern African Americans to the city.[29] City business and political leaders restructured the racial geography by demolishing and redeveloping central areas such as the Black Belt, the African American district on the South Side. Federal policy also drained white ethnic communities and hardened racial animosities by shifting new housing investment to places like Naperville and Downer's Grove at the metropolitan periphery, putting space between the races.[30] The University of Chicago used its position at the knife's edge of the war effort—leadership in the Manhattan Project that helped create the war-ending atomic bombs—to participate in, and at times lead, this process. University technocrats undermined racial integration in the community by creating local, state, and federal legislation and programs that prioritized the university over racial equality. The university sought to protect its interests and mission but meanwhile created blight, limited opportunity, and concentrated poverty in surrounding neighborhoods. Framing their efforts within the rhetoric of Cold War defense, administrators sought to maintain and expand a physical refuge from the black South Side. They would provide a training ground and experimentation laboratory for the next generation of Cold Warriors. University of Chicago leaders established a policy template that universities in cities around the country would adopt on their own campuses. In the process, they sparked strident opposition both in neighboring communities and within the university. The Woodlawn Organization came together with the help of Saul Alinsky's Industrial Areas Foundation to oppose university urban renewal. The local chapter of CORE, including University of Chicago students, protested and occupied administration buildings at the beginning of the 1960s.

Chapter 4 demonstrates how pioneering postwar expansion efforts were fully institutionalized in the 1960s and found even wider-ranging forms of opposition. Universities were key partners in a system of military Keynesianism, racial inequality, and anti-Communism that attracted a growing chorus of critics by the 1960s. The managed growth of postwar American liberalism preempted all manner of opportunities that American exceptionalist rhetoric seemed to guarantee. Social and economic opportunity for African Americans, varieties of political belief, and a diversity of personal lifestyles and expressions were up for strident, even violent debate, but the overriding system favored corporatism and benefits for white, middle-class nuclear families.

The public machinery of the state of California made the University of California, Berkeley, the center of the vision for economic growth and social progress that took precedence in the 1960s. Academic administrators and state politicians collaborated to coordinate a statewide system of higher education that provided broad access, funded by suburban expansion and defense contracting. The University of California included several campuses where scholars conducted world-leading research; state colleges emphasized undergraduate instruction; and local community colleges gave students their first step into higher education. Berkeley and its science research sat at the pinnacle of the whole enterprise of universal education and statewide investment in communities.[31]

The student upheavals that followed the expansion of the University of California system were confrontations with the contradictions and failures of liberalism. Berkeley students responded to episodes of university growth with a series of objections that called into question the very nature of their institution. Their school had become, like other universities, a key product of the Faustian bargain of twentieth-century development.[32] Mass education, urban renewal, the Cold War, and the promise of racial equality were all threads tangled together in the student and community protests of the 1960s in Berkeley. Campus building and neighborhood redevelopment were the physical realization of these priorities, poured, mortared, and hammered into the landscape of the Berkeley community.

In Chapter 5, we see how cities and universities undertook rapid transformations in response to the political, economic, and cultural tumult of the dissenting 1970s. American universities were centers of new thinking about markets, economic growth, and scientific commercialization, from Chicago School economics to biotech start-ups on the coasts. Economists, intellectuals, and policymakers considered university reforms to be opportunities to reverse the stagnation of the 1970s. The Bayh-Dole Act of 1980, for example, a mechanism for commercializing federally funded research and knowledge at universities, reflects this model: the marketplace rather than the public domain was the destination for knowledge. At the same time, lower tax rates, decreased regulation of financial investments, and an increased emphasis on philanthropy in American politics and society meant that universities of all types leaned more heavily toward privatization and the private institution model, funded by student tuition or donor gifts to endowments.

In Cambridge, Massachusetts, Harvard University and MIT both helped create the market model that dominates today. East Cambridge, the home of MIT, was heavily industrial and faced the challenges of urban disinvestment. Central Cambridge, site of Harvard Yard, was a genteel setting of expensive residences. MIT pursued a set of new research initiatives and corporate partnerships that would remake its surroundings, especially at Technology Square and Kendall Square, re-creating industrial Cambridge as a high-tech center of just a few dense acres of biotech research and computer services. MIT fought a battle over redevelopment with the Cambridge working class in the 1970s and, after a prolonged stalemate, eventually won. Harvard remade itself financially, expanding its endowment, already the nation's largest, from $1 billion in 1964 to $36 billion in 2005. But when it sought campus expansion in the 1980s, Harvard bought land across the Charles River, finding it easier to grow in a working-class area of Boston than in affluent central Cambridge.

Taken together, these stories illustrate universities' roles as both actors and stages in twentieth-century urban transformation, to employ a theatrical metaphor. Institutions of higher education are corporate bodies that function as legal persons, governed by boards and managed by administrators. In this role, they are able to borrow money, issue bonds, and charge fees; buy, sell, and develop real estate; and lobby government to advance and protect their interests. In addition, universities are places, forums where loose associations of people from many parts of society come together (or break apart), ostensibly to engage in, pursue, or facilitate the creation and attainment of knowledge. In the course of those activities, students, administrators, faculty members, and staff may individually or collectively act as political agents, as market participants, or as members of a broader metropolitan community in service of their ideals and interests. This book emphasizes the interaction between elites and the grassroots, illustrating the role of both institutions and individual actors in shaping higher-education legislation and policy, as well as specific development projects, combining both a "top-down" and "bottom-up" perspective in addressing this history.

Universities held an essential and growing role in the reproduction of American society and the development of human resources in the twentieth century. Their work in space, the campuses and buildings where scholars and students meet to research and learn, gave them motive to alter their local environments. The increasing resources devoted to higher education gave them the power to do so. However, the national and global mandates that provided and guided these resources meant that universities were decreasingly sensitive and responsive to the values and priorities of their surrounding communities. In effect, they were national and global institutions trapped in local places. This tension between the local and the global played out in creative ways for education but ones that could be harmful to the local communities. Architects and planners gave physical and symbolic form to these educational values and local tensions. To protect and expand their missions and resources, universities could create and exacerbate poverty, blight, racial segregation, inequality, and isolation in urban settings. Thus, these institutions reproduced American society—the problems and the promise—as they sought to create it anew. Universities were the classic American institution of the twentieth century. As they imposed their spatial ideologies on their local settings, they became the prime movers of urban development in the second half of the twentieth century.

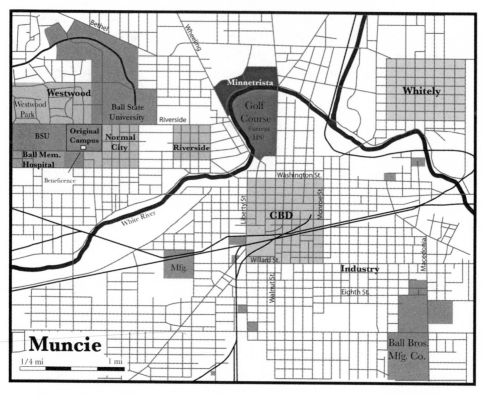

Figure 1. Muncie, Indiana. Map created by the author.

1 | The Gravity of Capital

On a Friday morning in September 1917, George Ball, manufacturer of the popular Ball glass jars, picked up the telephone to talk to his attorney. He approved his lawyer's bid on the property of a failed private teaching school at auction. Three bids trickled in over the morning at the courthouse: $35,000 . . . $35,100 . . . and $36,000. Only one bid came with the guarantee of a cash payment for half the amount that day—Carl Robe White's, offered on behalf of Ball. When the noon bidding deadline passed, the judge reaffirmed his condition and accepted George Ball's $35,100 offer for the property.[1] Later at lunch, Ball offhandedly remarked to his brothers in the family business, "[I] just bought a college."[2] The sale began the process that would establish the foundation of a major Midwestern university and shift the ground beneath the economy of Muncie, Indiana.

A few months later, state representative Charles McGonagle approached one of George Ball's brothers at a Rotary Club meeting. He offered to broker a donation of the college campus between the Ball family and the Indiana state government. The Balls agreed; the state created a new public institution on the site; and by June 1918, eight months after the auction, the Muncie campus of the Indiana State Normal School held its first classes.[3]

The Balls did not set out to remake Muncie, but the founding of the Normal School helped bring about powerful and wide-ranging shifts in the patterns of urban growth and economic development. Mass industrialization had formed the bedrock of the city's economy and culture. Having achieved industrial wealth, Muncie business and education leaders used the new school and its surrounding developments to set the city on a new path of century-long urban transformation. The creation of a postindustrial economic and physical landscape in Muncie was an attempt to boost the city to a leadership position in eastern Indiana, surpassing its local rivals with better education, greater cultural experiences, better health, and better jobs.

The founding of the Muncie branch of the Indiana State Normal School rendered spatial the logic of twentieth-century economic transformation. Investments in the college established a pattern of greenfield development and urban reorganization that helped redirect economic, residential, and civic investment from around the city to Muncie's northwestern quadrant. The Ball family created a new educational and health care institution adjoining it, the Ball Memorial Hospital, while Muncie's professional class slowly moved from their homes in the East End neighborhood to exclusive suburban subdivisions near the college's campus. With these changes under way, the city's political and economic leaders created civic institutions such as a laboratory school, an art museum, and public sculpture destined for northwestern Muncie. The city had been transformed into a consumer pleasure center. The college became a vehicle enabling a loose coalition of city elites to create a new urban vision characterized by a landscape of cultural production and affluent consumption. Higher education segregated the economic future of the city, separating the business class from the working class, whites from blacks, and the knowledge economy from the industrial economy.

Urban boosters and education leaders worked together in Muncie in a way we have rarely seen in the Progressive Era.[4] Yet George Ball's purchase of the college married the Progressive desire for urban order with the ambition for knowledge-based social improvement, setting off a series of spatial, technological, economic, and social changes that altered the logic of metropolitan life. This may not have been the most dramatic example of the founding of a college through a public-private partnership, but investments by the Ball family and other Muncie leaders were nonetheless emblematic of a larger pattern of educational growth, philanthropy, and urban boosterism across the country. Early in the century, Tempe, Arizona; Los Angeles; and San Jose, California, were all home to "normal schools"—two-year teacher's colleges. Those three became the institutions of Arizona State University, the University of California at Los Angeles, and San Jose State University, and are now major economic forces in their regions.[5] The founding and expansion of institutions like Ball State during the Progressive Era were the first steps in a new spatial political economy in the twentieth century that changed the face of urban America.

A Company Town

A natural gas strike in the 1880s fueled industrialization in Muncie. Entrepreneurs and immigrant laborers flocked to take advantage of the abundant natural resource that helped power the industrial transformation of the American economy in the latter half of the nineteenth century. Muncie's population quadrupled from 5,200 in 1880 to 20,900 in 1900.[6] Before the turn of the century, business interests were diverse and relatively small scale. One could find as many coopers and bootmakers working by hand on Muncie's Main Street as heavy manufacturers like carriage makers and castings companies, but the gas boom changed that.[7]

Natural gas brought Muncie its most successful industrial concern. Two brothers, Frank and Edmund Ball, had founded Ball Brothers Manufacturing Company in Buffalo, New York. They made glass jars that rural and small-town families used to preserve fruits and vegetables throughout the winter. When their Buffalo factory burned down in 1886, the brothers searched for a new location where the business would be less costly to run. Indiana presented such an opportunity. Gas for their glassblowing furnaces was plentiful and cheap. Muncie's business leaders offered the Ball Company free gas for five years and free land if the brothers moved their business west. The company, now under the management of all five brothers, struck a deal and set out for Indiana.[8]

The Balls manufactured lids and seals along with their jars. The matching components were more reliable than nearly any other product on the market. By the turn of the century, the company was part of a growing move in Muncie toward heavy industry and larger firms serving larger markets. Ball Brothers produced more than a third of the nation's canning jars, and the brothers were among the richest men in the state.[9] The brothers were renowned in the company's early years for peeling down to shirtsleeves, especially Frank Ball, and taking their turns at machines on the shop floor. Their unassuming manner won them admiration among workers, and the company came to be identified with the city as both grew in tandem. The Ball factories dominated Muncie's south side and poured smoke into the sky from the corner of 9th and Macedonia Streets (Figure 2).

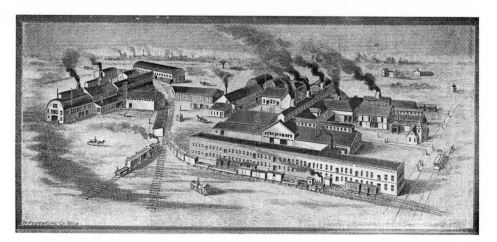

Figure 2. Ball Brothers factory. By the beginning of the twentieth century, the Ball Brothers glass jar company had become one of the top employers in Muncie and made the brothers among the richest men in the state. Ball State University Archives and Special Collections.

In this era, Muncie's development followed the enduring pattern of the walking city.[10] It was a replicable grid of streets, and only a few dozen blocks were accessible from the center of the city—those that could be reached on foot, with a horse-drawn vehicle, or those along the two main railroad lines connecting Muncie to the rest of the state and region. The Fort Wayne, Muncie, and Cincinnati Railroad ran north and south through Muncie with a jog in the middle of town. The Cleveland, Columbus, Cincinnati, and Indianapolis (CCC&I) rail line slashed from the northeast to the southwest across the city. Development clustered between the CCC&I lines and the White River to the north, although a few developments followed along the railroads and trailed the north–south line beyond the southern edge of town.

The mass industrialization of Muncie led to a population boom, growing levels of wealth and leisure, and ambition on the part of city boosters to rank as a leading Indiana city. Industrial development over the thirty-year period following the gas strike grew south of the city's rail lines. Working-class housing on the city's new south side accompanied this growth. It doubled the geographical size of Muncie in the first decade of the century, matching the growing population, which roughly doubled in the same period.

The business class leading the new manufacturing companies established their homes in the East End, a neighborhood just outside the central business district. This residential area offered easy access to Muncie's downtown, where residents could visit the city's leading banks, newspapers, and civic institutions, or could board trains at the station to take them to Indianapolis or Chicago.[11] The East End also kept business leaders near the city's south side, where they could supervise the operations of their factories. Journalist Emily Kimbrough was born in 1899 and grew up on East Washington Street in Muncie's elite section. At midcentury she wrote for the *New Yorker* and coauthored a best-selling memoir, but as a child she was part of a wealthy industrial family. Her book about her childhood recounts the appearance of automobiles in the city shortly after 1900 and her joyride around town in the city's first car. The trip included the rural outskirts of the city but never went as far south as Industry, the city's main working-class neighborhood.[12] Much of that farmland surrounding Muncie would be built up in the next few decades, not least owing to the success of companies like the Indiana Bridge Company, run by Kimbrough's father. By Indiana standards, the city was becoming an industrial juggernaut.

Philanthropic Interest in Education

In investing in the Normal School, the Ball brothers were following a trend established by the country's leading industrialists and philanthropists. Business leaders and Progressive Era reformers promoted education amid industrial growth, investing some of their surplus capital for the broader social good and working to mitigate class strife in labor relations. Higher education, especially, built upon new natural and social scientific knowledge and incorporated it into emerging fields of public and business administration. Andrew Carnegie created the Carnegie Technical Schools in Pittsburgh (now Carnegie Mellon University) to provide immigrants and working-class residents with engineering and mechanical training. John D. Rockefeller of Standard Oil gave hundreds of thousands of dollars to help found the University of Chicago. Leland Stanford of the Southern Pacific and Central Pacific Railroads commemorated his late son by founding the Leland Stanford Junior University in Palo Alto, California. Carnegie made a broader appeal to his wealthy counterparts on behalf of higher education in his essays "The Gospel of Wealth" and "The Best Fields for Philanthropy." In these widely read pieces, he suggested that the founding of a university stands "apart by itself" as the highest end of a lifetime of work and wealth accumulation.[13]

Real-estate profits were part and parcel to the development of educational opportunity, even from the founding of many institutions. Retail magnate Marshall Field joined John D. Rockefeller in donating to the University of Chicago, giving ten acres of Hyde Park land to it in 1890. He sold the university additional land a year later and then profited by selling more land holdings to the faculty, staff, and others attracted to living near a well-endowed institution on a picturesque campus.[14] Real-estate entrepreneurs Harold and Edwin Janss made a similar calculus in Los Angeles in 1924, selling the University of California hundreds of acres at bargain prices, thereby increasing the value of their nearby residential real-estate developments. The University of Michigan, the University of Illinois, and the University of California's original Berkeley campus all benefited from similar donations.[15]

The Ball brothers, in a sense, made good on an older real-estate gambit that brought higher education to Muncie. A group of local businessmen calling themselves the Eastern Indiana Normal University Association (EINUA) had optioned a tract of agricultural land beyond the northwestern borders of Muncie in 1898. The EINUA included, among others, George McCulloch, the city's leading transportation entrepreneur, and Frank Haimbaugh, publisher of the Muncie *Herald*. The growth coalition subdivided the land into three hundred lots and platted a development they called Normal City.[16] At the edge of this land, they founded the normal school to train young men and women to be teachers in rural schools. Their plan called for the sale of the residential lots to pay for development of the school's campus, based on an expected student body of 250. The EINUA projected the school to bring $75,000 of student and institutional spending to Muncie annually, a meaningful spur to the city's economy.[17] The Muncie Citizen's Street Railway Company, led by McCulloch, extended a streetcar line out to the new school, connecting Normal City to Muncie's downtown.[18] The Eastern Indiana Normal University was thus a mechanism for both rural and urban development. By training teachers to educate children in rural districts, the school would provide for the enrichment of rural life. By expanding the city's reach to outlying agricultural lands and increasing economic activity, the school would help the city grow, provide jobs, and improve human welfare.

The association created EINU as a for-profit enterprise. This proved an unorthodox choice that presaged nearly twenty years of fiscal tumult. For-profit institutions were part of the broad range of higher-education opportunities in the era, but they largely did not share the social responsibility and ambitions of nonprofit private and public colleges.[19] EINU began to offer classes in 1899 in

Figure 3. Eastern Indiana Normal University Administration Building. A real-estate scheme financed the founding of Eastern Indiana Normal University, including construction of its administration building. The building still serves as the administration headquarters for Ball State University. Ball State University Archives and Special Collections.

an impressive neoclassical building (Figure 3). The handsome brick structure could not guarantee its success, however. The school paired suburban development with educational growth, but the institution foundered, lacking students and prestige. The institution failed and was resurrected three times in the next eighteen years. In one unsuccessful scheme to reorganize the institution, representatives of the EINUA tried to convince leaders of nearby Taylor University to relocate to Muncie.[20] Taylor administrators demurred, and after its third bankruptcy, the Muncie school could find no new backers.[21]

After the institution failed for the last time in 1917, an Indiana court ordered liquidation to repay the school's creditors. The assets were worth more than $400,000 and included the administration building, a wood-frame dormitory for women, and about seventy acres of land. The creditors sought to recoup their investment with a plan to break up the properties and sell the land as individual parcels to the highest bidders.[22]

By that point, hundreds of residents lived in the suburban settlements of Normal City and Riverside. Alva Kitselman, the city's second leading industrialist, was the most prominent resident of the area. He moved from a house near downtown and built a twenty-six-acre estate the size of a city block in 1915, just three blocks from the east edge of the campus. Around his estate, an array of industrial and white-collar workers, from foremen to physicians to carpenters to salesmen, lived scattered throughout Normal City, but there was plenty of room for additional growth.[23]

The Ball Family Takes Over

The Ball brothers had created a neighborhood of architect-designed homes on the White River less than a mile east of the college, starting in the 1890s.[24] Years before, Lucina, one of two sisters to the five Ball brothers, had written them extensive advice about building homes. "It is risky building a good house in any place that may be made undesirable by some one putting up a poor class of buildings," she wrote. "Can't you get up a 'syndicate' to buy a whole square and build it all equally good, and so make your own surroundings. Houses moderately expensive, with neighborhoods fine and insured, would be a good thing."[25] Her counsel drew on models of classic suburban development schemes across the country and in Europe.[26]

The Balls faced the prospect of a Wild West of boom and bust and scattershot building in their neighborhood. Lucina's worry about a "poor class of buildings" nearby was an increasing possibility. The auction would open the normal school's land to individual development, lot by lot, if the creditors won and sold the land to clear their debts. Further, the municipality and plan commission would not be able to restrain new development because the area was unincorporated and lay outside the boundaries of the city of Muncie. Frank Ball set his lawyer, Carl Robe White, to acquiring the land, and on the day of the auction, George Ball took the phone call closing the deal.[27] However, the slighted creditors sued the Balls to recoup their investments and promised to hold up any development plans for years through lengthy litigation.[28]

Charles McGonagle saw a way out of the mess. McGonagle was a longtime Muncie politician and chair of the state's Ways and Means Committee, powerful enough to move policy through the legislature and enough of a Muncie booster to promote the city as an arm of government. In 1917 he led passage of a law empowering the state to accept land donations on behalf of colleges and universities.[29] McGonagle broached the subject to George Ball at a Muncie Rotary meeting in early 1918. The Muncie Rotary Club comprised the civic and business leadership of the community. George and Frank C. Ball were members and Frank's sons, Edmund A. and Frank E. Ball, would later become members.[30] McGonagle suggested that the governor and state legislature would be willing to accept a donation of the campus property and operate a branch campus of the Indiana State Normal School (ISNS, now

Indiana State University) based in Terre Haute. The representative contacted Governor James Goodrich and found him receptive to the idea of state-sponsored higher education in east central Indiana.[31] Goodrich and George Ball were both rising figures in the Republican Party; Ball would become a member of the Republican National Committee, while Goodrich would serve in the administrations of Warren G. Harding, Calvin Coolidge, and Herbert Hoover.[32] Establishment of a new public institution would serve the area's business and political interests, while strengthening the politicians' individual influence in their home region and their broader goal of collaboration between private enterprise and the state. Indeed, when state education administrators arrived in Muncie to inspect the property, the Muncie Commercial Club led a crowd of two hundred strong to celebrate the state officials.[33]

The Ball donation to the state was especially important to the family's interests because state ownership relieved the family of liabilities that came along with the school. Several creditors were irate about debts redeemed at less than ten cents on the dollar. They brought lawsuits to mitigate their losses, but under the agreement with the state, any lawsuits would have to be directed at, and defended by, the state of Indiana.[34] The ISNS board of trustees ratified the governor's bargain on the condition that Frank Ball serve as a trustee for the school. Ball agreed and sealed the political deal.

Muncie Politics

Rollin "Doc" Bunch, Muncie's mayor, was no fool. The leader of the city's Democratic machine realized he had to act when the development of desirable northwestern Muncie became an issue in his 1917 campaign for reelection. Normal City and Riverside were next to the Normal School, just outside the urban boundaries of Muncie. These neighborhoods escaped municipal taxation but contracted with the city for services such as water and sewer. In 1909 Muncie had annexed much of the industrial south side into the city. Thus, working-class homeowners in Industry paid more in property taxes than residents in the more expensive subdivision of Normal City.[35] Bunch benefited electorally from the annexation of Democratic south-side industrial workers. By keeping the Republican-voting, professional-class suburbanites out of the city's electorate, the mayor had consolidated political power in the midst of metropolitan growth.

The 1917 mayoral campaign was a classic contest pitting a progressive Republican challenger against a Democratic machine politician. Charles

Grafton, the Republican, made taxation and metropolitan equity one of the centerpieces of his run. Bunch drew support from the northeastern and southeastern areas of the city populated by working-class residents, both black and white. He also presided over a city payroll tens of thousands of dollars larger than any of his predecessors.[36] Grafton was an officer of a clay-pot manufacturer and lived in the city's East End. He attacked Bunch from different directions. He ran on a populist line in order to drive a wedge between the machine mayor and his working-class constituents. Grafton pledged that he would not allow the new educated and professional class of the northwestern suburbs to enjoy Muncie's urban amenities without contributing their fair share of taxes.[37] Then his campaign invoked the classic Progressive Era bogeyman of a saloonkeeper politician. Billy Finan was an Irish barkeeper who loomed large in the mind of Muncie Republicans. The longtime politician was a cog in the Indiana Democratic machine who had worked his way up to serving as a state nominating delegate, a position he held for several decades in the first half of the century.[38] A full-page newspaper advertisement in the city's Republican-leaning *Star* asked about annexation: "Why didn't Dr. Bunch and his council use this power? Because the residents of these suburbs were overwhelmingly 'dry' and Billy Finan and the crowd back of Dr. Bunch would sooner cut off their right hands than allow these people a vote on the 'wet' or 'dry' issue."[39]

Bunch recognized the political risk he faced in Grafton and moved to outflank his challenger. Pledging to capture taxes from the building going on outside Muncie's northwestern boundaries, Bunch initiated the annexation of the wealthier areas of the city.[40] In doing so, the mayor reaffirmed his populist credentials, declaring that he would not tolerate geographic inequality in metropolitan tax policy. Residents in working-class parts of the city picked up on his rhetoric against northwestern Muncie free riders and returned Bunch to lead the city for another term. After the election, the mayor followed through on annexation for the northwestern suburbs, and the city completed the process in 1919, along with Whitely, the working-class African American neighborhood to the city's northeast. This helped balance the more affluent voters of Normal City and Riverside.[41]

This political debate reflected an increasingly segregated city, separated by class, race, and geography. The new educational institution played a significant part in this geographic transformation. The business class, including Kitselman and the Balls, began to cluster around the college and create a leisure class with activities such as foxhunts and horse rides, with the Ball

Figure 4. Muncie fox hunt. The wealthy Ball family anchored high society in Muncie, organizing social events including fox hunts, as depicted in a 1937 Margaret Bourke-White photo essay on Muncie for *Life*. Margaret Bourke-White/Getty Images. Image from Special Collections Research Center, Syracuse University Libraries, Margaret Bourke-White Papers, Box 65, Folder 514, "Fox Hunt."

family at its center (Figure 4).[42] Few working-class families from south of the tracks could enter this social milieu or send their children to college in the hopes that they might enter that societal stratum or its equivalent. Industry and Whitely contained virtually all of the city's African American population. Industry was nestled near the Ball Brothers' manufacturing complex south of downtown and included the city's red-light district, known as "young Chicago."[43] Whitely, at the city's northeastern quadrant, had been planned as a white working-class suburb but became a black community when white buyers failed to materialize. African Americans moved north in the Great Migration and were willing customers for Muncie housing in Whitely.[44] As in many northern industrial cities, black workers and residents found themselves barred from living in many Muncie neighborhoods and from working jobs across the labor spectrum. Black men toiled in unskilled labor and factory work while black women served as domestic help in white homes. Institutions like the Muncie city directory upheld the color line, noting African American residents with an asterisk, lest an unsuspecting white shopper patronize a black business by accident.[45]

The Normal School

The term "normal school," common parlance at the time for a school that trained teachers, came from the *ecole normale* system that instituted teaching standards in France. As EINU and as ISNS, the Muncie schools offered teacher training in a two-year program. They reflected a precarious balance between civic enterprise and the conservative, normative impetus of the project of educating teachers.[46] The state renamed the school Ball Teachers College (BTC) in 1922 in recognition of the family's commitment and the school's growing curriculum. At older and larger institutions than BTC, small groups of students from a wide variety of backgrounds kept up an intellectual and political churn. At BTC, though, the career-oriented student body largely came from the region and was disengaged from student governance and electoral politics, which slowed development of campus life in the 1910s and 1920s.[47] A few years later, Ralph Noyer, the BTC dean, considered a rash of smoking on campus and speculated it came from student dissatisfaction with "the boredom of existence here."[48]

The college operated in the colorful context of a growing industrial city with numerous opportunities for indulging in worldly pleasures and vices. Throughout the 1920s, the large majority of students resided off-campus in Muncie, embedded in the urban realm of what was then a moderately sized, largely walkable city.[49] In the early years of the normal school, Doc Bunch suffered political storms for allowing some two hundred brothels and speakeasies to operate unfettered in Muncie.[50] However, the new urban pattern emerging in Muncie shaped the geography of vice. Normal City had been dry before its annexation, and Prohibition began shortly after its addition to the city, precluding the development of a pub culture near campus. Muncie's saloons were largely located in the center of downtown or in the working-class sections like Industry near the rail lines: even if they wanted to, students would have found it hard to get a drink before Prohibition in the new neighborhoods and commercial districts of Muncie.[51]

Higher education operated *in loco parentis*—"in place of the parent"—in part to protect students from these urban vices. By the 1920s, women's higher education had been stripped of its nineteenth-century radicalism, and women had been incorporated into the conservative, consumerist realm of collegiate life, in part by bringing women's housing on campus.[52] Women's dormitories predominated at colleges across the country, and administrators worked to re-create a domestic sphere on campus.[53] This was so important to the original Muncie normal school that the first building after teaching and office space at EINU was a women's dormitory.[54] Oversight of women's dormitories was more extensive and protective than men's off-campus housing. Women had curfews, for example, requiring them to be back at set times in the evening, where men did not.

Grace DeHority, the dean of women, enforced these restrictions. Deans of women made it possible for women to go to college and join the workforce by maintaining traditional social structures to calm conservative parents and provide a familiar environment. DeHority was a ruralite who made it off the farm because of her education and devoted her life to providing education to others. She came to Muncie in 1922 after she earned a bachelor's degree at ISNS in Terre Haute and taught junior high in her hometown. In addition to inspecting boardinghouses, DeHority expelled students for offenses from drinking alcohol to loafing. In one incident, the dean learned a student had "rather intimate connections" with a married man. She wrote the girl's parents to let them know and asked the student to leave school to "prove an unforgettable lesson."[55] DeHority expelled a man but not his girlfriend, both BTC students, when they stayed overnight together in Muncie, causing the woman to miss her curfew. She graduated; he did not.[56]

The African American experience at BTC mimicked that within Muncie— free from the constraints of Jim Crow but still segregated by state action. The first black student to graduate from BTC, Jesse Nixon, earned her degree in 1925. But African Americans were severely underrepresented at BTC, and the college relegated its black students to the margins of campus life.[57] Despite African Americans making up about 6 percent of the Muncie population in 1930, there were only a handful of black students at the college. They were not allowed in the college dormitories, fraternities, or sororities, and most lived in boardinghouses on the east side of the city. They also were shut out of the school's student social organizations, which were some of the key platforms for economic mobility in higher education.[58]

Campus Planning

Muncie industrial workers, black and white, read the world around them and realized that education was key to social and economic advancement—a path to the other side of the tracks dividing Muncie into north and south. Nationally, one out of twenty college-age adults attended college by 1920, more than double the rate from the beginning of the century.[59] The Muncie working class, however, had difficulty paying for advanced schooling and suffered from low educational expectations.[60] A pair of sociologists, Robert and Helen Lynd, studied Muncie in the early 1920s and published a best-selling book on the city called *Middletown: A Study in American Culture.* According to the Lynds, working-class families believed higher education provided a means of escaping lives of manual labor. "A boy without an education today just ain't *anywhere!*" lamented one Muncie man, but this realization alone could not get a man or woman through college.[61] The normal school had served obliquely as an instrument for the enrichment and protection of the business elites in the northwestern part of the city—the anchor to a real-estate endeavor—and directly as a means of class mobility and professional training unevenly shared by the business-class and working-class segments of the population living in their neighborhoods around the city.

BTC was growing, and an expanding institution needed a campus plan. The student body grew more than 450 percent over its first six years as a public institution, from 155 during the 1918–1919 school year to 833 in the fall of 1924.[62] College enrollment boomed nationwide, and annual college enrollments rose about 10 percent a year; but BTC grew faster than its counterparts elsewhere.[63] When the institution became Ball Teachers College in 1922, it began offering four-year degrees.[64] The state of Indiana approved new education programs, which brought more faculty, staff, and students to the campus.

Frank C. Ball used philanthropy and political clout to help the college in its new growth phase. In 1921 Muncie's state legislators appropriated funds for a new science building that would dramatically increase the college's instructional space. Governor Warren McCray, successor to James Goodrich, questioned the necessity of such an expense and worked to have it removed from the budget. Frank Ball caught wind of the proposed cuts and made a personal visit to Indianapolis to lobby the governor. The manufacturer won out as the governor shifted his position on the construction funds and signed on to state appropriations to the college for 1923.[65] Ball was not to be trifled with.

There had been a single neoclassical building and wood-frame dormitory on the campus when the Balls bought it. It could not contain the college's growing agenda. The institution turned to city planning, the progressive marriage of urban reform, scientific expertise, and the arts, to help provide for

Figure 5. Ball Gymnasium. The Balls' donation of several hundred thousand dollars helped give the university its first major athletics building. Muncie architect Cuno Kibele designed the gymnasium and continued his signature style that ran through many Ball-financed projects. Ball State University Archives and Special Collections.

and manage the growth of the college. At the turn of the century, this urban reform movement joined with the new architectural profession to create the field of city planning, developing urban space and employing civic symbols to promote the uplift of the American metropolis in concert with bourgeois elites.[66] Cuno Kibele was Muncie's leading architect and a member of the civic leadership. He designed commercial buildings downtown such as the Wysor Building and the Commercial Club block; residential buildings throughout the city, including additions to and redesigns of the Ball homes at Minnetrista; and industrial plants, including expansion of the Ball Brothers manufacturing plant.[67] Kibele was brought aboard to impose order on the campus. The college had averted the chaos that could have erupted around the bankrupt normal school, and Kibele's hire ensured the grounds and buildings would have the classic Vitruvian features of firmness, commodity, and delight (Figure 5).

Conservative forms molded BTC campus planning. Kibele provided a plan of development in 1921 featuring a partially enclosed lawn on a north–south axis, surrounded by a symmetrical quadrangle of buildings. The influence of the École Nationale Supérieure des Beaux-Arts in Paris dominated American architecture—training that emphasized grand, monumental designs and adaptations of classical and Renaissance architectural and planning principles.[68] A generation of Beaux-Arts architects had employed this spatial arrangement in cities and on college campuses. They drew on the Columbian Exposition of 1893 that crystallized and popularized Beaux-Arts planning and design in the United States.[69]

BTC leaders traveled to Chicago for inspiration. The master planning committee included Frank Ball, administrators W. W. Parsons and Linnaeus Hines, and a pair of other trustees. They visited Northwestern University in Evanston, just north of the city, and the University of Chicago on the South Side, where the Columbian Exposition had been held. The committee was impressed with Chicago and loosely adopted that city's university as their campus model. The institution was a national leader in research and civic engagement. Kibele's designs had established an architectural association between the college and the city's leading manufacturers and businessmen. Ball State leaders also emulated the works of the country's leading philanthropists, architects, and education institutions, making visible and tactile the alliance among business, civic, and education leaders.

Institutional Growth

After a decade as a public institution, BTC had solidified its position as a branch campus of ISNS, but Muncie boosters and politicos were determined it would be more than that. Lemuel Pittenger was a lawmaker and educator who held a long affiliation with the Ball family, playing an important legislative role in the development of the BTC campus. Pittenger followed Charles McGonagle's legacy when he became the Muncie state representative in the early 1920s and served as chair of the Ways and Means Committee for the Indiana State House, handling the state budget in the lower chamber. He helped BTC achieve independence from ISNS by developing separate budget appropriations for the Muncie institution, effectively ending Terre Haute's control over the junior campus.[70] When the president of BTC died suddenly in 1927, students led a successful campaign to have Pittenger named his successor.[71] With the Ball brothers' blessing, Pittenger served as president for fifteen years, continuing as an ally to the family.[72]

By 1925, enrollment at the college had nearly reached a thousand students, only sixty of whom could live on campus in the lone, wood-framed

Figure 6. Aerial view of the Ball Teachers College campus, ca. 1929. Several buildings begin to give form to the campus quadrangle. Aside from a handful of homes located north of the university, acres of open land extend into the distance. Ball State University Archives and Special Collections.

Forest Hall for women.[73] The Ball family addressed the problem, donating $300,000 for construction of a women's dormitory in honor of their late sister.[74] Lucina Hall was a Tudor Gothic brick-and-limestone structure designed by Indianapolis architect George Schreiber. Along with the administration building, the new dormitory served as the southern edge of the quadrangle. Housing over eighty students, it doubled the capacity of the college to house women students on campus. The measure, of course, expanded the reach of Grace DeHority and other college administrators to control the social lives of female students (Figure 6).[75]

In the final phase of building in the 1920s, the college abandoned the formula of private capital and public operational expenses in favor of wholly public expenditures, creating a new laboratory school directed by the college and the Muncie school district. BTC administrators lobbied the state for appropriations for the school, which would provide progressive education for Muncie students from kindergarten through senior high school. It also gave future teachers opportunities for the practice teaching required in the college curriculum. BTC leaders arranged with Muncie school officials to close a nearby grade school and have the new Burris School serve the population of northwestern Muncie, beginning in 1929.[76] The lab school, which drew on the ideas of education reformer John Dewey, was located on University Avenue, just across from Lucina Hall at the edge of BTC's campus. The school soon earned a reputation as the city's best.

College officials battled charges that Burris served only the wealthy business class. The new construction of the school, its excellent reputation, and the geographic district boundaries meant that professional-class families locating in northwestern Muncie could provide their children the city's best education on the public dime, right in the neighborhood where their business colleagues lived.[77] The school's first principal noted the Burris School also aided a group of poor rural families living in "Pigeon Roost," an undeveloped area beyond the college, and characterized the sons and daughters of Muncie's professional class as "average" and "typical" students; and, moreover, all would benefit from his strict discipline.[78]

The Gravity of Capital

When Burris attracted upper-middle-class families to the district, they wanted homes and neighborhoods as good or better than the ones they had left. Many came from the East End, the desirable enclave near the city's downtown that business elites had established before the turn of the century. The community was not so deeply rooted, however, that it could not be transplanted according to the Ball family's designs. The Lynds commented on the shifting geography of real estate in their 1937 follow-up study of Muncie, *Middletown in Transition*, asserting that the Ball family had "moved the residential heart of the city."[79] Where the elite section had been on the city's east side, later, "the aristocratic old East End, the fine residential section in the pre-motor period when it was an asset to live 'close in' and even in the early 1920s, runs a lame second to the two new [Ball] subdivisions in the West End, to which ambitious matrons of the city are removing their families." The Lynds, who had been friendly with the Balls during their stay in Muncie, connected the growth of the new subdivisions to the family's involvement with BTC and the college's transformation "into a cluster of beautiful buildings" as well as "the new million-and-a-half-dollar hospital, an outright gift to the city by the [Ball] family."[80]

Figure 7. E. A. Ball House, Westwood. A second-generation Ball family member developed two exclusive subdivisions at the edge of Ball Teachers College. His own home was among the finest and helped draw the Muncie business class to live in the northwestern area of the city rather than in the East End, which had been the traditional businessmen's enclave. Ball State University Archives and Special Collections.

The two new West End subdivisions were the work of Edmund Arthur Ball, Frank Ball's son. He bought a large tract of agricultural land north of the college campus in 1923.[81] Ball and a partner, Charles V. Bender, platted out a residential subdivision called Westwood. Ball built his own home there, where he lived with his wife and two young daughters. The subdivision followed enduring principles of suburban exclusion. Restrictive covenants on the property deeds explicitly forbade ownership or residence by minorities except as domestic servants, reserving Westwood for "the pure white race."[82] They also governed nearly every aspect of home building in the subdivision in ways that raised barriers to all members of the working class, including a minimum lot size of 7,500 square feet; property setbacks of 7 feet from each lot line and farther from the front line; and required review of architectural plans for any proposed structures.[83] Industrial workers would be hard pressed to buy the homes. Even apartment builders would be foiled (Figure 7).

The real-estate company drew upon the cachet of BTC in Westwood advertising. Education stood in as a class signifier, and the college's investments in planning and design provided value to the surrounding area.[84] Prospective buyers might consider college students unruly or politically charged and therefore undesirable neighbors. The college had social control over students in the dormitories, and the system of house inspections eliminated this threat from the local properties.[85] Following his success with Westwood, Ball established another subdivision, Westwood Park, right next door in 1939, with the same exclusionary laws.[86]

Muncie had a race problem that was especially pronounced in the 1920s. The Ku Klux Klan experienced a resurgence after World War I that corresponded to a flood of international immigration and increasing mobility for African Americans. Klan politics drew on a mix of racism, xenophobia, right-wing populism, and working-class insecurity amid dramatic social and economic change. The Klan was particularly prominent in Indiana, menacing black families in the region and influencing Muncie politics.[87] In one instance, white rioters assembled to intimidate a black Muncie mortician who was caring for the bodies of two lynching victims from nearby Marion. The city's black population and a handful of police officers prevented violence at the mortuary, but the Klan maintained significant power in the city in the 1920s.[88]

Muncie's Jewish population suffered at the same time. Affluent Jewish residents were shut out of home ownership in the city's elite neighborhoods, and their children battled anti-Semitism in the schoolyard.[89] Sherman Zeigler, a scrap dealer, grew up in Normal City and attended Burris, the campus laboratory school. As a child, he suffered harassment from Protestant children. In his teens, one of the city newspapers denied him a paper route "because they didn't want any Jews working on their paper," prompting Jewish retailers to withhold advertising in response. As an adult, restrictive covenants kept Zeigler out of a northwestern Muncie development immediately north of Westwood.[90]

Municipal zoning reinforced the privately created system of exclusion and institutionalized white supremacy on the landscape.[91] Zoning emerged as a means of protecting property values from the urban consequences of mass industrialization. It arose along with the city planning profession in the 1920s. The 1926 Supreme Court decision *Euclid v. Ambler* affirmed the rights of municipal governments to limit industrial development by real estate companies and generally ratified zoning as a form of the police power of the state—in this case, as a means of protecting high-class residential areas from the chemical and noise pollution of industry.[92] At the turn of the century, designers like Frederick Law Olmsted and his sons worked with cities to create rules that would support the bourgeois vision of suburban community design. Later, private real-estate investors such as J. C. Nichols in Kansas City and local entrepreneurs like Edmund A. Ball led the way, working hand in glove with municipal authorities to formalize such practices.[93]

Muncie's newly formed City Plan Commission administered a master plan that had divided the city into land-use districts, separating industry from business from residential areas. The town's code set its own minimum densities and lot sizes for some districts, reinforcing the intentions of the developers and serving as an economic barrier to keep minority and lower-middle-class aspirants from relocating to wealthy neighborhoods.[94] The resulting segregation along racial, class, and ethnic lines translated to social segregation. Muncie was renowned for high participation in community clubs, recreational organizations, and religious congregations, but the spatial concentration by class and race in a handful of more exclusive clubs reduced possibilities for class mixing and community influence by the industrial working class.[95] Higher education was becoming a means of social mobility, but the spatial logic of colleges and universities undermined that equalizing potential.

Founding a Hospital

Universities turned to medicine in the twentieth century, and the Balls followed the trend, creating a hospital to pair with the college. The 1910 publication of Abraham Flexner's *Medical Education in America and Canada* prompted educational reforms that would make medical training less plentiful and more exclusionary, but would also make education and treatment more scientifically based, advancing the transition of medicine from trade to profession and demanding facilities with up-to-date tools.[96] Lucius Ball, the eldest of the five Ball brothers, was a physician who joined the family business as the company doctor. He had helped found the Muncie Home Hospital, a modest, community-run institution, in 1905. Later, he and his brother Edmund B. Ball promoted the idea of a new, more modern facility rather than an expansion of the aging Muncie Home Hospital.[97]

Members of the Ball family provided the capital to create the hospital as part of an agreement that a government unit would take over and operate it once it was built. Edmund B. Ball negotiated with members of the state assembly to authorize the project. He died in 1925, but his will established a charitable foundation—now the Ball Brothers Foundation—to continue his philanthropic activities in Muncie, chief among them funding for the coming hospital. His surviving brothers, along with other medically minded civic leaders, formed an organization to create the hospital he had envisioned, the Ball Memorial Hospital Association.[98]

Frank C. Ball, one of the directors of the association, convinced the board to locate the hospital adjacent to the BTC, arguing that each institution would benefit from proximity to the other.[99] The college was not using the land south and west of the college quadrangle because the terms of the land gift to the state restricted it for educational purposes. The Ball hospital could use these dozens of undeveloped acres, however, because it would have a nurses' training program.[100] The college and hospital were like divisions of the same corporation, both under the direction of the Balls.[101]

Ball Memorial Hospital opened in August 1929 and intensified the economic transformation of northwestern Muncie. Cuno Kibele designed the buildings. In keeping with his preferred idiom, Kibele designed the façade in the Tudor Gothic style, symbolically lending the new institution maturity and authority, while it contributed to the modernization of health care, higher education, and the economy in Muncie. After funding the hospital's creation, the Balls provided funds for a women's dormitory for nurses in training—Maria Bingham Hall, built in 1930 and named after their mother. In sum, the complex cost $2 million to build, paid for by the foundation and the manufacturing company.[102] The hospital employed numerous physicians and trained scores of nurses annually in the course of its operations, concentrating knowledge and capital in northwestern Muncie when the staff helped populate the city's residential subdivisions around the campus.[103] The developments were mutually reinforcing, providing comfortable residential opportunities to a growing professional class in a move that put the housing market in concert with the job market (Figure 8).

Muncie in Transition

The opening of the hospital came at the end of more than a decade of dramatic economic growth and development. The Great Depression shifted the politics of Muncie and higher education, but did not divert the Balls from the overall strategy they had developed over their several decades in the city. The economic collapse provided opportunities for the Balls. They took over the main downtown department store and rescued three of the

Figure 8. Ball Memorial Hospital. The hospital brought modern health care to Muncie and symbolized the aesthetic, political, and economic association among the city, college, and Ball family. Ball State University Archives and Special Collections.

city's five banks from failure.[104] Like the wealthy Henry Potter in Frank Capra's film *It's a Wonderful Life*, the Balls had the means to save enterprises destabilized by panic or suffering from insolvency and illiquidity. When everyone else panicked, the Balls did not.[105] In numerous sectors— retailing, finance, and agriculture, as well as real estate and transportation— the Ball family scooped up enterprises overextended with debt or suffering from the economic downturn of the 1930s and accelerated the corporate consolidation of small-town life transforming the nation. The Lynds lauded the Ball brothers' "hard-headed *ethos* of Protestant capitalism," which lifted them to a status in the city "amount[ing] to a reigning royal family."[106]

The Balls and BTC's President Pittenger incorporated New Deal aid into their support plans for the institution. They jointly funded cultural development with an arts building that included studio instruction and a gallery that housed part of the Balls' art collection. Located on the BTC quadrangle, the Arts Building helped make the northwestern sector the cultural capital

of the city and the region in addition to the economic engine of Muncie. In
Middletown in Transition, the Lynds illustrated how dominant the Balls had
become by quoting a Muncie man speaking for the population dependent
on the Ball family:

> If I'm out of work I go to the Ball plant; if I need money I go to the
> Ball bank, and if they don't like me I don't get it; my children go to the Ball
> college; when I get sick I go to the Ball hospital; I buy a building lot or
> house in a Ball subdivision; my wife goes downtown to buy clothes at
> the Ball department store; if my dog stays away he is put in the Ball
> pound; I buy Ball milk; I drink Ball beer, vote for Ball political parties,
> and get help from Ball charities; my boy goes to the Ball Y.M.C.A. and
> my girl to their Y.W.C.A.; I listen to the word of God in Ball-subsidized
> churches; if I'm a Mason I go to the Ball Masonic Temple; I read the
> news from the Ball morning newspaper; and, if I am rich enough, I travel
> via the Ball airport.[107]

The account echoes the aggrieved workers of the company town of Pullman,
Illinois, two generations earlier, who claimed George Pullman's control over
their lives was so exploitative and total they predicted "when we die, we shall
go to Pullman hell."[108]

In May 1937, *Life* ran a photo essay by Margaret Bourke-White to coincide with the publication of *Middletown in Transition*. Her work depicting
Depression-era poverty had established Bourke-White as a central photographic interpreter of the American experience. Her photo essay emphasized
Muncie's class divide by running striking images of the poverty of south-
side workers opposite photos of an opulent Ball mansion at Minnetrista. The
grim, deteriorating peeled-away stucco and bare lath on worker housing "far
across town from the college" emphasized the city's geographic disparities.[109]
Readers saw the manicured lawns of BTC and brick-and-stone administration and teaching buildings in northwestern Muncie just a stone's throw from
Minnetrista. The *Life* feature proved exceedingly popular. Together, the photo
essay and the two *Middletown* books created Muncie's image as Everytown,
U.S.A. (Figures 9 and 10).

In September of the same year, the Muncie Chamber of Commerce in-
stalled a sculpture on the college grounds to honor the Balls. The statue,
Beneficence, by Daniel Chester French, conspicuously recognized the family's
philanthropy and tied it to their foremost community endeavors. In French,

Figures 9 and 10. Muncie, Indiana. *Life* published a photo essay by Margaret Bourke-White in 1937 to coincide with the publication of *Middletown in Transition*. Bourke-White captured the economic disparities in the city; her depictions of opulence, greenery, and open space in northwestern Muncie (*above*) were starkly contrasted with the crowding and deterioration of working-class southern Muncie (*below*). Margaret Bourke-White/Getty Images.

Figure 11. *Beneficence.* Business leaders in Muncie commissioned a sculpture by Daniel Chester French to symbolize the relationship among the Ball family, the college, and the city. The sculpture, at the southern edge of campus, faces the city of Muncie. Ball State University Archives and Special Collections.

Muncie business leaders selected an artist whose work embodied the grandest of civic and national statements. Responsible for *The Republic*, the main sculpture at the Chicago Columbian Exposition, and the seated Lincoln sculpture in the Lincoln Memorial, French had been among the foremost American sculptors for nearly half a century.[110]

Beneficence affirmed the spatial relationship between the Balls and the northwestern quadrant of the city. The college placed the bronze statue on the southern edge of the original Ball State quadrangle, positioned within a semicircle of five Corinthian columns representing the five Ball brothers. Facing out from campus, the winged woman reached out to Normal City and the rest of Muncie in welcome. She held the gift of education in one hand. Located at the edge of the Ball State grounds, the statue symbolized the prodigious philanthropy the family had offered the city and made clear the connection between campus and community in Muncie, with the Ball family the beating heart of every major Muncie institution—public, private, educational, and commercial (Figure 11).

The interdependence between the Ball family and the city's elite institutions was entrenched as a major feature of civic life and had begun with the teachers college as the key catalyst. The four bodies—the Ball family, the city itself, the Ball Memorial Hospital, and Ball Teachers College—seemed to be joined as they looked to rise from the Great Depression. The future of the college, the hospital, and the city were secure with the continued support of the Ball family, while the Balls' work and Muncie life were enhanced by the growing influence of the hospital and the college that had started the whole transformation. The Ball family had come to Muncie for natural gas, and they returned some of the wealth gained from manufacturing glass jars to the city that helped enrich them. They had molded Muncie through their support of the college and the hospital and through real estate development. Indiana governor Clifford Townsend, attending the dedication of *Beneficence*, claimed, "No Hoosier thinks of Muncie without thinking of the Ball family and its influence in the community. Their philanthropy has been both intelligent and generous."[111] One worker, quoted in *Middletown in Transition*, sarcastically affirmed the Balls' power, noting that they were such an exceptional group of businessmen they were "about the only people I know of who have managed to augment their fortune through the art of philanthropy."[112]

The Balls had turned Muncie from a small industrial town into a small, but real urban center. At the dedication for *Beneficence*, Glenn Frank, the former president of the University of Wisconsin, enthused, "Through hospitals, they have ministered to the body, through schools, to the mind, through religious agencies, to the spirit, and through the arts, to the senses. And, in all this, they have given of themselves as well as of their means."[113] Just as important, Muncie elites compounded that capital investment with real estate developments that redirected patterns of urban growth and catalyzed a new metropolitan economy for the city. In that sense, the Balls did not dominate Muncie, but their influence was essential. Through charitable and business decisions over a half-century, the Balls, the McGonagles, the Kitselmans, the Pittengers, and other leaders in the region led the Progressive reordering of urban America that was under way in cities large and small. Higher education led the entire process. Muncie was more than Everytown in the minds of *Life* editors and the Lynds' readers. It was Everytown in the sense that cities around the country would display similar patterns of real-estate transformation, beginning with a college.

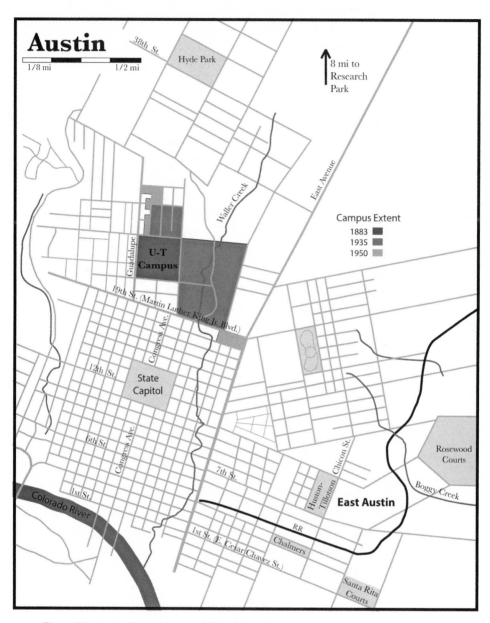

Figure 12. Austin, Texas. Map created by the author.

2 | The City Limits

The evening of May 27, 1923, an oil driller's bit passed the depth of three thousand feet after nearly two years of drilling into arid West Texas land near Odessa. Gas bubbled up into the Santa Rita well, named for the patron saint of impossible causes, and the drillers stopped their rig, realizing they had found oil where investors had been searching since 1919. The drillers hurried to lease more lands nearby before the news broke. The next morning, crude oil erupted from the well and sprayed over the top of the derrick: the drillers' bet paid off. Oil honeycombed the land, and the strike instantly made the acreage, which belonged to the University of Texas (UT), worth hundreds, even thousands of times more than when the school leased it as ranching land.[1]

Federal policy and new technology made crude oil an essential commodity in the American economy. Transportation policy shifted early in the twentieth century from emphasizing rail to automobility. Gasoline-powered internal combustion engines moved goods and people from farm to market, from city to city, and from producer to port. American oil consumption increased steadily throughout most of the twentieth century, and the University of Texas sat on a large pile of royalties that grew larger every year.[2]

That wealth held the potential to lift the University of Texas, and the city of Austin with it, to a new elite rank. However, its Southern, segregationist practices and its national aspirations were in conflict. In the midcentury decades, the university's northern peers increasingly looked askance at Jim Crow segregation, and national policy chipped away at it until, by the mid-1950s, explicit segregation was no longer viable policy for either a great university or a major city.

Discussions of segregation and the influence of the civil rights movement on higher education often center on legal battles and flash points like the one that erupted over James Meredith's enrollment at the University of Mississippi in 1962: famous clashes over enrollment decided in favor of integration.[3] George Wallace's 1963 symbolic blockade of the door of the University of Alabama promised "segregation now, segregation tomorrow, segregation forever" and propelled him to national prominence as a part of the "massive resistance" movement.

Urban development, however, was also a key mechanism of racial segregation—a "passive resistance" counterpart. Robust suburbs at the metropolitan periphery of cities like Atlanta and Detroit were often populated by and usually limited to white, middle-class professionals.[4] Universities helped drive this suburban growth at midcentury. On the outskirts of Chicago, the University of Chicago helped build and manage a national research laboratory in DuPage County after World War II that led to growth in the nearby suburbs of Naperville and Downers Grove. Stanford University in Palo Alto, California, created a research park that was central to the development of Silicon Valley far outside the largest Bay Area cities of San Francisco and Oakland.[5] The state of New York incorporated the University of Buffalo into its state higher-education system and created a new, second campus in suburban Amherst, exacerbating urban disinvestment and peripheral expansion in Buffalo. In all of these places, suburban growth exacerbated racial segregation, and universities were part and parcel to suburban growth. In Austin, understanding the the relationship among segregation, metropolitan growth, and higher education is essential to understanding the development of the city.

The University of Texas helped pave the way in the 1930s and 1940s to a new kind of sprawling, segregated metropolis, just at the moment Austin was becoming a major American city. In this era, the university drew on federal resources to promote growth in Austin, reinforced Jim Crow in central Austin before the antisegregation *Sweatt* and *Brown* cases, and, fueled by oil, helped drive a less explicit metropolitan segregation afterward. Suburbanization, highway building, and metropolitan expansion after World War II provided opportunities to sidestep political opprobrium and seemed to leave behind the legacy of Jim Crow, especially after a losing court battle over segregation. Postwar metropolitan growth allowed UT leaders to partner with Austin's civic elite and develop sprawling greenfield and automobile-oriented sites that were functionally segregated by race while they advanced a race-neutral ideology of scientific discovery, regional economic growth, and consumer choice in the national interest. University president Theophilus Painter, politicians James "Buck" Buchanan and Lyndon Johnson, mayor Tom Miller, publisher Charles Marsh, and chamber of commerce head Walter Long—all worked together to draw federal funds, to bring economic growth to Austin, and to make it one of the boom cities of the twentieth century. Many large cities during the century lost population, tax base, and civic optimism as they suffered from urban crisis. Austin was one of the winners, with a growing population and a tech economy that made it a model for other cities at the end of the century.

The University Landscape

The University of Texas opened in 1883 after the state's constitution authorized the creation of a "university of the first class."[6] The impoverished state could not provide the resources necessary to realize this ambition, and the modest income from the West Texas ranch lands limited the university's growth. Dirt paths crisscrossed campus as students wore down the grass and their trails became permanent, dusty walks. At the turn of the century, a Victorian-Gothic structure, built wing by wing in the 1880s and 1890s, was the university's signature building, but after just a few decades, it seemed antiquated and unfashionable.[7] The need for classroom space was so dire that a set of rickety wooden structures built during World War I remained for more than a decade, stretching in lines across the campus.[8] Students reviled them as "the shacks," and campus wags joked that the university featured "shackeresque" architecture. A faculty member called them "hideous and uncomfortable, the shame of Texas."[9] The university sought to use oil revenues in the 1920s to begin expanding, bypassing a constitutionally created endowment fund. The state attorney general challenged this action, prompting the state supreme court to acknowledge that "a shackless campus is much to be desired," even though it ruled in favor of the attorney general (Figure 13).[10]

In 1928 the university constructed a new sculptural gateway on the campus as a monument to the Southern Lost Cause. Statues of George Washington, Jefferson Davis, Woodrow Wilson, Robert E. Lee, James Hogg, John Reagan, and Albert Sidney Johnston lined the main campus walkway from the south. A dispute that began in 1919 had led to their erection, as two regents, George Brackenridge and George Littlefield, battled for control of the campus location and its appearance.[11] Brackenridge was a northerner, a Republican, and a longtime UT Regent. He was a banker who had made a

Figure 13. "The Shacks" in Austin. The University of Texas suffered from limited state funding from the time of its creation, relying on the leasing proceeds of ranch lands in West Texas. These buildings were constructed for temporary purposes in World War I but continued to be used for more than a decade. Austin wags dubbed the buildings "the Shacks." The discovery of oil on the ranch lands gave the university the resources to remake its campus despite the economic crisis of the Great Depression. UT Texas Student Publications, Prints and Photographs Collection, di_06442, Dolph Briscoe Center for American History, University of Texas at Austin.

fortune evading the Confederate blockade on cotton exports during the Civil War.[12] He donated land along the Colorado River to accommodate a new, larger campus for the university, but Littlefield, a staunch segregationist, Confederate veteran, and native Texan, opposed the move. Littlefield had fought and been wounded in the Civil War and was saved by his slave. After the war, Littlefield moved to Austin along with his wife, Alice, and Nathan Stokes, the slave who remained as a servant for more than fifty years.[13] The Northern–Southern dynamic of the campus debate set the tone for decades of imagining the future of the UT campus.

George Littlefield donated $250,000 for a fountain and the sculptures that would embellish the approach from the state capitol, symbolize the university's commitment to the Lost Cause, and keep the main campus in central Austin. Littlefield and Brackenridge both died in 1920, and Texas politicians battled over the plan to relocate the campus to the banks of the Colorado. With the key patron for relocation dead, city business interests rallied to keep the university downtown. The campus remained centered on the original forty acres, just a few blocks north of the state capitol, while the university used the Brackenridge tract as a golf course it leased to the city of Austin until the 1970s.[14]

The sculpture commission conformed to a broader agenda within Texas to emphasize a Confederate identity for the state after Reconstruction.[15] Littlefield had contracted with Pompeo Coppini, an Italian sculptor based in San Antonio. Coppini provided the design, even though his vision did not entirely conform to his patron's. The sculptor hoped to show how World War I unified the national rift of the Civil War, while Littlefield sought images of Southern heroes.[16] The Southern military and political heroes depicted in the statues (as well as Woodrow Wilson, a Southern segregationist) made a clear statement, visually and symbolically asserting white supremacy to the next generation of Texas leaders. Thus, the Confederate veteran's gift affirmed Texas as a self-consciously Southern state and implicated the university as a fundamental part of this racially segregated ideological project. Jim Crow, however, would not be limited to symbolic statements, either on campus or in the city of Austin (Figures 14 and 15).

Segregation in Austin

Austin in the 1920s was a small capital city perched on the verge of tremendous growth. It was bigger than Muncie, Indiana, but smaller than El Paso and Fort Worth, Texas cities that were double and triple Austin's population, respectively.[17] Railroads, including the International–Great Northern and the Southern Pacific railways, passed by lumberyards and warehouses along Third and Fourth Streets and crossed the Colorado River west of the Congress Street Bridge. These rail networks connected Austin producers and merchants to regional and national markets for agricultural goods such as animal hides and pecans.[18] The national highway system touched urban Austin in name but hardly connected points within the city, let alone across the state. State institutions besides the university provided employment stability, including the school for the blind in the city proper and military camps in the region. Most of the business economy in Texas, the nation's fifth most

Figure 14. Littlefield Fountain. Pompeo Coppini sculpted Littlefield Fountain as a gateway from downtown Austin and the state capital to the campus. It was a symbolic statement depicting Columbia aboard a ship representing the American project. Along with a series of statues of Southern and Confederate heroes, the fountain represented the resolution of sectional difficulties but affirmed the university's commitment to white supremacy. Flickr https://www.flickr.com/photos/kewing/8702417281/sizes/l.

Figure 15. Jefferson Davis statue. The president of the Confederacy, Jefferson Davis, was one of the Southern heroes depicted in statues at the campus gateway. Larry Murphy, UT News and Information Bureau, Prints and Photographs Collection, di_02469, Dolph Briscoe Center for American History, University of Texas at Austin.

populous state, flowed elsewhere, however. Oil money funneled through Houston and banking through Dallas; Galveston had long served as the state's chief port. As the Texas capital, Austin's top commodity was politics. Like the state's position in the region, it served as both a geographically central point and a metaphorical one where east Texans of the Old South mindset brokered compromises with politicians from the urban centers, the ranching hill country, and the agricultural panhandle.[19]

Census Day 1930 documented the segregation of the era. Two white Austin census takers, Bessie Carpenter and Flossie Pluenneke, traveled to different parts of the city and wrote down demographic data for Austin residents. Carpenter was the wife of an auto salesman and mother of two children, an eleven-year-old boy and eight-year-old girl; they lived in Nowlin Heights, a comfortable subdivision of white residents near the university campus, and owned a home worth $5,000, which put it among the top third of Austin homes.[20] Over the first two weeks in April, Carpenter started going door to door, taking the census from the southeastern corner of campus, snaking through a white working-class neighborhood that shifted to white collar farther north. Walking the surrounding blocks on the eastern and northern edges of campus, she knocked on doors of homes almost exclusively filled with white residents. Along the way, she moved through just one black neighborhood centered on Swisher Street. It was one of the few remaining clusters of African Americans outside East Austin that had once been dominant areas of black life.[21] Carpenter also surveyed a handful of isolated Hispanic households in the course of her work. Most rented modest apartments, while a handful of the black Austinites on Swisher and Cole Streets owned their homes. Though her house was in the top third in Austin, it was more expensive than all but two Mexican American–owned homes in the city, and fewer than thirty African American families owned houses more valuable than her comfortable but by no means ostentatious house.[22] The fruits of a growing economy were out of the reach for almost all of the city's black and Hispanic population.

Flossie Pluenneke, who surveyed East Austin, rented her home in Hyde Park, an exclusive development far north of the UT campus.[23] She and her husband, a physician, had a fourteen-year-old daughter. Platted in the 1890s, Hyde Park had been a suburban neighborhood with Victorian and Craftsman homes at the very outskirts of Austin, but by 1930, it was well within the city limits. Most residents were white-collar professionals—the two neighbors across the street were a lawyer and a pharmacist—and of its 1,500 residents, the only one who was not white was a live-in domestic worker, Rose Gooden, a black cook who worked for a prosperous lawyer.

Pluenneke's daily path illustrated the city's racial stratification. She began her two-week walk on the 1800 block of East Avenue, the large north–south street that was one of the city's transportation arteries and the boundary between East Austin and downtown. The first block of East Avenue was all white—clerks and grocers and office printers—except for one black family. A block south, every house on both sides of East Avenue was occupied by African Americans who worked in the service class. As she moved farther into East Austin, the most heavily segregated of the city's African American neighborhoods, her path snaked around the city's black schools and churches and a handful of Hispanic neighborhoods in East Austin, a neighborhood of cottages and small bungalows. Pluenneke tallied black income and jobs in Austin's Jim Crow society that were lower than whites' and reflected constrained job opportunities. Indeed, more than 85 percent of working black women held jobs as maids, cooks, servants, or laundresses for white families or white institutions.[24] Black men hardly fared better: two thirds of the black workforce in Austin were either laborers, porters, servants, cooks, waiters, chauffeurs, or launderers.[25] In a city with two African American colleges in East Austin, even those with higher education had low-prestige jobs. Black home values were also lower than those of white-owned homes, thwarting a key means of accumulating wealth and concentrating that disadvantage in black neighborhoods. The census revealed the spatial aspects of racial segregation as well as its social and economic implications.

Residential racial segregation was part and parcel of the project of urban development in Austin. In the 1920s, it was a city in transition. Civic leaders pursued a Progressive-type agenda of good government and urban order, including adoption of a council-manager form of government in 1924, establishment of the Austin City Plan Commission in 1926, and a civic improvements campaign called "Onward Austin" that drew on emerging ideas about economic development and urban planning practice. The civic agenda included the preservation of segregation but advanced in fits and starts. The Austin Chamber of Commerce helped promote passage of the Love Bill, which enabled Texas cities to pass racial segregation ordinances.[26] Throughout the 1920s, Southern cities including Dallas and New Orleans established such measures. When they failed legal challenges, Southern city leaders needed to find new methods of segregating.[27]

Austin turned to city planning to institutionalize separation of the races. In 1927, the city plan commission invited Will Hogg, chairman of Houston's plan commission, to discuss a plan for Austin. Hogg had gone on record with the Houston commission: "Negroes are a necessary and useful element of the population and suitable areas with proper living and recreation facilities should be set aside for them. Because of long established racial prejudices, it is best for both races that living areas be segregated."[28] Yet explicit racial zoning had been deemed unconstitutional, and so it would not be among Austin's instruments of urban development.

That same year, the plan commission hired Koch and Fowler, a Dallas engineering firm, to create Austin's first master plan.[29] Traffic and transportation, public services, land use—for the first time, all of these would be considered in concert, and the planners would present a unified vision for the city's future. The university contributed its expertise to the endeavor through an alumnus, Hugo Kuehne, who served as a local representative for the plan and later helped create the UT architecture program.[30]

Koch and Fowler's 1928 plan proposed a service district in East Austin where the city would locate public facilities for African American residents. The report recommended that "the nearest approach to the solution of the race segregation problem will be the recommendation of this district as a negro district; and that all the facilities and conveniences be provided the negroes in this district, as an incentive to draw the negro population to this area."[31] In the 1910s, white residents of West Austin had fought a bitter battle against an African American school there, arguing that black residents would follow black schools.[32] Koch and Fowler turned that logic around in their 1928 plan, which went public as a special insert in the city's leading newspapers in February.[33] The press discussed Austin's "racial segregation problem"—not the inherent unfairness of it or its cost to society, but the barriers to effective segregation. Even though the city's Hispanic population, at greater than five thousand, was more than half the size of black Austin, far less anxiety attended segregation of the city's Hispanic population. Largely Mexican American, they lived in two neighborhoods, one at the foot of Congress Avenue near the Colorado River, and one in the southern part of East Austin. There was no planning effort to concentrate the city's Hispanics in either of the two districts. The color line was drawn more boldly between black and white than it was between brown and white.[34]

Koch and Fowler's report planned a segregated city that would at least double its size, reaching three to five miles outside of the boundaries in 1928.

Civic leaders accepted the plan and set an election for city bond issues worth $425 million in the spring of 1928 to fund the infrastructure improvements it called for, including road paving, more and better school buildings, and parks and leisure spaces. The business community was squarely behind the "Onward Austin" campaign that would guide development for several decades.

Everett Givens saw the bond election as an opportunity. Givens was a dentist and business leader, one of only seven black medical professionals in the city.[35] He was a native Austinite but had gone to Howard University for his dental training, returning to Austin to practice.[36] "Insofar as you could say that [black] Austin had a political boss when I came here . . . it was Dr. Everett Givens," a political rival later remembered.[37] A longtime Austinite called Givens "a bronze mayor."[38] Givens was part of a generation of black leaders who sought equalization long before integration rose to the fore of the civil rights movement.[39] He had inherited the mantle of black leadership from an earlier generation; the philosophy of Booker T. Washington had guided those predecessors, who advocated self-improvement rather than radical social change.[40] While Givens made greater demands on Austin's leaders, he did not question the fundamental logic of segregation.

Bond elections empowered black voters, and this was a rare moment to exercise their political clout. Whites largely excluded African Americans from Democratic primaries, which were the de facto general elections in the one-party South.[41] They could intimidate voters or exclude black citizens from being members of a private political organization. Bond issues, however, were general-election votes ostensibly guaranteed to majority-aged citizens. Poll taxes, however, constrained the franchise to more affluent and business-friendly parts of the black electorate. Passage of a bond required a supermajority, a two-thirds "yes" vote. These elections were often closely divided, making African Americans—nearly 20 percent of the city's population—a key swing constituency. A bond election had failed in 1926 without black support, and the city's boosters would not let that happen again. They also consulted retired postal clerk Dudley Woodard about the black community's likely response to the bond issue. Woodard estimated that 95 percent of black voters would go along with the property-tax increase if they received infrastructure improvements from the program.[42] East Austin desperately needed road improvements. Only three streets east of East Avenue were paved, and the rest were packed dirt and gravel. East Avenue itself, the main thoroughfare on the eastern side of the city, was hardly paved and had no paving at all north of 19th Street.[43] Boggy Creek, a small tributary to the Colorado River, ran across roads and through backyards to make a swampy mess of impassable streets and marshy lots.[44]

Everett Givens also prodded city leaders to devote some of the bond-funded infrastructure to East Austin, to which they agreed. An activist recalled some decades later that Givens "got where he could get. . . . He believed in not stirring up things. Keeping people quiet. 'Let me take care of it.'"[45] Addressing a crowd of his friends and neighbors at a public outreach meeting in April 1928, Givens said, "We believe in the bonds, and all that we ask is that we get a dollar's worth of value for every dollar spent."[46] Woodard also held promotional events for the bond election, convincing black voters to approve the measure.[47] The bond program particularly appealed to the property-owning class of Austin African Americans who could pay the poll tax: the improvements would make their land more valuable.[48] Austin's African American wards supported the bonds overwhelmingly, which passed strongly all across the city.[49]

The dual-track infrastructure of Austin would not have been possible without capital from financial markets drawing investment from outside Texas. The city marketed the bonds in New York, and notices ran in the financial papers.[50] Thus, the financialization of public infrastructure and the implementation of an openly segregationist plan spread north. Violence in the form of lynchings, house bombings, and race riots were clear and localized ways that whites maintained the color line in communities.[51] Financial instruments disguised culpability for the color line. Government bonds spread responsibility for Jim Crow—and profit from it—to investors around the country.

By 1929, Austin had millions to spend, and the infrastructure plan began to work. The black community got its paved roads in East Austin, a public library branch, and a public school.[52] The city's black elites already lived in East Austin, and with each passing year after 1928, more African Americans moved to East Austin from their enduring neighborhoods of Wheatsville northwest of the UT campus, Clarksville west of downtown, and South Congress across the river. Ada Simonds, whose family moved from Clarksville to East Austin early in the century, remembered the segregation worked "because people are going to go live where the facilities are. The family needs recreational resources, the family needs educational resources, they need a place for a church. . . . You'd be closer to the church. You'd be closer to this and to that and to the other."[53] The racial geography became even more segregated under the Koch and Fowler plan, making the city's

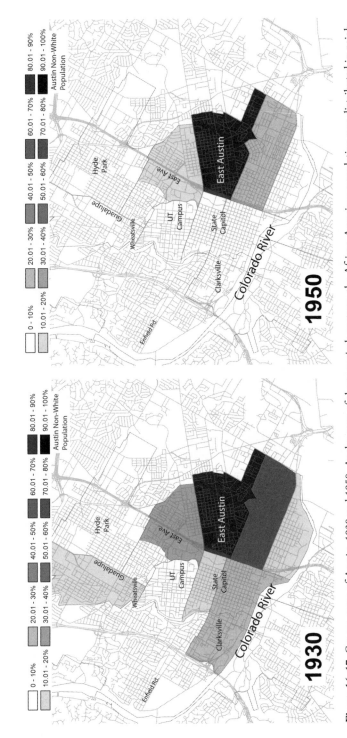

Figure 16, 17. Census maps of Austin, 1930 and 1950. At the turn of the twentieth century, the African American population was distributed in neighborhoods throughout Austin, including Wheatsville and Clarksville. A city plan in 1928 and infrastructure program sought to segregate African Americans in East Austin, draining them from the mix of traditional neighborhoods throughout Austin. Maps created by the author. Census data from University of Minnesota Population Studies Center, www.nhgis.org.

white sections whiter and black neighborhoods blacker.[54] Segregationist city planning first redrew the color line on city maps, then slowly on the city landscape, house by house and block by block (Figures 16 and 17).

Rivers of Oil

Back on campus in 1930, the university was ready to build. Texas A&M and the University of Texas had waged an institutional feud from 1923 to 1930 over royalty payments for the oil. The state legislature required drillers to pay one-eighth the value of the oil to the university, to be deposited in a fund for investing in the university's buildings and grounds. Texas A&M had appealed for a portion of the oil proceeds because they were technically a branch institution of the University of Texas.[55] After much negotiation, in January 1930, the UT Regents settled the dispute with the directors of A&M, agreeing to give A&M one-third of the royalties and freeing the funds from litigation and negotiation. The Texas state legislature institutionalized this agreement in 1931.[56]

William Battle knew the value of architectural symbols and concrete buildings. He had played politics effectively when he served as an acting UT president from 1914 to 1916, overseeing the creation of UT's architecture building, Sutton Hall, designed by Beaux-Arts architect Cass Gilbert. Battle was a professor of Greek and Latin, was familiar with classical forms, and was a key go-between to the city's business class through the Town and Gown social club, a collection of the city's leading citizens. He was one of ten UT presidents and numerous university officers who were members of Town and Gown at some point in the organization's first fifty years.[57]

University development policy was often debated and negotiated in civic groups and alumni organizations, keeping college life and city life in synch. Battle maintained relations with commercial, legal, and political leaders like Walter Long, of the city's chamber of commerce, on behalf of the university.[58] Long served for decades as the public face of Austin's business interests and credited the campus building program as a key bulwark against the Depression. The chamber promoted the idea of UT investing its oil money in higher-yield securities so that more revenue would lead to a larger building program. Enabling amendments to the state constitution passed handily, and UT construction proceeded apace.[59] Among academics and civic boosters, there was little doubt that the interests of the city and the university were one.

Tom Miller, Austin's long-serving mayor throughout the midcentury decades, made the university-city nexus a metropolitan political issue in his first run for office. He wrote in a full-page newspaper advertisement in 1933, "I will further cordial relations between the city government and State and University authorities. I am also conscious of the great asset in material and cultural value of all the other great schools of Austin."[60] To a broad phalanx of political, business, and social organizations, the effects of the university on the city were clear, and there was a consensus that the two should work together: the growth of one should spur the other.

In 1930, university officials expected UT would prosper despite the nation's deepening economic depression. The university's oil lands had produced about $3 million in revenue, and Texas was poised to build with its share.[61] Like the city, the University of Texas sought a new master plan to accommodate its future growth. This expansion would encompass more than a dozen new buildings and facilities. Battle led the university's committee on campus grounds, and he recommended Philadelphia architect Paul Cret for the campus plan, a marker of UT's ambition to rank among the nation's top universities.[62] Cret was a Frenchman who headed the University of Pennsylvania's architecture school. Through his private firm, he designed buildings and monuments across the United States and Europe. The architect was born in France and trained at the École des Beaux-Arts in Paris. He brought the aesthetics of European architectural refinement to Texas. Battle termed him "a man of great ability, the highest training, and notable taste."[63] All of his work for UT would be cloaked in the style and ornament of the Spanish Renaissance Revival.

Cret delivered the master plan in 1933. It showed axial arrangements and pathways bounding and connecting rectilinear campus zones consistent with Beaux-Arts principles. He adapted it to the local conditions by creating multilevel terracing to accommodate the sloping Austin landscape. He developed schemes for new buildings, and, when selected as the architect for individual buildings, Cret provided designs and ornamentation that alluded to and, in some cases, rivaled *palacios* in sixteenth-century Spain (Figures 18 and 19).[64]

Cret's master plan for the University of Texas was urban planning ideology writ small. The Beaux-Arts tradition and City Beautiful movement emphasized urban order by creating grand boulevards, using visual symbolism, and harmonizing the chaos of large and growing cities. Cret's plan reinforced gender and racial segregation on campus and in the city by creating campus zones that prescribed areas of activity and reinforced geographic concentrations. It

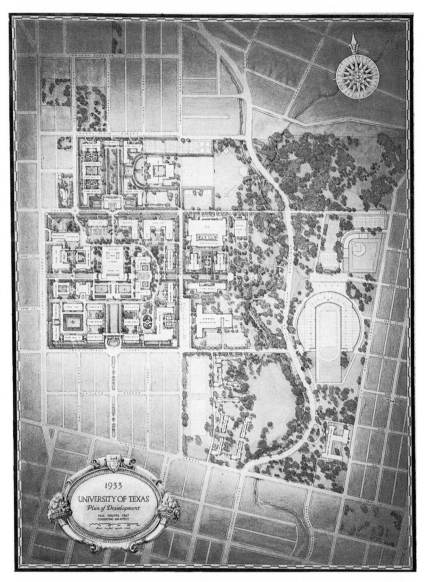

Figure 18. Paul Cret campus plan perspective. Paul Cret, a leading Philadelphia architect, created a Beaux-Arts master plan for the University of Texas campus. Flush with revenue from leases on the oil lands, the university commissioned Cret to design more than a dozen buildings between 1930 and 1945. In this era, the university fulfilled its ambition to become a "university of the first class." University of Texas Buildings Collection, Alexander Architectural Archive, University of Texas Libraries, University of Texas at Austin, Paul Philippe Cret Collection, Project # 241.

Figure 19. An overhead view of Cret's design. University of Texas Buildings Collection, Alexander Architectural Archive, University of Texas Libraries, University of Texas at Austin, Paul Philippe Cret Collection, Project # 241.

called for UT's white female students to live and study as far on campus as possible from segregated, black East Austin.[65] The zone in the northwestern corner of campus included women's dormitories, the women's gymnasium, and a building for home economics. Cret located the zone near two existing dormitories created for women in the 1920s, the Scottish Rite Dormitory and Littlefield Dormitory. A Masonic organization had built Scottish Rite just off the northern edge of campus to provide housing for the daughters of masons at UT. The Littlefield family had donated funds for a dormitory for first-year female students, built at the corner of Twenty-Sixth (now Dean Keeton) and Whitis, and it was the northwestern anchor for the women's zone. To the southeast of campus, Cret's plan also used the existing Texas Memorial Stadium, along with new parking, men's housing, athletic fields, and open space, as a buffer between East Austin and campus.

Cret's plan followed leading planning practice. The top guide on college design, Charles Klauder's *College Architecture in America*, indicated, "Girls especially like to carry on all the activities of home life under their own roof." Klauder recommended closed, "homelike" dormitories with as many amenities as possible provided on the premises. This would preempt "the inconvenience, loss of time and exposure of making an outdoor journey" for women.[66]

Thus, the design called for dormitory groups with house mothers and deans of women supervising them. Students also lived in nearby female rooming houses in respectable neighborhoods like West Austin. Claudia Taylor, the future Lady Bird Johnson, while an undergraduate in the 1920s and 1930s, lived in a women's rooming house on West 21st Street near the western edge of campus.[67] Formerly the home of a prominent family in one of the more desirable neighborhoods in nineteenth-century Austin, the building was inspected by university administrators to "enforce certain standards relative to sanitation, health and social environments."[68]

These designs and policies enabled the college to regulate the behavior of its female students and had the progressive effect of making parents and administrators comfortable permitting women to seek higher education. Predominating mores often precluded women from pursuing degrees at all. At the end of the nineteenth century, women's attendance at American institutions of higher education was rare, radical, and highly constrained.[69] Bureaucratic controls such as deans of women, housing inspections, and house mothers, as at Ball Teachers College in Indiana, maintained campus discipline and standards for chaste and nurturing environments, encouraging conservative communities to send their daughters to university. Cret even recommended the university build a wall or fence around the women's dormitory group, which would mimic Ivy League institutions.[70] UT did not build the wall, but the administration recognized that growth in higher education could exacerbate social tensions and sought designers who brought physical solutions to these problems.

A New Deal for Austin

The national economic crisis raised the stakes for UT expansion. Across the country, the contagion of the economic crisis had spread from finance to higher education. College and university enrollment declined nationwide nearly 10 percent from 1931 to 1933, back to its 1925 level.[71] That enrollment drop seemed even more dramatic since it followed a decade of continual growth. Admissions officials across the country flipped from seeing rising numbers of more than 50,000 new students per year in the late 1920s to confronting drops of about 50,000 students per year in the early 1930s.

The construction industry had collapsed and found no help on college campuses. Nationally, construction spending dropped from $11 billion in 1928 to $3 billion in 1933. Employment fell from 2.9 million in the summer of 1929 to 1 million in 1933, and, according to one assessment, nearly three-quarters of the construction workforce was out of a job.[72] At the end of the Roosevelt administration's first hundred days, Congress passed the National Industrial Recovery Act, which created the Federal Emergency Administration of Public Works, more popularly known as the Public Works Administration, or PWA. It stepped into the breach with grants and loans to public institutions, putting architects, engineers, surveyors, and construction workers back to work.[73]

Franklin Roosevelt laid out his approach for spending billions of dollars for public works in his first inaugural address. He proposed "to put people to work . . . but at the same time, through this employment, accomplishing greatly needed projects to stimulate and reorganize the use of our natural resources," balancing and developing rural and urban markets for agricultural and industrial production and consumption.[74] The university construction subsidies of the PWA not only put unemployed architects and building contractors to work; it also helped expand institutions that were becoming central to the future of American intellectual, scientific, and economic development.[75] Roosevelt trumpeted the federal investments in higher education, saying in 1936, "I am proud to be the head of a Government . . . that has sought and is seeking to make a substantial contribution to the cause of education, even in a period of economic distress." He noted the central role of "bricks and mortar and labor and loans."[76]

New Deal funding for higher education helped achieve two key goals: reorganization of the nation's political economy and development of new means to achieve federal ends. PWA funds for universities and National Youth Administration jobs for students were investments in middle-class institutions and in the future of new white-collar workers. These college students were business people and industrial engineers in the making, budding members of the medical and legal professions, and workers who would staff the administrations and bureaucracies of public and private institutions, using the skills and ideas learned in their college days. The New Deal helped keep students in college courses during the Depression, but it also made more and bigger classrooms to hold them, helping expand the capacity of higher education in the 1930s by approximately one-third.[77]

At the same time, New Dealers worked through nonfederal channels as much as possible to provide this aid. The PWA supported private enterprise with grants for hiring workers and firms rather than employing laborers directly. While the Roosevelt administration was stimulating and reorganizing the use of American resources, it was recruiting a wide array of institutions to more directly and intensely create, exploit, and provide these resources, from education to housing to infrastructure to financial instruments. Colleges and universities came to constitute a "parastate," an intermediate means through which the federal government could mold students into citizens and provide them services, while remaining at arm's length.[78] The New Deal became less visible, and, while federal aid became more important to higher education, this support was often masked and not recognized as such. These two features, the investment in capacity and the use of nonfederal means, combined to lay the foundation for a new economy after World War II, led by an increasingly educated workforce that was, ironically, less committed to the pillars of New Deal liberalism, including collective bargaining in the industrial sector, as time went on.

The spatial nature of these investments could boost or burden local communities as the federal government worked with local partners and channeled aid to a chosen set of institutions. Congress created the Federal Housing Administration (FHA) in 1934 to help stabilize and expand housing markets across the country. The agency wrote a manual for mortgage underwriters in order to standardize procedures for receiving a federal mortgage guarantee. The FHA favored stable, white, middle-class neighborhoods for committing its funds and incentives. In the manual, FHA experts specifically invoked the beneficial effects of colleges, which worked to protect and buffer desirable areas. The manual noted that "a college campus often protects locations in its vicinity" and compared it to other protective measures and natural features that would "prove effective in protecting a neighborhood and the locations within it from adverse influences . . . includ[ing] the infiltration of business and industrial uses, lower class occupancy, and inharmonious racial groups."[79] Through the FHA, the Roosevelt administration made this protective feature of higher education an operational feature of its housing policy. Investments in universities like the University of Texas were acknowledged to increase urban segregation by protect neighboring white homeowners. Each new building at UT advanced the cause of segregation in higher education and in Austin.

Federal funds and oil revenue allowed the university to become the "university of the first class" the Texas constitution had promised. Between 1930 and 1940, UT built fourteen structures designed by Paul Cret. Oil royalties were deposited in the Permanent University Fund and could be dispersed from the Available University Fund. In 1929, the latter fund held $800,000

Figure 20. Library Building Tower. The Library Tower and Main Building at the University of Texas was financed with a combination of oil revenue and New Deal aid. It was the second largest Public Works Administration grant for a university building in the country, with Hunter College in Manhattan receiving the largest. Walter Barnes Studio, Prints and Photographs Collection, di_04018, Dolph Briscoe Center for American History, University of Texas at Austin.

for construction and would accrue millions of dollars a year by the end of the 1930s.[80] The PWA required local matching contributions for most projects, and UT could easily make these contributions.[81] The PWA provided grants and loans for seven UT buildings, including the signature Main Library building, five dormitories, and a laboratory building. PWA aid totaled more than $2.7 million, making the University of Texas one of the largest recipients of building aid in the country. The Main Library and administration tower was the second-largest allotment for a single building in the country.[82] The University of Texas tower reached twenty-eight stories and 307 feet in height, nearly the equal of Austin's state capitol building (Figure 20).[83] The ultimate consequence of federal aid to higher education in this era was to create more capacity at colleges and universities like the University of Texas. PWA and WPA funds made it easier and more democratic to pursue higher education—largely for whites—and provided investment in new research endeavors and professional schools.

The New Deal helped the University of Texas and other institutions like it indirectly as well, by boosting Lyndon Baines Johnson's career. Perhaps more than any other Austinite, Johnson recognized how the Roosevelt administration could help the city bring about a new metropolitan order. He built his congressional career on his ability to work Washington connections and bring federal resources to the Texas Tenth District, especially as part of an urban development agenda for Austin. Johnson brought federal slum clearance funds to East Austin, plowed into three segregated public housing projects. Rosewood Court was built for black residents, Chalmers Court was for white residents, and Santa Rita was for Latino residents. Johnson arranged for loans and grants to the Lower Colorado River Authority for dam construction, electrification, and flood control, putting people to work and bringing electricity to the hill country outside Austin. The congressman also coordinated the development and exchange of military assets, as with the land that became Bergstrom Air Force Base and then Bergstrom International Airport.

For politicians like Johnson, investments in higher education were one part of an urban development strategy. The land and plans and brick and mortar that went into construction had the same kind of employment impact on a college campus as they would in building a public housing complex. Austin leaders arrayed those investments within the city, whether public housing or college dormitories, to harden the spatial and social system of racial segregation. Thus, the city's African Americans might benefit from federal slum clearance, but white college students at segregated universities like Texas received the education subsidies of relief jobs and affordable dormitories that would allow them to become middle-class professionals. Slum clearance projects like Rosewood Court continued the system of geographic segregation; so even when Austin's black population gained from the New Deal, those gains were bounded in ways that continued to limit their prospects.

Changes in World War II

Roosevelt's reform impetus took a different turn as the administration mobilized to prepare for war in Europe. "Dr. New Deal" became "Dr. Win-the-War," in Roosevelt's phrase, as mobilization for World War II brought the military to campus.[84] The federal government had grown in unprecedented ways in the course of the New Deal, but the Roosevelt administration pivoted from economic recovery to military mobilization. These often haphazard experiments in statecraft nonetheless evolved during the war as the federal government increased its control over society. They changed the nature of the federal government and its relationship to the American people through rationing, taxation, and new levels of spending, to name just a few areas. The American military's struggle to scale up training of personnel after the bombing of Pearl Harbor led to the creation of numerous education programs in partnership with colleges and universities. Higher education had struggled to rebound from diminished enrollment during the Depression and faced a loss of students again. Colleges sought ways both to support the war effort and to keep their enrollments up. President Roosevelt requested that the secretaries of war and of the navy "have an immediate study made as to the highest utilization of the American colleges," and the U.S. Navy stood out for creating several wartime programs to train its officers, including the V programs involving thousands of students.[85]

Research funding brought the war into the campus laboratory, a war of the minds waged on campuses against the Axis powers. In Washington, Roosevelt advisor Vannevar Bush counseled the president on the creation of the National Defense Research Committee and its successor, the Office of Scientific Research and Development, to "correlate and support scientific research on the mechanisms and devices of warfare."[86] The varied types of military research amounted to a war of the minds waged on college campuses against the Axis powers. The Manhattan Project developing the atomic bomb is the most prominent in public memory, but research projects led to military applications large and small and built up the American war machine. At UT, the physics department established the War Research Laboratory in 1942 to coordinate contracts with the Office of Scientific Research and Development and home to projects that calculated ordinance trajectories and improved gunsights for B-29 bombers.[87] Charles Boner, a physicist with expertise in acoustics, worked on sonar technology at Harvard University and at UT directed a naval ordinance research project, then the Defense Research Laboratory after the war's end.[88]

University support for war research was a welcome constant and source of stability on campus because the war years were a period of political upheaval. The UT Board of Regents, named by the governor, had become increasingly conservative and clashed with campus faculty and the university president over anticommunism, academic freedom, and liberal politics. At the end of the 1930s, conservative governors W. Lee "Pappy" O'Daniel and then

Coke Stevenson succeeded the liberal James Allred. This shift changed the composition of the university's governing board because every two years the governor appointed three new members to the nine-member governing board.[89] The New Deal was on the wane.

In the 1940s, the Board of Regents took an active role in scrutinizing faculty teaching, student behavior, and administrative activities, finding fault with critiques of capitalism, with homosexual activity, and with efforts to promote academic independence from politics. Liberal members of the faculty were identified for dismissal and accused of supporting communism and socialism based on their support for public utilities, their teaching about communism in classes, and their defense of organized labor. Conservative regents D. F. Strickland and Orville Bullington worked to gain direct control of hiring, firing, promotion, and compensation changes of individual faculty members, with some success. The Regents attempted to fire several tenured professors in economics, unsuccessfully, then in 1943 succeeded in firing several untenured professors who supported organized labor and the New Deal.[90]

The political tensions came to a head in 1944 when UT President Homer Rainey, an education scholar, confronted the regents about this interference with a public list of accusations. The Regents dismissed him and replaced him with Theophilus Painter, a genetics scientist. Upon Rainey's firing, thousands of students marched to the state capitol in a protest over intellectual autonomy, carrying a coffin to symbolize the death of academic freedom. Painter was a compromise-oriented faculty member and administrator who eschewed controversy and worked to broker an agreement between Rainey and the Regents before the president's dismissal. After Rainey's tumultuous tenure, Painter kept the university in step with the Regents, working to administer their mandate rather than contest their actions. The Regents' replacement of an education professor with a hard scientist illustrated a more robust commitment to scientific research but also reflected their interest in a technocratic form of university administration rather than Rainey's independent-minded governance and his overt engagement with the politics of higher education.

Balcones Research Center

In the fall of 1945, university administrators and Austin leaders prepared for the world that would emerge after the war—unprecedented numbers of veterans, crowded housing, and rising material consumption. The war's end also meant disposition of federal surplus materials. Outside Austin, a magnesium plant became one of the most coveted surplus properties in central Texas, attracting the interest of public authorities, state bodies, veterans groups, universities, and private business interests.[91] The magnesium was used for lightweight metal alloys in airplane manufacture and for the creation of incendiary bombs, dropped in both the European and Pacific theaters. The War Production Board had closed down the Austin plant in late 1944 when the need for magnesium waned.[92] Lyndon Johnson had been key to the magnesium plant's development three years earlier. In the summer of 1945, he sprang into action again, contacting the University of Texas, Austin mayor Tom Miller, and Chamber of Commerce secretary Walter Long to spur redevelopment efforts and reaffirm the importance of the plant to the Austin area.[93]

The magnesium plant, known as Plancor 265, was part of the web of federal development efforts for central Texas and the Austin area. The Lower Colorado River Authority (LCRA) had built the Tom Miller hydroelectric dam on the eastern edge of the city to provide the area with electricity; it needed customers for the resulting energy bounty.[94] Magnesium production was an energy-intensive process, and the power authority was eager to keep up demand for electricity through private industrial clients after the war.[95] Thus, the existence of this web of development relationships established for crises—the LCRA, the Plancor 265 plant, and wartime industrial production—became its own justification for maintaining the institutions after the war. The university, the central actor in Austin economic growth, stepped to the fore.

Lyndon Johnson and UT president Theophilus Painter found a way to bridge the divide between Austin business leaders and the university. They arranged transfer of the magnesium plant to UT. Johnson advocated for the transfer of the plant grounds, buildings, and equipment from the federal government to the university for a nominal fee.[96] Painter put this project in the national interest, suggesting that military-funded research projects would pay for the university's use of the property.[97] UT scholars and administrators had developed a plan for the grounds including university housing, radio research for the navy, a missile research project for both the army and the navy, and an ordnance accuracy project for the Army Air Corps, among others.[98] Johnson's office lobbied federal agencies on behalf of the University of Texas and helped arrange a deal when UT bid for the magnesium plant property. Johnson helped negotiate an agreement with the Surplus Property

Board in the spring of 1946 and leapt into action to block the University of Minnesota when administrators sought to purchase equipment from the plant separate from the real estate. The University of Texas would lease the property for three years at an annual rate of one dollar and make all its own improvements, expenditures amounting to $75,000.[99] The federal government entered into a purchase agreement for the property, a twenty-year contract in which the university's payments were to be made through "educational benefit" rather than cash payments of $1.5 million on the facility.[100] This amounted to an accounting trick, making the property transaction a federal grant arranged by then Senator Lyndon Johnson and his protégé in the House, J. J. "Jake" Pickle.

The militarization of the UT campus during World War II brought development to the outskirts of Austin after the war. The creation of the research center was possible because of a plan for building a new highway that would connect the city to peripheral developments. From the outset, federal research contracts sustained the Balcones Research Center (BRC), as it was named. The center featured a wind tunnel used to test the shape and flight of missiles and shells. In 1949, the university established a service agreement between the UT Bureau of Economic Geology and the U.S. Geological Survey to perform research designated by the federal government, setting graduate students to the task of geological analysis.[101] This partnership helped identify possible points for extracting oil, minerals, and other natural resources—just one of the ways the federal government helped fuel the ongoing dependence on fossil fuels. In just a few years, fifteen of the BRC's nineteen labs conducted federally supported research.[102] The director of the BRC, J. Neils Thompson, was a civil engineering professor who had worked for the Texas Highway Department testing road materials during the Depression. He also served as the vice president of economic development for the Chamber of Commerce and was a leader of the chamber for much of his life.[103] Thompson regularly emphasized the academic value of the site, but his overlapping roles illustrated how closely Austin's economy was linked to academic research at the University of Texas. Ribbons of concrete highway bound the city's economy to one of its new, outlying engines.

Ribbons of Concrete

Across the country, highway building was a key item on the agenda for regional and national economic growth. Labor unions, road contractors, auto companies, and policy makers comprised a growth coalition that had spatial and transportation emphases.[104] The postwar economy would move on rubber tires along concrete highways. Through World War II, though, Austin was hardly connected by car to the rest of America. A handful of rail lines rolled through town, but they could not adequately provide for automobiles, a transportation mode that grew precipitously with federal support. Only 3 percent of county roads were paved by 1932, and only a single U.S. highway, 81, reached Austin.[105] The administrations of governors James "Pa" Ferguson and then his wife, Miriam "Ma" Ferguson, had been rife with corruption, and the federal government cut off matching highway funds from Texas in 1925. By the late 1930s, federal highway designations made it to Austin, but even U.S. highway numbers did not guarantee high-quality paving from border to border of Travis County. The university had taken possession of a magnesium plant marooned in a sea of rural land. It was so far in the hinterland that the distance over dirt and gravel roads to the new research center on the former site of the magnesium plant was at first an obstacle to discovery.[106] Austin's rustic transportation network was due for an upgrade.

Walter Long took the lead in the city's highway advocacy efforts and sought to keep Austin at the center of the region. Long put economic growth foremost on the chamber's agenda. In an automotive age, road quality was essential to business. Travis County farmers could serve customers with farm-to-market highways, trucks could haul freight throughout the region, and the city could better connect and expand south of the Colorado River with more and larger highway bridges over the river. The Chamber of Commerce maintained priority lists for road paving and expansion for decades, and advocated for improved roads at every turn.[107] Long appeared before state, county, and local boards to remind policy makers of where the Chamber of Commerce stood on such projects—squarely in support. Indeed, he had to. Road and highway building was largely a decentralized county obligation, so Long and his fellow highway advocates had to mobilize local political will in all places and at all times.

East Avenue became central to the city's growth and divided Austin as it enabled urban expansion. Until the 1920s, the main north–south paved highway through the city was on the western side, running on Rio Grande Street. The 1928 city plan had found East Avenue's two-hundred-foot right-of-way too good to waste. The Koch and Fowler plan claimed "East Avenue is destined to be the backbone of all traffic in the eastern portion of the city." This destiny may not have been apparent to most Austinites. Prior to the

Depression, only a few blocks were paved, and, for several years, much of the ample right-of-way was filled with bales of cotton.[108] Using proceeds from the 1928 bonds, Austin paved East Avenue up to Manor Road near the UT campus, and the highway department rerouted State Highway 20 along the new, modern boulevard. Cars followed the concrete, and East Avenue's destiny as a backbone to the transportation system was far more likely. For the next two decades, the expansion of East Avenue was a continual process. City leaders sought a larger, faster, and higher-volume auto connection to the outskirts of the growing city and proposed an interregional highway on the East Avenue right-of-way, a local precursor to the interstate highway system.

The new highway would open outlying rural areas to suburban development and help connect central Austin to the research center. More than five miles away from Austin's edge, the research park had leapfrogged the typical process of incremental development: an economic center had been pulled to the periphery. It would take nearly a million dollars to make good on the gamble on the outlying research center.

To raise the needed funds, Miller returned to the foundational mechanism for funding urban growth—municipal bonds. The city council set an $18 million bond for May 1946. It was the largest bond total in Austin history, including almost $1 million to pay for development of the interregional highway.[109] Austin leaders proposed the investments in highway infrastructure at the same time as the research park; both were parts of a new vision for economic and metropolitan growth that centrally featured the University of Texas.[110] Voters approved all $18 million worth of proposed bonds, but only after the city council chose to use the majority standard rather than the typical two-thirds supermajority.[111]

Metropolitan growth was a unifying affair and shifted civic discourse away from Jim Crow segregation in central Austin to new possibilities unbounded by race at the undeveloped periphery. Labor, minorities, and the Austin business class all stood to benefit from the bonds and urban development, and offered their support for schools, fire stations, and the highway. Miller recruited Austin minorities into the effort and called the interregional highway a "must" project.[112] It would provide industrial development to East Austin and would divert traffic from West Austin's older, wealthier, and whiter neighborhoods.[113] Largely surrounded by rural land, Austin had almost no suburbs to speak of. Hyde Park had been Austin's first suburban development and helped establish the direction and pattern for future growth outside the municipal boundaries. The city created a process for regular annexation and slowly incorporated new peripheral growth into the city proper in concentric rings.[114]

New construction techniques and modernist aesthetics shaped the design of the interregional highway.[115] It would take commuters and motorists passing through Travis County up above the rooftops of East Austin homes, as reinforced concrete pylons lifted the highway into the sky. An undulating system of berms, underpasses, and off-ramps created development and traffic barriers between East and Central Austin. Its construction required a wide right-of-way and complete acquisition and destruction of homes and properties in its path—overwhelmingly black homes.

Long before the construction of federal interstate highways, the legacy of the interregional highway was tinged with racial inequality. Homer Thornberry, an Austin city councilman in the late 1940s, negotiated with property owners to acquire their land. He later won a congressional seat and was named to a seat on the federal bench. "In a way," he said about Austin's black population in an oral history, "I think they felt probably that it would benefit them." Civic elites expected slum clearance and infrastructure investment to improve the neighborhood, as they had Depression-era construction, road paving, and public housing projects. These would help fulfill the long-held goal they had of equalization in a segregated society. Thornberry acknowledged that the project had spent millions for little return for East Austin; poor conditions continued to predominate. "It's still closed off in many ways. You can just leave the Interregional and drive Twelfth and Eleventh, the roads there and see still that is not [a] happy place to be."[116] The interregional highway drained resources from the neighborhood, redirected metropolitan business and real estate investment to the city's north, and reinforced the geographic color line in Austin with berms and bleak underpasses, just as the battle for civil rights in higher education reached UT's forty acres.

Sweatt v. Painter

Federal investment in Southern cities revealed a profound contradiction in the postwar order. In state capitals and booming cities (e.g., Atlanta, Georgia; Montgomery and Birmingham, Alabama; and Jackson, Mississippi), civic leaders invested public resources to create economic growth and individual opportunity for whites.[117] These investments were unequally distributed and, in some cases, were explicitly denied to African Americans and other minorities. The University of Texas was becoming a leading Southern institution—in part, owing to direct federal aid such as PWA and War Assets Administration grants. Austin, as well, was a growing city benefiting from indirect aid to the region, including LCRA grants and highway spending. As a public enterprise, the university was a special pressure point in the long battle for civil rights. The Texas constitution had established separate tracks of college education for whites and blacks by forbidding black attendance at UT and the College of Agriculture and Mechanics (now Texas A&M). Instead they created Prairie View State Normal and Industrial College for African Americans (now Prairie View A&M).[118] Since there was no separate option for graduate or professional school, equal or otherwise, Texas was failing the standard set by *Plessy v. Ferguson.*

The state NAACP organized to take on the University of Texas and to desegregate higher education. They raised funds and sought a qualified applicant to apply to the UT law school for their case, and worked with the national organization to devise a legal strategy. Heman Sweatt, a Houston postal worker and Wiley College alumnus, volunteered to serve as the law school applicant and presumed plaintiff. Sweatt had no interest in law school per se, but the application process for that program was more transparent than that of other graduate and professional programs.[119] The postman and NAACP representatives met with university president Theophilus Painter and other state officers on February 26, 1946. The delegation made the point clearly: Texas was failing to fulfill its constitutional obligations and to serve the state's population. "We want to know what the committee has done. What is available now? Not tomorrow, next week, or next month. We need training for our returning GIs and our children who must compete with others in their own state for jobs with inferior education."[120] Both Huston-Tillotson College, the consolidated college in Austin, and Prairie View A&M, the state's land-grant institution for African Americans, were principally concerned with training teachers. They had little to offer those interested in graduate education. Painter accepted the application and deferred a decision until the attorney general issued a ruling. Sweatt filed suit against the university in May 1946.

Facilities, faculty, and students were at the heart of the desegregation lawsuit. The national NAACP had developed a legal strategy with shifting bases to attack the system of segregation in public education, from seeking state support, to promoting roughly equal access, to attacking segregation as creating inherently unequal facilities.[121] Legal principle required that the state provide educational opportunities for blacks that were "substantially equivalent" to those available to whites at the University of Texas. The state had no law school open to African Americans at the time, but the trial judge at the state level ordered the dismissal of Heman Sweatt's suit if Texas could provide one within a few months.[122] Seeking to comply, the University of Texas Regents solicited a $100,000 appropriation from the state legislature for a temporary school in Austin, a few blocks south of the main UT campus. When state lawmakers agreed, UT rented the basement of an Austin office building between the campus and the capitol. Thus instruction began at the newly created Texas State University for Negroes. The short-term setup at the law school consisted of the space rented from an oil company, a table and some chairs, and faculty and staff shared by the University of Texas law school, as well as nine hundred books, some of them donated from UT alumni.[123] A handful of local black residents applied and enrolled in the school, satisfying the trial judge who ruled in favor of the university in 1947.[124]

Social and economic mobility for African Americans were at stake in the case, while a key redoubt of white supremacy was under attack. Sweatt and NAACP strategists, including Thurgood Marshall, refused the state's efforts as unsatisfactory tokenism, appealing the case to the U.S. Supreme Court.[125] The stakes for maintenance of the dual track system of public education were significant and clear throughout the South. State attorneys general throughout the region banded together to file an amicus curiae brief, arguing on the side of the state of Texas, lest their own graduate schools be desegregated in the event of a ruling for Sweatt.[126] Northern legal educators aligned with the NAACP, including a committee of law professors at Yale, Harvard, and the University of Chicago who filed an amicus brief in Sweatt's favor.[127] In Texas, the legislature intensified its investment in an alternative education track, creating a permanent version of Texas State University in Houston in 1947, appropriating $2 million for facilities and $50,000 a year for its operations.[128] However, given the legal education provided to whites at dedicated, architect-designed buildings in the heart of a Beaux-Arts campus in the state capital, with a library that offered tens of thousands of volumes and an alumni network that ran both broad and deep, the school was certainly not approaching equal in terms of institutional wealth.

The U.S. Supreme Court ruled unanimously in favor of Heman Sweatt in June 1950. The court offered the NAACP another major victory in the battle to desegregate public education. "We won the big one!" Thurgood Marshall claimed at a victory rally that summer.[129] Sweatt enrolled at the UT Law School in September 1950 along with six other African American classmates (Figure 21). When Lyndon Johnson assumed the presidency in

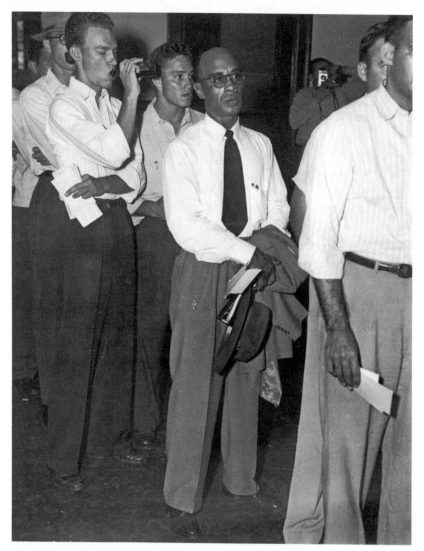

Figure 21. Heman Sweatt stands in line to register for law classes at the University of Texas. UT Texas Student Publications, Prints and Photographs Collection, di_01127, Dolph Briscoe Center for American History, University of Texas at Austin.

1963, he named Marshall the U.S. solicitor general, then in 1967 nominated him to the U.S. Supreme Court, in large part for his work fighting for civil rights with the NAACP.

Heman Sweatt could attend integrated law school, but he still had to live in segregated East Austin.[130] Sweatt and his wife rented an apartment in a large Victorian house in a black working- to middle-class neighborhood on the same block as Dudley Woodard, along with another black classmate who registered after the decision.[131] The house on East 12th Street was a handful of blocks from the Rosewood public housing complex, and poverty still abounded in East Austin. Just a year earlier, black Austinites had complained of deplorable East Austin conditions before the City Council: the dream of equal public facilities promised by the 1928 public works program had died. East Austin had a higher population density than any other section of the city, and municipal reports detailed poor conditions on nearly every measure— crowding, access to private bathrooms, absentee ownership, infant mortality, and tuberculosis rates.[132] The racially bounded real estate market did not work for black Austin, and Supreme Court decisions could not remedy the surreptitious patterns of the private sector. In *Brown v. Board of Education*, the Supreme Court would establish the principle that separate facilities were inherently unequal and could not be maintained in public education. The less explicit forms of segregation that cornered African Americans like Sweatt in neighborhoods deprived of capital and healthy facilities would survive even longer.

Sweatt left law school without a degree after two years, but the door to higher education he and the NAACP had pried open would remain so. UT's law school had long fed white alumni into positions of state legislative and executive power, and its white graduates filled the most elite positions in the state and across the country. In the uncertain years until the *Brown* decision, African Americans could not be excluded from this network of influence by direct means of the state.[133] George Washington Jr., the first black law graduate at UT, completed his studies in 1954. The spaces of higher learning were no longer black or white, but the color lines in Austin's racial geography were being redrawn even more starkly.

New highways in the city were one sign of changing times. On March 29, 1962, the city dedicated the downtown section of IH-35, the interregional highway that rose above Central and East Austin and became part of the interstate system (Figure 22). The length of the interregional highway outside downtown Austin had been easier to build. Demolition of East Avenue before construction of the raised highway had taken a great deal of time and money. IH-35 towered above East Austin, and cars zoomed through the city on their way north toward the Balcones Research Center, the new residential developments, and shopping developments. The expressway symbolized the arrival of midcentury modernity in Austin.

Figure 22. Highway dedication, Austin. In 1962, Texas celebrated the opening of the downtown section of Interstate Highway 35 in Austin. A state official cut a "ribbon of girls," the women in plaid skirts to the right. Afterward, a motorcade drove north on the highway past the main University of Texas campus, visible in the background on the left of the image, to the outskirts of the city near the new research park, which would economically flourish with improved transportation access. TxDot Photo Library, Crowd at the Opening of IH 35, Austin, 3-29-62, image 6448.

The BRC was a magnet that drew like-minded private enterprises. By the early 1960s, the BRC employed upward of a thousand people. In 1967, IBM located a manufacturing plant and engineering center on the same road a few blocks from the BRC to build the popular Selectric typewriter. IBM was the classic postwar electronics and computing company—part and parcel of the Cold War space race and, with General Motors, the post–World War II American economy. These investments in research and production, and receipt of federal grants and contracts north of the city, helped catalyze a shift in the Austin economy. In a 1962 promotional publication on the BRC, Walter Long enthused that an "old farming section of several thousand acres north and northwest of Austin [was] rapidly filling with homes, even up to the fence surrounding the old Magnesium Plant. Millions of dollars in value have been added to the tax rolls of the city."[134]

This outlying growth—sprawl, even—created jobs and created demand for more gasoline and petroleum. At the same time, the university allied with oil companies to store and conduct research at the BRC on oil-field cores, columns of rock drilled from the earth illustrating the stratigraphy and geological history of Texas oil lands.[135] The research park was part of a cycle in which oil companies expanded their research and development in partnership with the university, then promoted and facilitated auto-oriented development and a motoring ideology. This process expanded urban boundaries and created a new type of metropolitan segregation far different from Austin's version of Jim Crow early in the century. Land development at the outskirts and easy escape from the city's center to suburban homes by whites meant residential racial segregation was *worse* in Austin in 1960 than it had been in 1930.[136]

Austin was a city without suburbs, annexing new subdivisions and open space at its edges on a regular basis. The city council moved municipal boundaries again and again toward the research campus, and Austin provided urban services as the city grew. The new business executives and technology researchers populating the research parks sought higher-level and more exclusive amenities. Residential growth in the northern part of the city intensified as developers built homes near job centers. The university and its professional programs continued to expand to provide all of these services and amenities, contributing to a cycle of economic development. The city itself more than tripled in population, from 53,000 in 1930 to 186,000 in 1960, and the reach of the university expanded in both power and geography as an integral part of the Austin economy.[137]

A flow of federal money mixed with a stream of West Texas oil revenue at the university changed the spatial organization of the city and the nature of the Austin economy. The renewal and ascendance of the University of Texas in the 1930s, 1940s, and 1950s brought with it serious efforts to reinforce racial segregation in urban space, maintaining municipal strategies of earlier decades, and to perpetuate a social system of racial apartheid embedded in the higher-education system. When the civil rights movement challenged the legal system of segregation at the university's law school, civic leaders and education administrators continued to pursue development within the university and the city in such a way that when the legal system was overturned, spatial segregation remained firmly entrenched within the expanding boundaries of Austin's city limits.

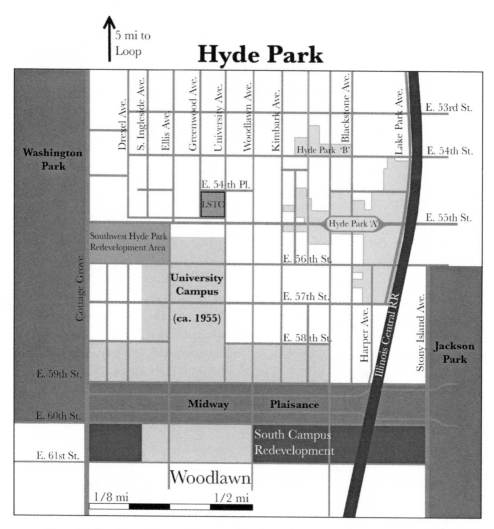

Figure 23. Southeast Chicago. Map created by the author.

3   Origins of the University Crisis

The destruction of Hiroshima and Nagasaki at the end of World War II was the triumph of Chicago. The Manhattan Project had gathered the world's leading physicists at the University of Chicago's Metallurgical Laboratory, where they conducted the first controlled nuclear chain reaction in 1942 and enabled the creation of the atomic bomb. The day after the United States dropped the first atomic weapon on Hiroshima and leveled the city, the country's newspapers blared excited headlines, and the city's leading daily proclaimed Chicago the "Scientific Center of the Universe."[1]

This close relationship between scientific research and higher education found a forceful advocate in Vannevar Bush, an engineering professor at the Massachusetts Institute of Technology (MIT) who served as a presidential adviser during the war. Bush led the Office of Scientific Research and Development, and in July 1945, he published a report on scientific policy entitled *Science, The Endless Frontier*. In it, Bush advocated for the provision of federal resources to continue building the research relationship between the federal government and higher education. "Government, like industry, is dependent on the colleges, universities, and research institutes to expand the basic scientific frontiers and to furnish trained scientific investigators."[2] He proposed a federal agency to fund scientific research, one that would become the National Science Foundation, one of the key sources of research support in the postwar era.

In the aftermath of the war, the University of Chicago was poised to build on its role in the signature scientific war effort and consolidate its position as a global leader in research for the postwar era. Now that federal support for academic science would be institutionalized, University of Chicago administrators solidified the institution's achievements by creating research institutes to house physicists such as atomic scientist and Nobel laureate

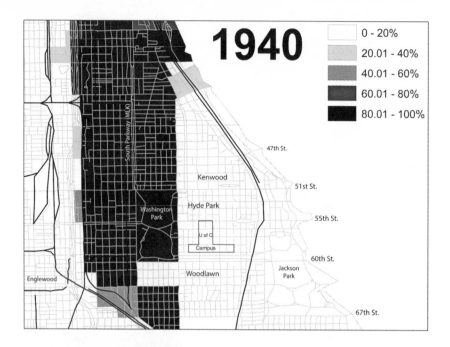

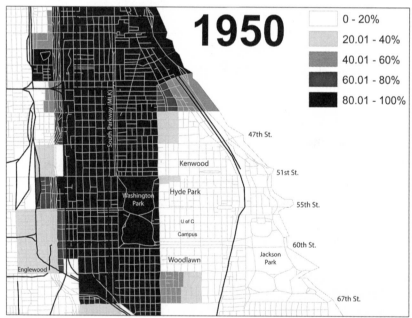

Figures 24–27. Census maps of the University of Chicago area, from 1940, 1950, 1960, and 1970. At the outset of World War II, African Americans in Chicago were bounded in a small area of the city known as the Black Belt, the edge of which ran near Washington Park and the University of Chicago. During the 1950s, an influx of new arrivals, redevelopment in the Black Belt, and economic advancement by black Chicagoans led them to move into border neighborhoods. University of Chicago administrators and Hyde Park

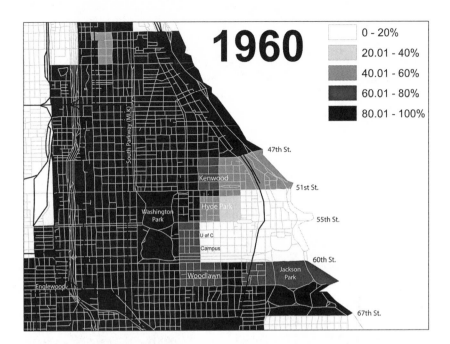

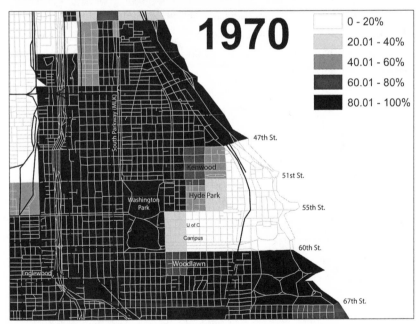

residents responded by taking dramatic measures to stop the demographic wave washing over Hyde Park and to preserve a largely white, professional-class community buffered from Woodlawn south of the Midway Plaisance. The maps indicate the proportion of black residents in census tracts. Maps created by the author. Census data from the University of Minnesota Population Studies Center, www.nhgis.org.

Enrico Fermi. Faculty and university planners prepared for an influx of students eager to study after fifteen years of economic depression and conflict.[3] The University of Chicago's future was as bright as the blinding atomic blast it had helped create.

Just a few years later, the onset of the urban crisis in southeastern Chicago distressed city leaders, shocking university administrators and creating panic in the 1950s. Although exultant at the conclusion of World War II, administrators felt threatened by a postwar demographic chain reaction playing out in Chicago (Figures 24–27). The waves of the Great Migration, the movement of African Americans out of the Black Belt into nearby neighborhoods, and the accompanying public response endangered the university's reputation as a school for the region's intellectual elite. Universities throughout the Northeast and Midwest felt the same effects of this transformation and the deterioration of central cities, having been starved of investment in the Depression and crowded with new arrivals during and after the war. In New York, Columbia University struggled with changes in neighboring Morningside Heights and sought aid for redevelopment, creating Morningside Heights, Inc., led by financier David Rockefeller, who was an important conduit to the University of Chicago.[4] New York University followed suit with slum clearance and redevelopment in Greenwich Village.[5] Civic elites in Cleveland worried about the area surrounding Case Institute of Technology (now Case Western Reserve University) and funded an urban renewal plan and University Circle, Inc., a redevelopment organization, to channel investment.[6]

These changes contributed to declining undergraduate enrollment and faculty retention problems, and University of Chicago administrators responded by physically remaking the surrounding neighborhoods. They drew on modernist design ideas and employed federal policy programs to maintain the university's prestigious role as a leader in global research and graduate education. The university and its allied organization, the South East Chicago Conference, led or supported the Hyde Park A & B federal slum clearance projects, urban renewal plans in the Hyde Park and Woodlawn neighborhoods, and redevelopment and expansion of its own campus. Mid-century leaders Lawrence Kimpton, George Beadle, and brothers Julian and Edward Levi sought to socially and economically manage the university's surroundings to produce an affluent, largely white island amid the expanding Black Belt. Chicago drew on its particular history and institutional assets to develop a national template for university expansion and urban redevelopment that for decades guided colleges and universities across the country. The university was the jewel of a leading industrial city that had amassed political and financial capital through exploitation of natural resources around the Midwest. Few American institutions had the reputation, clout, and resources to lead this effort, but when Chicago stepped to the fore, many universities followed.

The university remade southeastern Chicago in this moment of crisis in pursuit of institutional security and academic prestige. Its redevelopment actions exacerbated racial inequalities and subverted the liberal and democratic ideals fundamental to the Cold War era's struggle for global power. Indeed, the university's protective and preemptive actions seemed to contradict its own ideals. At midcentury, the neighborhoods surrounding the university were often poor or working-class communities that felt the push of the bulldozer and the crash of the wrecking ball far more viscerally and tangibly than any scientific or humanistic advance the universities made. Redevelopment caused rifts within the university and between local communities that hardened over the decades. An institution at the heart of the global and urban liberal order sacrificed its African American neighbors in order to advance world-leading research and to provide a more comfortable environment for its predominantly white faculty and students. This internal tension between two parts of the liberal coalition broke open cracks of urban renewal, one of the cornerstones supporting the edifice of midcentury liberalism.[7]

Community

Chicago's Hyde Park neighborhood was ground zero for the urban crisis detonating in university communities. It had been founded in the 1850s as a resort outside of the city, then became a prosperous railroad suburb, and finally was incorporated into Chicago in a large 1889 annexation of what is now the South Side. The neighborhood won renown in the 1890s as the home of the University of Chicago and location of the Columbian Exposition, the 1893 world's fair that featured the White City, the neoclassical grounds orchestrated by Daniel Burnham.[8] By the middle of the twentieth century, the neighborhood was left leaning and ethnically and culturally diverse. Chicago students and graduates were active in the local theater community, and residents remember it as a chaotic mix of artists, leftists, intellectuals, and bohemian hangers-on.[9] "Hyde Parkers," as residents called themselves, were highly educated, politically involved, and engaged in an array of creative endeavors.

Walking the blocks around the university campus, to classes or to a small local theater, one could feel the tension between the city's aging past and the institution's confident future. Hyde Park suffered from disinvestment during the Depression and World War II, exacting a toll on the infrastructure and condition of the community. The deterioration seemed both to enable the neighborhood's creative bohemianism and to signal an impending, precipitous decline for the community. Some of the last remaining structures from the Columbian Exposition era stood as both fact and symbol of Hyde Parkers' distressed neighborhood. They represented a dramatic fall from the height of Progressive Era visions of urban reform. On 57th Street, just to the east of the university campus, a set of concession buildings from the fair, glass-front, one-story structures with wedding-cake detailing, seemed long past their best days. They had become an artists' colony, cheap structures housing beatniks, bohemians, studios, used bookstores, and diners that brought diversity to the community, alternately characterized as eccentric and unsafe (Figure 28).[10] This jumble of dilapidated structures and uses held the promise of creative rebirth, a movement that would take hold in American cities in the last two decades of the twentieth century. The 57th Street Art Fair began here in 1948 and gave renowned sculptor Claes Oldenburg his commercial start.[11] Sixty years after the Columbian Exposition, however, the decay of these buildings was more symbolically powerful than their actual deterioration. Having been part of an epochal event that helped inspire an age of urban reform, the crowded buildings and flaking paint gave the impression of lost opportunities rather than the future of the American city. Like the remnants of the world's fair that coincided with the opening of the university, the neighborhood's most glorious years seemed to have dissolved from an idealistic dream into a shabby reality.[12]

Demographic changes in the city gave urgency and meaning to the perceptions of deterioration. The Great Migration brought tens of thousands of African Americans to Chicago, where they crowded in tightly bounded areas. The expansion of the region's economic and transportation infrastructure began a centrifugal process that moved white residents, high-paying jobs, and investment out to the metropolitan periphery. The city's black population grew from 233,905 in 1930 to 492,265 in 1950, and they sought the comforts and opportunity of postwar life.[13] Middle-class, working-class, and poor African Americans had arrived in droves throughout the first half of

Figure 28. Chicago's 57th Street Art Colony buildings. These structures, remaining from the 1892–93 Columbian Exposition, became increasingly contentious sites as community residents complained about crime and blight. They were demolished in 1961. Special Collections Research Center, University of Chicago. 57th Street Art Colony I, Series II: Buildings and Grounds, University of Chicago Library, Special Collections Research Center, Archival Photographic Files apf2-03965.

the twentieth century. After World War II, they sought to move beyond the boundaries of the Black Belt on the South Side, where restrictive covenants and white violence had kept the city's black population pinned for decades.[14] During the 1940s, several of the neighborhoods with the fastest-growing black populations in the city were on the South Side in close proximity to the University of Chicago, including Woodlawn, south of the Midway Plaisance, a strip of land between 59th and 60th Streets, and Kenwood and Oakland, north of Hyde Park.[15] In neighborhoods throughout the city, white residents feared a shifting of the community boundaries that had endured for decades and blamed African Americans for deterioration of infrastructure or changes in neighborhood character.[16]

This tinderbox of racial tension ignited in 1952 with a home invasion in Hyde Park. Early in the morning of May 11, an intruder described in the press as a "thin-faced Negro gunman" broke into the house of scientist Samuel Untermyer and his family. Untermyer was a Manhattan Project nuclear physicist from the plant at Oak Ridge, Tennessee. He was working to develop the successor to the university's Metallurgical Lab, the federal nuclear complex at Argonne Forest west of the city in rural DuPage County. The Untermyer residence was in the heart of Hyde Park, just two blocks from the university campus and two doors down from Enrico Fermi's home. The attacker held the couple at gunpoint, stole thousands of dollars worth of jewelry, and kidnapped Samuel Untermyer's wife, Joan, sexually assaulted her, and left her in a parking lot a few miles away.[17]

The community panicked. The event amounted to a physical attack on the university's signature achievement and its continued ambition as a global leader in science. The new chancellor, Lawrence Kimpton, stepped up to face the crisis.[18] Kimpton's predecessor, Robert Maynard Hutchins, had lost control of the surrounding neighborhood, but Kimpton had a plan to reassert university dominance. Hutchins was a legal scholar, public intellectual, and head of the University of Chicago from 1929 to 1951. He had maintained a strained relationship with surrounding communities, supporting restrictive covenants and racial segregation. These legal clauses on property deeds maintained racial boundaries by forbidding the sale of property to non-whites. The U.S. Supreme Court had struck down restrictive covenants in their decision on *Shelley v. Kraemer* in 1948, eliminating a state-sanctioned power from Northern segregationists' repertoire, leaving Hutchins and others unsure how to proceed.[19] The university trustees drew from the well of the university's greatest triumph when they hired Kimpton. A longtime administrator with a doctorate in philosophy, he had helped lead the Chicago segment of the Manhattan Project during World War II and had seen the university at its apogee of national importance. Kimpton considered neighborhood conditions an existential crisis for the institution, requiring a dramatic response.

The chancellor created the South East Chicago Commission (SECC), a nonprofit corporation external to the university, though Kimpton served as its president. The University of Chicago contributed much of the SECC's operations budget in its early years and the commission largely served a university agenda. Over time, the organization became known as "the urban renewal arm of the university."[20]

The SECC identified police protection and real estate exploitation as key to university's problems.[21] It would work alongside the three-year-old Hyde

Park–Kenwood Community Conference (HPKCC), a citizens' organization that used block clubs and neighborhood organizing to try to stave off blight, apartment conversions, and "overuse of property."[22] The SECC's citizens' committee identified these concerns and added police ineptitude and corruption to their list of issues in a May 1952 report that signaled the beginning of a new university neighborhood strategy. In the report, released to the public, the group pledged "to keep close check on the sale of real estate within our area" and to "raise hell" at the prospect of illegal conversions, vowing that "nobody is going to make a fast buck at the expense of our community."[23] The group implicated the Democratic political machine as controlling the police and failing to deter petty crime, policy wheels, and other forms of crime and graft. "Police enforcement, particularly against gambling and tavern violations, is lax," they claimed, adding "the city administration in many departments is inefficient, dominated by self-serving political influences."[24] The SECC pivoted from specific crimes threatening persons to crimes against a more nebulous community well-being, identifying illegal apartment conversions as a key threat to the community and echoing the critique of the HPKCC.

Police enforcement and property conversion were ostensibly color-blind measures. The HPKCC, led by executive director Julia Abrahamson beginning in 1951, adopted the goal of creating "a stable interracial community of high standards." This would include professional-class African Americans as homeowners and full community participants, even suggesting they would accept small amounts of largely black-occupied public housing in a few neighborhood locations. The HPKCC worked on both the social front and the policy front. They included role-playing activities to help prepare white members to approach, introduce themselves to, and befriend black neighbors.[25] Their policy agenda did not include policing but focused on real estate use and enforcement of laws against the excesses of capitalism. They emphasized illegal tenure conversions from owner occupancy to rental units and landlords' splitting of large apartments into tiny kitchenette units that led to overcrowding and neighborhood stress.

These measures, as well as the SECC priority of police enforcement, held profound racial implications for the area. The SECC report admitted "our area has a special police problem because of the geographic proximity of a large number of people who are economically underprivileged and ill-housed." Hyde Park abutted the Black Belt, but linking crime and poverty in this way sidestepped the continuing legacy of racial segregation. Illegal housing conversions in Hyde Park and other neighborhoods near the boundaries of the Black Belt were largely aimed at providing residences to two groups. The first was black households displaced by urban redevelopment at Lake Meadows or by Chicago Housing Authority projects. The second was the growing black population coming from southern states, and which was still prevented from living in most neighborhoods in Chicago. The university shared the blame because it had supported restrictive covenants in Washington Park, Oakwood, and Woodlawn and undermined market forces that might have alleviated the crowding, poverty, and poor housing that Hyde Parkers feared.[26] Chicago had a growing total population and a growing black population. Among the key goals of preventing the conversion of grand apartments to kitchenettes was to keep low-income African Americans out of Hyde Park and black children out of its neighborhood schools. From the outset, the SECC and university leadership concentrated on crime and property, but they avoided publicly discussing the racial nature of the university's actions and the self-inflicted origins of its wounds.

Julian Levi was the man to translate the university's concerns into community plan and action at the SECC. A Hyde Park attorney and businessman, he became the SECC executive director in 1953, a post he would hold until 1980. He was well connected to the business community and the university administration. Levi sold his interest in a printing business and took up leading the SECC, returning to the family business—helping lead the University of Chicago. He had lived in Hyde Park his whole life and understood the neighborhood dynamics in detail. His grandfather, reform rabbi Emil Hirsch, had been a university professor. His brother, Edward, was dean of the law school and would eventually become university president and U.S. attorney general.

The administrative position on race was conflicted, to others and to itself. Robert Hutchins, Kimpton's predecessor, admitted he couldn't understand it. He once wrote that the ideals of university academic policy should be set aside when considering real estate policy. "I have always been perplexed by the problem. . . . I think they are different, but don't ask me why."[27] As a faculty member, Edward Levi had worked against Jim Crow segregation and had helped write an amicus brief supporting the NAACP in *Sweatt v. Painter*. Later, as president, he and his brother exploited racial fear and inequality to guard and build the prestige of the university. The university named Julian Levi an urban studies professor in the university's law school in 1963, in large part based on his experience leading renewal in Hyde Park. Kimpton and

Levi—and, by extension, the university and the SECC—worked hand in glove during the 1950s, communicating several times a day and enjoying an easy familiarity that strengthened their collaboration.

Enrollment Crises

A prime example of the problems facing Kimpton and Levi was the enrollment drop in the fall of 1953. Worries about crime in Hyde Park were not the only factor. College enrollment was stagnating across the nation, as the number of World War II veterans funded by the G.I. Bill, a strong source of enrollment from 1945 to 1950, had fallen off. Further, low birth rates in the 1930s had a distinct effect on Chicago's applicants, and the Korean War was drawing down the student-age male population.[28] At the University of Chicago, just eighty-seven first-year students enrolled for classes in 1953, down 50 percent from the usual numbers. Undergraduate enrollment overall had declined about 40 percent from 1950, signaling problems for the future of the institution.[29]

Programs across campus were suffering because of the drop in enrollment. College reforms during Hutchins's tenure had only made things worse. Hutchins and Chauncey Boucher, dean of the College at the University of Chicago, had led dramatic academic reforms and separated the college into upper and lower divisions in 1931. They emphasized general education in the lower division, including the university's renowned core curriculum. Under this system, the lower division of the college began to accept students at the end of their sophomore year of high school.[30] Hutchins believed that if students completed their general education early on, by the final two years in the college, they could emphasize research and work more closely with faculty. This innovation ruptured the relationship between the university and the elite schools of the region that had traditionally supplied a large segment of the University of Chicago undergraduate population. The university was stealing students from the high schools.

The loss of undergraduate tuition revenue contributed to a significant operating deficit. In a memo, the dean of students in September 1952 noted both factors in the analysis of declining enrollments, writing that "the decline of the University neighborhood has been widely discussed and the sharp decline in enrolment of women students in the College reflects the resulting fears concerning safety. . . . The public schools have failed to co-operate with the College of the University, Public school associations continue to express doubt about the wisdom of the academic structure of the University of Chicago."[31] He elaborated, "Since 1931 few high school teachers have been prepared at Chicago; we have few representations of our College in the public high schools," and "high school teachers among our alumni . . . were outraged at the notion that the last two years of high school were a waste."[32] High school administrators, many of whom had been loyal alumni of the university that was the "teacher of teachers," considered the new college system a challenge to their educational authority and stopped recommending the university to their promising students.[33]

The enrollment crisis and the urban crisis combined to become a larger university crisis. George Watkins, a university vice president, later called Hutchins's college restructuring "a disaster," but administrators at the time blamed the transformation of the South Side.[34] Levi put the issue in more cynical terms, noting "men and women of good will . . . applaud the 'noble experiment' [of racial integration] while at the same time they caution their daughters not to go to the University of Chicago lest they be raped on the streets."[35] Pointing to Hyde Park and asserting the incompatibility of university life with a slum neighborhood, Kimpton starkly told Chicago's Board of Aldermen that "the very life of the university is at risk."

The memory of the old University of Chicago could not have offered much comfort. The predecessor institution had been cofounded by Senator Stephen A. Douglas and chartered in 1856, but had folded in 1886 owing to financial difficulties.[36] The university board had given its name to Rockefeller's institution, and, to administrators and trustees fighting for the university in the 1950s, victory and stability in this university could not have seemed a certainty.

Urban Redevelopment

Leadership at the university sought a dramatic, sweeping strategy that would secure its surroundings and reputation. In the 1950s, there were few models for dealing with the challenges that came to be known as the urban crisis. Nineteenth-century patterns of urban development based on boosterism and growth had little to offer cities facing losses of human and investment capital to suburbanization. The City Beautiful movement had worked to tame urban disarray—a surplus of economic and human vitality—rather than decline and deterioration.

Slum clearance was a new and viable idea. The Housing Act of 1949 provided resources to cities to demolish blocks of urban land affected by blight and to rebuild larger, planned projects. Urban renewal and urban conservation followed from the Housing Act of 1954. It featured the strategy that an area or a city could be made new again by redeveloping the most problematic parcels or blocks and by reinvesting in the rest of the area to keep it from becoming blighted. Leaders like Levi groped for the emerging strategy of centrally planned urban redevelopment that would dominate planning for the next two decades. But it was unclear how these relatively untried programs would work in a complex university community.

Julian Levi grasped both the challenges the university faced and the wide-ranging means available to take control of the area. In a 1954 memo, he delineated the SECC's priorities, urging Kimpton that the university had to "maintain and create the kind of community within which students and faculty wish to live"; "to protect the operations of the institution itself"; and "to protect and develop major real estate holdings already within this area." Among other measures, this required "that [Hyde Park] must be rid of slum and blight which will attract lower class Whites and Negroes."[37] In the most explicit statement of their collaborative vision, Levi wrote,

> The general planning objectives to be sought in the preparation of plans of the University Community under the Neighborhood Redevelopment Corporation Law are the following:
> 1. The development of the concept of a unified University of Chicago campus, involving the development of an integrated community characterized by limited traffic access, broad community landscaping, etc.
> 2. A drastic reduction in density, to be obtained by the demolition and destruction of over-aged apartment buildings throughout the area and their replacement by single residence, town house, and duplex structures.
> 3. The establishment of a homogeneous, economic, middle class or better level within the community.[38]

Making the university the centerpiece of a low-density, exclusive Hyde Park would involve a planning effort that matched development in suburban communities on the fringes of metropolitan Chicago—low-density zoning meant to restrict low-income and largely minority populations. In order not to lose population and faculty to suburban communities, the University of Chicago would have to resuburbanize Hyde Park, rolling back more than a half-century of development. To do so, Levi and the university administration would employ an unprecedented variety of tools, including campus expansion, publicly supported urban redevelopment, private real-estate development in the local community, and intervention in the private rental and finance markets.

A key element of the SECC and University of Chicago program was the influence of its trustees. Chicago's industrial, commercial, political, cultural, and intellectual leaders numbered among the university's alumni, patrons, and trustees. The businessmen who led the university were heirs to the commodities fortunes—the flows of iron, timber, livestock, and grain, as well as retailing and media empires—that had made the city an industrial powerhouse. They had made or inherited their fortunes while such wealth and clout were still concentrated in local businesses, families, and individuals. They included meatpacking heir Harold Swift; steel executive Edward Ryerson; retailer and publisher of the *Chicago Sun-Times* Marshall Field III; his son, Marshall Field IV, successor at the *Sun-Times*; Laird Bell, a Chicago lawyer on the board of Weyerhaeuser, the timber corporation; and J. Howard Wood, publisher of the *Chicago Tribune*. Their support provided national strength and Republican connections, a useful counterpart to the city's Democratic political machine of ethnic whites.[39]

Administrators often made the case that student security was their ultimate goal. Julian Levi and Lawrence Kimpton claimed that the very foundation of the University of Chicago was in jeopardy, asserting that neighborhood problems endangered the university's students and scholars whose work would lead the nation to greater prosperity and scientific achievement.[40] Kimpton emphasized in a speech, "It is extremely important that we maintain a community in which our faculty desire to live and in which our students will be secure."[41] They reiterated at conferences and public hearings that the university's problematic local context threatened Chicago's position as a national leader in education and research. The university had a hard time competing against institutions such as Stanford, Princeton, and the University of Michigan in wealthier, whiter, and more spacious settings with less severe problems of race, poverty, or expansion. Levi claimed, "If we are really serious about the next generation of teachers and scholars, lawyers and doctors, physicists and chemists, then we have got to worry about the adequate housing of the graduate student. . . . We cannot have it both ways. We are either going to have graduate students, who produce leadership for the next generation . . . or we are not going to achieve these results because we are unwilling to disturb existing owners and populations."[42] Graduate students were the future of national greatness. The faculty members were leading technicians and engineers in the Cold War. With these two precepts, university administrators convinced leaders of the community, the city, and the nation that a university-led redevelopment effort was good for Chicago and good for the country, as it would be in cities nationwide.

The university started its efforts at city hall but found Mayor Martin Kennelly's administration uncooperative. Levi later recounted, "We simply could not operate by cajoling the city of Chicago, by pleading with them. We had to somehow or other develop a position that really required them to respond whether they wanted to or not."[43] The reform-minded Kennelly, successor to notorious machine mayor Ed Kelly, simply would not trade political favors to build a police station or increase the number of officers in Hyde Park.[44]

Levi shifted to the state level and lobbied Illinois legislators for new powers. Changing the law would give him leverage with the city administration. The lawyer negotiated with Illinois politicians to amend the 1941 Neighborhood Redevelopment Corporation Act to grant powers of eminent domain to a private redevelopment corporation.[45] The 1953 statute revisions meant that the University of Chicago could create a private redevelopment corporation and, if it convinced or comprised 60 percent of landowners in a given area, could take a designated area by eminent domain and start bulldozing.[46] No longer would the university be forced to beg the city for favors; instead, it could initiate its own slum clearance projects and avoid political obstacles.

Richard J. Daley, who took office as mayor in 1955, was a far more congenial political ally than his predecessor, Kennelly. When one of the city's most prestigious institutions sought municipal support for its urban renewal efforts, the mayor pledged his help. Daley was eager to attract federal money to pay for construction jobs, planners, surveyors, and consultants. Levi, Kimpton, and Daley agreed the university and the SECC would finance and conduct all the planning involved in creating the Hyde Park slum clearance and urban renewal plans. The university thus controlled public input and development priorities in Hyde Park throughout the whole process in the 1950s.[47]

The racial dynamic of supporting the Hyde Park plan raised political difficulties for Daley. His record on race was mixed. The Bridgeport neighborhood of his youth featured gangs of Irish American boys violently policing the color line. Daley refused to push the city's anti-integrationist whites to accept mixed-race housing in residential areas like Bridgeport or in housing projects in South Deering. Ethnic tribalism died hard, but Daley was a practical politician and African Americans were becoming a loyal constituency of the Democratic party. The mayor balanced between the two groups, accepting the support of the city's Democratic black political leaders and pledging sympathy to the black electorate, while supporting white-led slum clearance and urban renewal.[48]

Planning expertise was key to remaking the city. The midcentury liberal ideal featured a modernizing ethic and universal standards. The planning profession happily provided that expertise, combining the scientific marshaling of data with artistic aesthetics.[49] The university formed a planning office in 1954 and drew upon the connections of its trustees to receive a $100,000 grant from the Marshall Field Foundation in New York.[50] The University of Chicago hired the region's most experienced redevelopment planner, Jack Meltzer, to lead the office. Meltzer had been a planner on the Michael Reese Hospital near the Illinois Institute of Technology (IIT), and the two institutions had worked together to reshape the Bronzeville neighborhood a mile north of Hyde Park.[51] The university planning staff consulted closely with the SECC to plan physical redevelopment of the university area. In some cases, the city would contract with the University of Chicago office to perform planning work for the Daley administration.[52]

The university and SECC had the staff and powers of eminent domain in place and were able to drive urban renewal in southeastern Chicago for the next two decades.[53] The first major project was west of campus in Hyde Park. Following the amendments to the Neighborhood Redevelopment Corporation Act, the university formed a corporation—whose officers included Julian Levi, university vice president for business William Harrell, and university trustee Howard Goodman, among others—to take property to prevent blight rather than to eliminate buildings that already had become blighted. They designated a four-block area south of East 55th Street and east of Washington Park, on the border between the campus area and western Hyde Park, for seizure.[54] The South West Hyde Park Redevelopment Corporation (SWHPR) acquired fourteen acres through eminent domain and proposed clearing the land and selling it to the university to build married-student housing.

Neighbors opposed the use of eminent domain but could not stop the university. St. Clair Drake was a Roosevelt University professor, University of Chicago PhD, and coauthor of *Black Metropolis*, a study of African American life in Chicago. He complained that such seizures were unjust to residents who could not live in the "Golden Square," the more affluent areas east of the university campus. Discrimination and economics kept African Americans out of the Golden Square. Drake himself had tried and failed multiple times to buy property there.[55] The SWHPR reached the threshold of agreement of 60 percent of property owners, in part because it owned a large proportion of the land. The SWHPR cleared the land south of East 55th Street between Cottage Grove and Ellis Avenue, but did not immediately redevelop it. It held the land for more than a decade before the university shifted its athletics field to the site.[56]

Next, the university turned to slum clearance in Hyde Park and flexed its political muscle with the U.S. president. Inland Steel executives Clarence Randall and Edward Ryerson were university trustees, prominent Illinois Republicans, and strong Eisenhower supporters. Rumors circulated that Ryerson was up for a cabinet position after the 1952 election, but it was Randall who ended up in the administration, serving as an economic adviser to President Dwight Eisenhower with an office in the Old Executive Office Building. On July 13, 1954, Randall requested a meeting between a University of Chicago team and President Eisenhower to discuss slum clearance funds for two projects north of campus, Hyde Park A & B.[57] Eight days later, on July 21, a contingent of university trustees and administrators sat in a meeting with President Eisenhower in the Oval Office. Levi remembered, "They had everybody who could say 'no' there. We walked out of the meeting about forty-five minutes later assured of the contract." Afterward, they met with administration housing officials where they received verbal approval of $15 million for redevelopment. Levi lamented that their proposal had not been aggressive enough: "The fact is, I'm starting to realize what you could do. . . . We should have been here with the whole package."[58] Even he and Kimpton underestimated their abilities to sway policy makers. It would not be their last trip to Washington.

Hyde Park A & B brought large-scale demolition to the neighborhood. The slum clearance projects passed at the local, state, and federal levels in the winter of 1954–55. The university razed blighted areas on East 51st Street and at East 55th Street near the Illinois Central Railroad (Figures 29 and 30). Don Blakiston, who had earned a PhD in sociology from the University of Chicago, worked for the SECC and brought his expertise in urban criminology to bear on Hyde Park. Blakiston was "humorless, dour, and anything

Figure 29. Hyde Park A&B (East Hyde Park) before land clearance. At East 55th Street looking west from the Illinois Central Railroad tracks toward the University of Chicago campus, the area could be seen as chaotic, crowded, and filled with aged buildings that attracted unsavory businesses such as taverns and speculators who would convert apartments to kitchenette studios. Special Collections Research Center, University of Chicago, Hyde Park, Series II: Buildings and Grounds, University of Chicago Library, Special Collections Research Center, Archival Photographic Files apf2-03950.

but particularly friendly," but he mapped crime and blight statistics with aplomb to make the case for the specific boundaries of the two projects. Dozens of shops, scores of apartment buildings, and neighborhood institutions fell to the wrecking crew, including the Swedish Methodist Episcopalian Church, the African Methodist Episcopalian Church, hotels, theaters, garages, and laundries.[59]

By the time Hyde Park A & B broke ground, demolition of entire neighborhoods had lost political favor, and urban renewal succeeded the slum clearance approach as a tool of redevelopment. Urban renewal, institutionalized in the National Housing Act of 1954, allowed more targeted, specific demolition of buildings paired with revitalization of a much larger designated area.[60] These changes allowed the university to take on all of Hyde Park and

Figure 30. Hyde Park A+B (East Hyde Park) during redevelopment. East 55th Street was widened and routed around the University Park condominium towers (under construction in the photo), designed by I. M. Pei and Associates. Buildings on the northern side of East 55th were demolished and redeveloped with wider roads and more parking as part of the Hyde Park A slum clearance project. Special Collections Research Center, University of Chicago, Hyde Park, Series II: Buildings and Grounds, University of Chicago Library, Special Collections Research Center, Archival Photographic Files apf2-03954.

part of Kenwood in a new urban renewal proposal, their third major project, focusing redevelopment on numerous scattered sites between 47th Street in Kenwood and 59th Street at the Midway Plaisance. In the name of area conservation, 20 percent of structures within the Hyde Park–Kenwood plan area would be demolished, rather than the 100 percent clear-cutting of slum clearance.[61] In Hyde Park, where the residential architecture was often grand—including buildings by Frank Lloyd Wright, Solon Beman, William Le Baron Jenney, and Henry Ives Cobb—community members warmed to the preservation and rehabilitation parts of urban renewal.[62]

Preservation built support among Hyde Park whites, but the university began to face opposition to redevelopment on racial grounds. The *Chicago*

Defender, the nation's leading African American newspaper, as well as the Catholic archdiocesan council on urban conservation, lined up against the plan. They argued it would halt the citywide process of integration in Chicago by prioritizing the maintenance of a middle class, largely white enclave in Hyde Park.[63] "The Negroes who will be displaced by the demolition of housing, some of it good and sound, will be relocated . . . in the already overcrowded ghettoes," argued the *Defender*, while "new housing . . . will go mainly to the upper income whites who can best afford to pay the high rents. The lily-white islands east of the University of Chicago must remain lily-white according to the dictates of Julian Levi . . . and Lawrence Kimpton."[64]

The university responded that its redevelopment was race neutral. In fact, the university emphasized, most of the residents displaced in the Hyde Park A & B clearance projects would be white.[65] However, new development in these transitional areas was subject to the latest zoning ordinances. This reduced the density of development and mandated significant increases in off-street parking, thereby preventing the in-migration of poorer, especially black residents. It effectively created a barricaded island against the demographic wave washing over the South Side of Chicago. Members of the HPKCC were critical of Levi and the SECC for working solely in the university's interest, not in that of the broader community.[66]

The politics of redevelopment among Hyde Parkers were conflicted. The renewal plan needed the support of the HPKCC since it was the most active neighborhood group and the earliest to address racial transition.[67] The organization's relationship with the university was complex. The group included Hyde Park professionals and faculty such as Harvey Perloff, Sol Tax, and Louis Wirth, who worked with university administrators on neighborhood issues. The HPKCC emphasis was on the social side of urban conservation. They developed an active set of block organizations and recruited neighbors into a social network throughout the community. While the HPKCC nominally sought an "interracial community," it embraced historic preservation and building rehabilitation as a means to achieve "high standards"—i.e., a class-based standard that effectively excluded all but a few African Americans.[68] The HPKCC, as well as many local community members and politicians within the affected neighborhoods, supported the urban renewal plan in negotiations.

Leon Despres, City Council alderman for the Fifth Ward Hyde Park–Woodlawn area, supported the plan as well. Despres was subject to the political will of the liberal, professional-class constituency of groups like the

HPKCC because he was not a machine politician. Despres depended on members of local liberal groups rather than municipal employees and ward heelers to get out the vote at election time.[69] He expressed reservations about the renewal plan while ultimately supporting it, which was key to its passage for the Fifth Ward.

The HPKCC had minimal influence on other SECC efforts and development policy more generally. Among all the clearance, renewal, and development activities the university undertook in the 1950s and 1960s, the 1958 urban renewal plan was the only measure requiring broad community support. Thus it was the HPKCC's only key role in the redevelopment process over two decades. The university and the SECC had allowed local residents little input into development of the plan created by Meltzer, essentially removing community members from the university-centered planning process.[70] Indeed, the SECC billed itself as an organization comprising locals and neighborhood groups to offer it credibility. But a board member accused Levi and Kimpton of running the organization behind closed doors and using community members as merely "a sounding board" for what were essentially university plans.[71] These tensions within the community grew more fractious.

The Campus Plan

In the fall of 1954, University of Chicago administrators and trustees also began working to replan, redevelop, and expand the university's campus. They sought both to reestablish the university's preeminence as a major research and educational institution and to contribute to the redevelopment getting under way in Hyde Park. The expansion of professional schools and the hospital, for example, would require additional real estate and new buildings. In effect, the neighborhood transition and apparent deterioration facilitated campus expansion and redevelopment by reducing potential public opposition and creating a buyer's market for real estate.

The trustees wanted the nation's best architect to drive the vision for the university grounds, in concert with slum clearance and urban renewal plans.[72] The governing board selected Eero Saarinen, passing on Ludwig Mies van der Rohe, Edward Durell Stone, and Frank Lloyd Wright, the key luminaries in American architecture. Saarinen had won international renown for his corporate campuses reimagining business and industrial designs, such as the General Motors Technology Center in the Detroit suburb of Warren and IBM headquarters in suburban New York.[73] Saarinen delivered the master

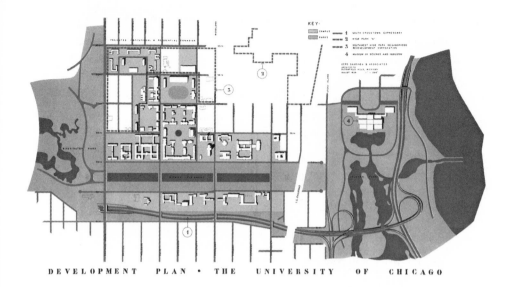

DEVELOPMENT PLAN • THE UNIVERSITY OF CHICAGO

Figure 31. Saarinen and Associates' master development plan for the University of Chicago. The proposed South Crosstown Expressway runs east–west to the south of campus, and would have required demolition of numerous buildings in Woodlawn to separate the expanding campus from the neighborhood. Special Collections Research Center, University of Chicago, Kimpton Administration Papers, Box 230, Digital file: asas-02442.

plan to guide development in the spring of 1955. The SECC's work on the Hyde Park–Kenwood urban renewal plan at the same time provided a seamless transition between on-campus and off-campus development (Figure 31).[74] Setting the stage for the next decade of university activity, the campus plan called for demolition along East 55th Street and construction of new university buildings. This paired with university expansion on campus land south of the Midway, which separated the university from the Woodlawn neighborhood.[75]

Saarinen's plan proposed an expressway south of the Midway Plaisance to wall off the campus from the increasingly African American Woodlawn neighborhood. The east–west highway would remove traffic from the Midway, moving it to a limited-access connection between Lake Shore Drive to the east and South Parkway to the west (now Martin Luther King Jr. Drive). Building the highway would require demolition of numerous buildings between 60th and 62nd Streets. "This drive serves two important purposes," University of Chicago vice president for business William Harrell said. "Since we do not control the area south of 61st Street, the drive will serve as a barrier to encroachment from that direction."[76] Saarinen's plan and design of buildings, the slum clearance projects, and urban renewal activities would dramatically alter the character and physical experience of life in Hyde Park, Woodlawn, and on the university campus to make it more automobile friendly and less dense.

Women's space, in particular, was of paramount concern in campus planning. Saarinen's design for Woodward Court, a new women's dormitory that opened in 1958, provided a cluster of residences near the middle of campus. Administrators had long felt female students would be safer from both the crimes and vices of the surrounding community if they were housed centrally.[77] Located on the southeastern corner of East 58th Street and South Woodlawn, Woodward Court was sited next to Ida Noyes, an existing women's dormitory to the south; across the street from the Rockefeller Memorial Chapel to the west; near a residential neighborhood of upscale homes, including Frank Lloyd Wright's Robie House, to the north; and by the private Laboratory Schools to the dormitory's east.

The organizing principle of the design was a courtyard that would mimic the nearby quadrangles. The space would open to Ida Noyes to the south, where undergraduate women could easily move on foot between the two buildings. However, the complex would turn its face from the neighborhood to the north, providing no entry to the dormitory from East 58th Street. The design instead called for an entrance only from the courtyard and through the central dining building. This central part was referred to in planning meetings as "the control unit."[78] Residential wings extended around the control unit, offering a modern version of the nearby neo-Gothic forms of enclosure as the building reached out its massive arms to surround the courtyard, sheltering the undergraduates in a stone-armored volume.

An interior ethos of domesticity attempted to allay students' or their parents' fears about safety by overwhelming them with protection and luxury. Proctors oversaw the residents' activities, and the dormitory provided well-appointed lounges for social and domestic space, interior and exterior protected space for women and the university.[79] At the University of Chicago, as at Ball Teachers College and the University of Texas decades before, the goals of programming secure domestic space governed the planning of women's residences.

Pierce Hall, a men's dormitory built in 1960, sat as a counterpart at the northern edge of campus. The project fulfilled urban renewal plans to replace taverns, flats, and shops on East 55th Street and to separate students from the life of the street. The university bought a block of land on the south side of East 55th between Greenwood and Woodlawn from the city that had been home to a mélange of single-story retail shops, six-flat residential buildings, and mixed-use structures up to four stories tall.[80] The university hired Harry Weese to design a residential tower. The Chicago architect had been a student of Eliel Saarinen, Eero's father, at Cranbrook Academy of Art and shared fundamental design ideals with the university's planner.

The dormitory altered the formerly close-knit relationship between the block's buildings and the street. Harry Weese's ten-story tower concept centered on the creation of interior social spaces to replace the varied private commercial venues and concentrated students into a medium-rise residential tower.[81] The design included limestone bay windows that harkened back to Chicago-style commercial architecture. But it lacked entrances onto East 55th, instead facing the building toward Woodlawn Avenue, a side street. It channeled pedestrian circulation to the southern side of the complex, which opened onto a small courtyard and an open playing field on campus. This redevelopment removed the attraction of diverse uses and services from this block of East 55th, and the new design disrupted pedestrian traffic on the street, intensifying the isolation of the campus from its northern neighbors as it drew student activity indoors.[82]

Private Capital

Construction required capital, and the return of prosperity in the 1950s led to a new source of support for higher education: capital campaigns. Gilded Age support from the likes of John D. Rockefeller, Andrew Carnegie, Cornelius Vanderbilt, Johns Hopkins, and Leland Stanford led to the founding of a number of leading institutions in the nineteenth century, but the more equitable postwar distribution of wealth made it necessary to attract a broader base of support for private institutions. Prominent among potential donors were members of the growing corporate executive class and a relatively new source of funds—private foundations. The crisis of the Great Depression and increased taxation levels during and after World War II led to the creation of the Field Foundation, which was a supporter of the University of Chicago, and the Ford Foundation, which would become one.[83]

Philanthropic investment was key to the university's urban renewal program. To raise the funds for an ambitious private market intervention, in

1955 Lawrence Kimpton organized a three-year capital campaign of $32.7 million, one of the largest in the history of higher education. Of that total, approximately $6 million would go to the neighborhood program—more than $3 million to build Pierce Hall and Woodward Court and about $3 million for off-campus buildings.[84] The funds allowed the university to buy off-campus apartment buildings and to tie campus growth to urban renewal. University of Chicago leaders and the SECC had become far more aggressive about properties on the private market. The board of trustees established the Midway Properties Trust to own the local real estate, removing it from the university budget and allowing the trustees to borrow against its value.[85] Later, they organized University City Realty Company. It attracted private investment capital for a corporation that would manage apartments designated for university students and buildings for general Hyde Park residency consistent with the university's management plan.[86] The university organized these two companies with moderate start-up capital. Administrators needed an influx of new funds to take on their neighborhood ambitions. The university brought the capital campaign to a successful close in 1957, and shortly thereafter started to buy and build with their new millions.

With this cash in hand, university leaders began to draw upon the experiences of other local and national institutions to learn what strategies had proven successful in battling the specter of blight and deterioration. Higher-education institutions had long since developed formal and informal networks to share knowledge about educational and administrative best practices and mutual interests. Michael Reese Hospital in Chicago and Columbia University in New York, for example, had also led urban redevelopment efforts and kept in touch with Chicago leaders. David Rockefeller, who had earned his PhD in economics from Chicago and was a grandson of John D. Rockefeller, was a key connection to the Columbia effort, where he helped lead their redevelopment.

University of Chicago administrators also sought counsel from leaders at the Illinois Institute of Technology, located two miles north of the campus, where the Bronzeville neighborhood seemed a threat to administrators despite being the capital of the black metropolis.[87] After one meeting, William Harrell wrote a confidential memo to Kimpton detailing the role of existing housing in controlling the Bronzeville neighborhood around IIT. "In an effort to maximize income, IIT attempted, with the cooperation of the city authorities, to correct only the most flagrant violations of the city ordinances. This policy was followed because IIT was primarily interested in obtaining control of the land and did not have a long term interest in retaining the improvements."[88] Without the burden of maintenance, IIT realized a profitable return on their invested endowment, even in the least desirable housing in areas already considered blighted. Harrell went on, "A total of about 90 acres of slum properties have been purchased by IIT. A large part of the properties so acquired have now been cleared and the land is or will be used for expansion of the campus." He concluded, "IIT did not create the slums, but did take advantage of the situation," and suggested that Chicago do the same, in concert with a program of eminent domain, demolition, and redevelopment.[89] The University of Chicago's innovations were to use philanthropic funds and student housing to enable this community management process.

The university acted as aggressively to manage the South Side real estate market as they had to redevelop sites. Administrators emphasized that slumlords menaced them with "threat properties"—buildings they threatened to sell to white speculators with black tenants—in order to command a high purchase price from the university.[90] Far more frequently, however, Don Blakiston searched out real estate in the city's newspaper listings, and the university bought any properties that advanced their program.[91] The university's allied real estate arms would arrange for purchase when Blakiston saw a building owner stop advertising in the *Tribune* and take out an ad in the metro edition of the *Defender,* the city's leading black newspaper.

In many cases, the university purchased buildings around Hyde Park and drew revenue from renting the properties, leaving some in states of disrepair as IIT had done and renovating others as apartment buildings for upper-level university students. After a decade of these activities, the university owned or controlled more than 120 buildings—nearly 2,500 housing units—in the campus area, almost 10 percent of the rental units in Hyde Park.[92]

When Julian Levi could not buy the properties he wanted or worried about, he intervened in the financial transactions of private parties. He pressured local banks and insurance companies to deny loans and investments to buyers he did not approve of or whose plans he feared were not consistent with his own development plans.[93] At times, the university paid landlords rent to hold apartments empty in the summer so that African Americans could not lease them in months when student demand declined and vacancies opened up.[94] Levi was particularly sensitive to the impact of racial demographics at local schools, arguing that when Hyde Park's primary and secondary schools became majority African American, it would provoke white disenrollment and movement out of the neighborhood.[95] "Kosminski school, which serves this area [from 47th to 55th over to Cottage Grove] is now predominantly Negro," he wrote in 1955, and argued that black inmigrations were "endanger[ing] Philip Murray and Kenwood Schools."[96] Unwilling to abide by the tendencies of the local housing market, the university worked to control the local economic landscape of real estate in addition to the physical development landscape.

Federal Policy

On October 5, 1957, the nation woke up to the news that the Soviet Union had launched a satellite into space. Opinion leaders and policy elites panicked. Senate Majority Leader Lyndon Johnson predicted that if the Soviets continued to dominate the space race, they would soon "be dropping bombs on us from space like kids dropping rocks onto cars from freeway overpasses."[97] He ushered through passage of the National Defense Education Act (NDEA) in 1958 to help bolster American science.[98]

The NDEA made urban policy more central to fighting the Cold War. The elite institutions that could train the nation's leaders in math, science, and engineering were, for the most part, located in cities. Institutions like the University of Chicago, Columbia University, the University of Pennsylvania, Johns Hopkins University, the University of California–Berkeley, the University of Texas, Harvard University, and MIT were too important to the nation's well-being as members of the "military-industrial-academic complex" to succumb to the blighted future of the urban crisis.[99] The urban setting of the University of Chicago became a threat not just to the college's survival but to the global struggle to advance democratic capitalism.

Lawrence Kimpton and Julian Levi lobbied for an urban planning counterpart to the NDEA as a means to allow Chicago and other schools to expand their campuses to fulfill the growing federal higher-education mandate without obstruction by deteriorating neighborhoods and slumlords. Kimpton served in 1957 and 1958 as the president of the American Council on Education and as a board member of the Association of American Universities, the two most important lobbying organizations for higher education. He was in regular contact with top administrators of other major universities and helped set the national agenda for higher education. In 1957, the Association of American Universities created a committee to study the problems of urban universities, sharing information among institutions such as Chicago,

Columbia, Penn, and Washington University in St. Louis. This coalition of institutions created a plan to promote a federal program to aid universities in urban redevelopment.

The universities wrote the federal legislation that would give them leverage with urban politicians and force a reordering of municipal urban renewal priorities.[100] Levi coordinated the congressional lobbying effort and hired former Housing and Home Finance Agency general counsel B. T. Fitzpatrick to write the final text.[101] The Section 112 credits program, named for the new section inserted into the amended Housing Act of 1949, reflected the new importance of higher education to cities and the importance of cities to American power.

The politics of elite education aided university urban renewal lobbying. In the U.S. Senate, urban renewal legislation fell to the Committee on Banking and Currency. The Democratic side, which held the Senate majority and ran the committee, was chockablock with higher-education loyalists. They included Paul Douglas, the former University of Chicago economist and Chicago alderman who still lived in Hyde Park; John F. Kennedy, a loyal Harvard alumnus who served on the university's governing Board of Overseers; and Joseph Clark, the former Philadelphia mayor who earned his law degree at the University of Pennsylvania and was also a Harvard alumnus and member of its Board of Overseers. State universities were also represented on the committee: Senator John Sparkman, a loyal University of Alabama alumnus, chaired the committee and heard from the statewide institution that urban renewal could help the university in places like Birmingham.

In congressional testimony, Levi and other university administrators affirmed what supporters of the NDEA had already asserted over the last year—that universities were essential to the well-being of the nation. Charles Farnsley, University of Louisville trustee and mayor of Louisville, Kentucky, went even further in his testimony, suggesting "if the universities are required to abandon our urban areas, the universities will survive but our cities will not."[102] Posing higher education as an antidote to urban disinvestment, Farnley went on: "If the university is the only thing you can work for and it is respectable to live near, and if you have the professors living back down there, that will help bring back the middle class to the city."[103]

The legislation passed in early 1959. Numerous universities, including Harvard and MIT in metropolitan Boston, Penn and Temple in Philadelphia, and New York University and Columbia in New York, drew upon these urban renewal programs in pursuit of an urban vision for the educated class, creating a robust, postindustrial urbanism in which jobs, housing, and services were clustered around universities instead of factories.[104]

Julian Levi became a nationally known figure in urban redevelopment and higher-education circles. Having learned how to use trustees and sway legislators, he began to speak around the country and to consult with higher-education institutions and hospitals, providing advice on how they might best win and use urban renewal funds for their hospitals and campuses. Levi advised leaders in Boston and Pittsburgh, and created reports that circulated the country. He detailed the University of Chicago success story, illustrating how it had risen like a phoenix from the ashes of the urban crisis.[105] His consulting work helped solidify the university's actions as a model for other institutions and explained how to replicate their efforts at universities throughout higher education.

South Campus

The university's two avenues of city-renewal politics and campus expansion intersected at the Midway Plaisance. The Midway had served as a recreational and carnival-type space during the 1893 Columbian Exposition. The university had expanded onto several parcels across the Midway in the six decades since the fair but was poised for a dramatic expansion that would require all the land in a mile-long strip between 60th and 61st Streets running between Washington Park on the west and Jackson Park on the east.

The Section 112 credits program gave the university the leverage Julian Levi sought—and intended to use. As the creator of the program, Levi had ensured that it would especially suit the University of Chicago's purposes. Any qualifying expenditures a university made near an approved urban renewal plan area—up to seven years before the approval of the renewal plan—could be counted by the municipality as a local contribution to trigger a federal match, typically at the rate of two to one. City administrations could use the credits in urban renewal projects anywhere within their municipality, not solely in the approved urban renewal plan near the university. This meant that cooperation between a university and a city administration could lead to windfalls of millions of federal dollars without the city spending a dime. Thus, the University of Chicago was able to entertain, under the provisions of the law, a proposal from Sears Roebuck and Company to give $2 million to the university to spend on urban renewal near its Hyde Park campus, triggering $6 million in federal credits that could be used on an urban

renewal project in Lawndale on the city's West Side where Sears was headquartered and tripling the power of what the corporation could achieve with
direct investment in redevelopment alone.[106] In Chicago, Mayor Daley ran
both the city administration and the Democratic machine almost as a unit
and regularly sought revenue for additional workers and programs. The Section 112 program would give the city millions without burdening taxpayers.

In 1960, a majority of the land in the strip south of the Midway was not
in university hands. The university had spent $6.9 million in eligible contri-
butions for acquisition and demolition in the area, on buildings like Pierce
Hall and Woodward Court. The city of Chicago stood to reap approximately
$14 million in credits from the federal government.[107] The Chicago Land
Clearance Commission, the municipal office created to implement slum clearance and urban renewal programs, felt pressure from the mayor's office and
had no practical alternative but to approve the university proposals. Levi remembered, "Phil Doyle of the Chicago Land Clearance Commission bitterly, bitterly resented this approach. . . . The reason being that he felt in
effect the University was hustling the city agencies, wasn't giving them their
discretion. We were forcing the issue."[108]

The South Campus strip was the first application of the Section 112 legislation, a plant expansion that simultaneously buffered the university from
Woodlawn and asserted the university's clout with the city administration.
By 1960, 84 percent of Woodlawn was African American, and 31 percent of
its housing stock was deteriorating (27.4 percent) or dilapidated (4.0 percent),
versus 22.9 percent African American and 15.3 percent problematic housing
for the city as a whole. African Americans constituted only 37.7 percent of
the population in Hyde Park and had been diverted from the university
neighborhoods in the earlier urban renewal efforts.[109] South Campus was Julian Levi's opportunity to make concrete his recommendation to Lawrence
Kimpton in 1954: "Make it amply clear that the area from 60th to 61st is
ultimately an area of University interest and dominance."[110]

The politics of growth liberalism was changing by the late 1950s and early
1960s, and dissenters had begun defecting from the postwar liberal coalition. One of the focal points of this dissent was urban renewal.[111] When policy makers and the urban proletariat realized the promise of postwar growth
would not be evenly shared, a new coalition of individual political and cultural critics and grassroots organizations began to realign and mobilize
against urban growth and redevelopment policies. Key advocates of modern
housing such as Catherine Bauer Wurster, who had worked to popularize

European ideals of social housing in the United States, began to launch critiques of the public housing and renewal program, calling it a "dreary deadlock."[112] In the case of Southeast Chicago, the University of Chicago had so successfully insinuated itself into the municipal vision for economic growth and the national agenda for technological and capitalist triumph that it became inextricably caught up in the web of political mobilization, public policy, and redevelopment finance.

Neighborhood groups in Woodlawn feared a major urban renewal project south of the Midway would harm their local community more than the university's efforts in Hyde Park had done. A coalition of religious leaders sought aid, over Levi's objections, from Saul Alinsky's Industrial Areas Foundation (IAF) to organize in opposition.[113] Alinsky, a Chicago alumnus with a degree in sociology, had made his name by helping organize citizen groups in the Back of the Yards neighborhood near the Union Stockyards. He lived in Hyde Park and had been peripherally involved in community protest of the Hyde Park renewal plan.[114] The IAF began mustering opposition to the university while helping build a black grassroots organization to serve as a countervailing force against the university.[115]

Alinsky had developed a successful template for community organizing that he employed in Woodlawn. He thought the university's land grab would succeed eventually but used the issue to "rub raw the resentments of the people of the community," helping build a neighborhood organization by playing up issues of conflict.[116] Alinsky and his chief Woodlawn organizer, Nicholas von Hoffman, helped a coalition of neighborhood institutions, from church congregations to businessmen's organizations, coalesce under the umbrella of the Temporary Woodlawn Organization (TWO).[117] When Fifth Ward alderman Leon Despres tipped off von Hoffman to a South Campus construction proposal before the Chicago Plan Commission in December 1960, TWO appeared with approximately forty local residents to question the redevelopment approval, and the proposal ground to a halt.[118] City officials were surprised by the display of public engagement by African American residents of Woodlawn, dramatically overestimating the crowd at "hundreds, you might as well say a thousand."[119] Though Julian Levi expected a quick agreement, the individual proposal took several months to enact. South Campus, however, remained a contentious political issue delayed by politics and process for several years.[120]

Woodlawn activists pursued a broader agenda for community development. TWO, led by pastor Arthur Brazier, used the community spirit stirred by the South Campus urban renewal proposal to address school segregation and retail exploitation, and to build solidarity with Southern civil rights efforts. TWO brought Southern Freedom Riders to Chicago in 1961 and Southern Christian Leadership Conference leader and Chicago Freedom Movement member Ralph Abernathy as the guest of honor when TWO became a permanent organization.[121] In parallel to the work of the HPKCC, where women played prominent roles, TWO recruited and empowered the women of the community to take on the key issues of the neighborhood. They formed "truth squads" of mothers to document crowded conditions at black schools and excess capacity at white schools and identified crooked grocers who used weighted scales in neighborhood shops. TWO's greatest threat to the established order was a voter registration drive that built a black vote independent of the influence of South Side Congressman and machine loyalist William Dawson.[122] This engagement led several University of Chicago and Hyde Park–area theological students to begin organizing with TWO, fulfilling their personal and vocational interests in community service.[123]

Student Action

David Wolf and his group of friends could not get an apartment, and they suspected it was because one of them was black. The University of Chicago freshman and his classmates were turned away at building after building when they searched in the spring of 1961 for an apartment for the fall. Wolf's father, a labor organizer, advised that if they wanted to show racial discrimination, they needed a paired-applicant test, where a white applicant and a black applicant would independently inquire about a vacancy in the same building. They took his advice, and as a result, the Congress of Racial Equality (CORE) found a pattern of racial discrimination by University Realty Management Office, the company that managed the off-campus properties owned by the University of Chicago. In the 1950s, U of C students had supported the Hyde Park urban renewal effort, but the Civil Rights movement prompted students to take racial inequality more seriously.[124] Later in 1961, members of CORE confronted George Beadle, Lawrence Kimpton's successor as university president.[125] Beadle had maintained Kimpton's initiatives, and Levi remained in position at the SECC. Beadle defended the university's practice as incremental progress, claiming the university worked to proceed "as fast as we can to attain integration as soon as we can."[126]

Figure 32. Bernard Sanders (right) and George Beadle (left). Congress of Racial Equality (CORE) students occupied the University of Chicago Administration Building in January 1962 to protest housing segregation. CORE member and future U.S. Senator Bernard Sanders appeared at a press conference with university president George Beadle to discuss the occupation and university response. Danny Lyon, Magnum Photos.

The students were not satisfied. At a meeting in January of 1962 at the new Woodward Court dormitory, CORE members voted to occupy the administration building and the realty office to protest the housing policy. On January 23, a group of thirty-three people, mostly students, occupied the offices of the university administration building and the office of University Realty Management Office, which handled the university's off-campus residential real estate (Figure 32).[127]

The occupation revealed significant tensions among the institution's administrators, faculty, and students. A week before, students at Southern University in Baton Rouge, Louisiana, had staged a mass protest against racial segregation in that city. The Southern University president, Felton G. Clark, had suspended twenty-three students following the protest. It was one of the first civil rights protests directed at a university; the protest in Chicago was the first directed at a university itself for discriminating. Demonstrators remained in the administration building around the clock, seeking meetings with university administrators. Police arrested several at the realty office. Debate raged for more than a week.[128] The *Chicago Tribune* scoffed that the students "no doubt fancy themselves intellectuals" but called the sit-in "un-intelligent."[129] The *Defender* called the sit-in "the only intelligent, rational way of making the University of Chicago realize its moral responsibility to the surrounding community."[130] Faculty largely opposed the obstruction of the university's business. Students split on the protest and the broader issue of campus housing policy.[131]

After thirteen days of protest, President Beadle threatened to suspend the students from the university.[132] CORE ended the sit-in when Beadle agreed to create a faculty committee to study the issue. Julian Levi had often joked to Kimpton that faculty research in the Hyde Park community was irrelevant, but in one of the university's most critical moments, it was an essential tool—as a stalling tactic. The university commissioned professors from law, sociology, and business programs to study local housing and write a report.[133] A month later, the committee issued a document that exhibited the influence of university faculty who were involved in the HPKCC, such as Harvey Perloff, Sol Tax, and Herbert Thelen. It echoed the HPKCC goal of "an interracial community of high standards," and the committee recommended a more active role by the university, including research on group dynamics and advocacy of open housing.[134] These actions—incremental, technocratic solutions tilting slightly liberal—undermined the position of CORE, which pushed for more engagement with administrators after the report's release. Students found they did not have the support of the moderate faculty, who prioritized research and working within existing organizations like the HPKCC over direct action. University leadership had neutralized student opposition to university segregation and the overall neighborhood management program by returning to a shared, fundamental university priority: research.

The issue would not stay buried. Just a few months after the demonstration, the city's Commission on Human Relations wrote to request a public commitment against housing discrimination. Ely Aaron, the commission's executive director, asked the university to forbid discriminatory local landlords from advertising in university venues. University administrators were determined to keep the issue in the background. They debated the proposal and decided not to respond.[135] The dean of students sought to comply but William Harrell overruled him. Harrell wrote, "Certainly, we can ill afford to undertake the responsibility for telling our neighbors that they should not discriminate."[136] In Harrell's telling, university administrators, who could seize land, demolish buildings, force the hand of the city's powerful mayor, and meet with the president of the United States about their conservation and redevelopment schemes, claimed it could not risk the bad will of local landlords. He did not admit that local landlords' discrimination aided and advanced the university's own neighborhood initiatives.

Urban Politics

The university could do more than create and pass plans and programs. It learned how to navigate the growing opposition to urban renewal and redevelopment. Later, in the spring of 1962, voters denied a city urban renewal bond issue at the ballot box, leaving the Daley administration wanting for local redevelopment funds and empowering the university.[137] That year, a plan to redevelop a block across East 55th Street from the University of Chicago campus also met neighborhood opposition. The university coordinated with the Lutheran School of Theology in Chicago and planned to expand its redevelopment buffer around campus. The two schools faced down holdouts by threatening to build the new, modern building *around* the last remaining apartment building (Figure 33).[138]

TWO and the university both recognized they were playing with a strong hand—the university because it could bring millions of dollars to redevelopment efforts in need; the community group because satisfying the demands of loyal Democratic voters would remove the political obstacle to passage of the plan. The liberalization of the restrictions for Section 112 credits meant a dramatically increased number of credits for the city of Chicago. Julian Levi predicted an agreement with university chancellor George Beadle. Indeed, in the spring of 1963, Daley, Levi, and Brazier met at City Hall and negotiated a settlement the mayor announced in July. The Woodlawn neighborhood actually demanded a *broader* urban renewal plan that would include investments as far south as 63rd Street, provide public housing, and not displace residents. TWO also negotiated significant input into the plan but compromised from a position of self-determination—one of the organization's rallying cries—to representation on a citizen planning committee. In return, the university would finally get all of the land between 60th and 61st Streets, from Cottage Grove to Stony Island. Ironically, the delay and more vigorous independent action by the university yielded the city more credits—$20 million by 1964 versus the $14 million initially considered in 1960.[139] Municipal finance counted far more than protest or political activism. With the South Campus agreement, the university had nearly fulfilled the initial vision created by Levi and Kimpton in 1954.

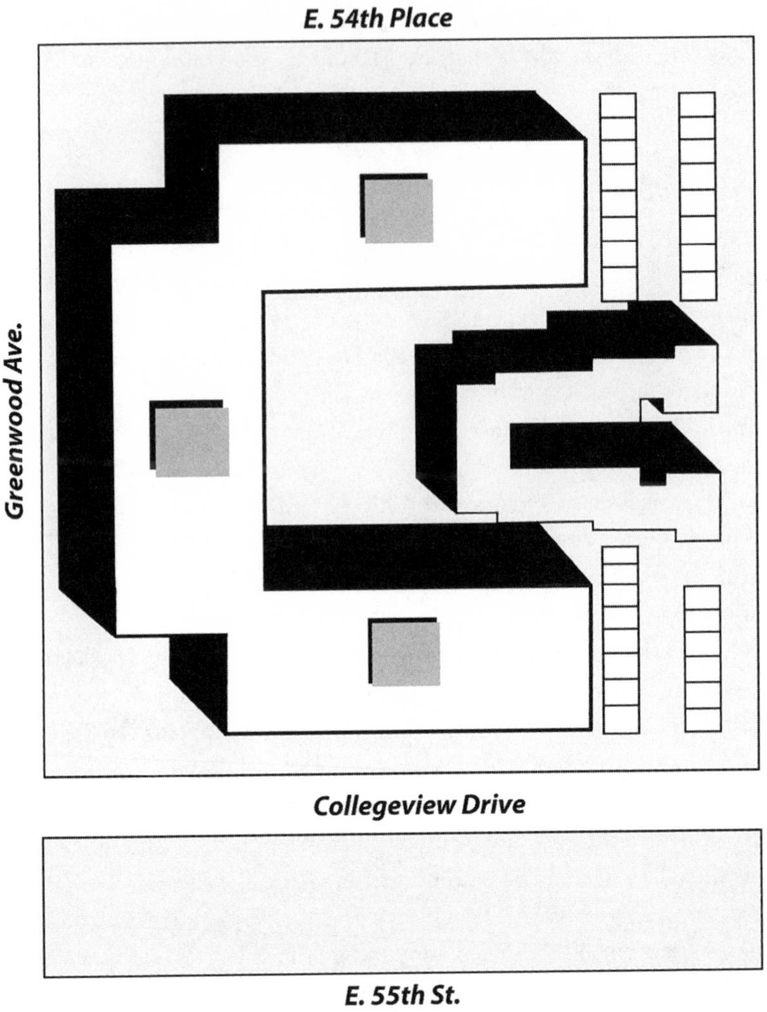

Figure 33. Lutheran School of Theology design. For the proposed site for the Lutheran School of Theology (LSTC) in Chicago, architecture firm Perkins+Will released a design that would surround the last holdout building on the block and isolate it from the neighborhood. Members of the building cooperative relented and exchanged property with the University of Chicago for a different building. The LSTC building design was subsequently rotated ninety degrees counterclockwise before construction. Image created by the author, after a Perkins+Will image published in the *Chicago Maroon*.

Administrators had learned to preempt political surprises and, in order to expedite future development proposals, created a general development plan for South Campus. Rather than face the possibility of political opposition for each new building, university officials proposed a multiphase plan over many blocks in Woodlawn that, when approved, would provide all necessary authorization for the University of Chicago to proceed with construction. Once again, Julian Levi led university officials in creating the development plan, gaining final city approval in 1966.

When the plan went before the city, the proposed ordinance saw no opposition and passed without even press notice. TWO had criticized the university's plans in 1960 and had found fault with the manner of seizure and the university's interest in isolating itself from the neighborhood. The organization had never opposed university developments per se and made no complaints now. The university had learned a valuable lesson about shaping the built environment. Zoning, which could seem one of the most tedious and trivial of all forms of government regulation, in fact represented the victory in a political battle by other means. Zoning was the bureaucratization of development politics, a means of hiding a transformative urban agenda by burying it in reams of arcane city code.

By the mid-1960s, the University of Chicago had reached the limits of its own resources and had arrived at a crossroads in Hyde Park and Woodlawn. In the early years of Beadle's administration, he publicly discussed the possibility of moving the campus to the Chicago suburbs. The president and trustees decided to organize another capital campaign, one even larger and more ambitious than Kimpton's effort of the 1950s. The university had overcome its enrollment crisis of the early 1950s, and student numbers at the undergraduate and graduate levels were high.[140] Having saved the university in the 1950s, university leadership then sought to envision what a new University of Chicago would look like—larger, better funded, and even more central to the future of the city and region.

The Campaign for Chicago, announced in 1965, aimed to complete the transformation of the university and Southeast Chicago. The campaign was then the largest capital campaign in the history of higher education. The development staff planned to draw on more than 19,000 alumni in the Chicago region and had particular interest in more than 1,000 prospects for gifts of $100,000 or more, signaling a repaired relationship with the city and region after the Hutchins years. The $160 million goal dwarfed the previous campaign record, Duke University's $102 million campaign, announced just two months before Chicago's.[141] Of the university's $160 million goal, $88 million was slated for physical plant improvements, including $5 million devoted to acquisition of the rest of the land between 60th and 61st Streets.[142]

The laying of the cornerstone of the Regenstein Library on November 15, 1968, was an auspicious day for the university. It represented the promise of its plans for redevelopment and growth along with the tensions of its position in metropolitan Chicago. In the course of the capital campaign, the Helen and Joseph Regenstein Foundation gave $10 million, the majority of the funding for a new library devoted to graduate research. The library site was the heart of campus, replacing the university football field, where the original Manhattan Project uranium-pile chain reactions took place. In turn, athletics facilities would shift to the western edge of campus located at Cottage Grove and East 55th Street—the site of the original South West Hyde Park Neighborhood Redevelopment Corporation's graduate student housing proposal. Recentering the university's brain also involved establishing a grassy buffer on the western part of Hyde Park and fulfilled the university's first steps, taken nearly two decades before, to remake the area. The afternoon ceremony included addresses by Robert Streeter, the dean of the humanities; Joseph Regenstein Jr., the son of the industrialist who had amassed the fortune enabling the family's gift; and Edward Levi, the University of Chicago president who had just succeeded George Beadle. The ceremony was held on a chilly Friday as part of the week of events for Levi's inauguration. The new president proudly claimed, "I cannot imagine an event in the history of The University of Chicago which is more important than this one," gesturing at an institutional history that was bound up with his family's history.[143] He and his brother had spent nearly two decades working to secure the institution their grandfather Emil Hirsch had helped create.

The ceremony was a celebration of promise and plans for the future but revealed a profound failure. Administrators had wanted a dinner and an evening ceremony in the new law school building south of the Midway, including a reading by author and faculty member Saul Bellow. The major donor, Helen Regenstein, vetoed an evening event. She was not about to ask her acquaintances among the Chicago elite to go "down into that dangerous neighborhood at night."[144] Despite two decades remaking the city's South Side, the university could not remake the opinions of Chicago business elites and North Siders like Regenstein. To them, Hyde Park and Woodlawn were still too dangerous after dark.

That enduring opinion was another category entirely from the concrete changes that the university had brought to the neighborhoods. With millions of dollars of private investment, federal urban redevelopment and renewal funds, and philanthropic donations, the University of Chicago's postwar neighborhood plans demolished scores of buildings, acquired dozens more, and included the construction of several new buildings on its own expanded campus. In the process, university administrators had bent municipal, state, and even federal law to its own purposes in order to facilitate redevelopment. University of Chicago administrators also worked with universities around the country in similar efforts and created a template for institutional expansion and university-led urban redevelopment. In the case of Chicago, the imperatives of institutional preservation and national competitiveness took precedence over considerations of remediating local racial inequality.

By 1968, universities and higher education had earned prominent places in American society and successfully argued that their expanded mission required expanded resources, key among those academic space. Drawing on its prominent position at the end of World War II, the University of Chicago illustrated that an institution of higher education could use federal funds for more than research to contribute to economic development. The school administrators had shown that if it chose to take on the challenge, an institution of higher education had the tools to fundamentally remake an urban area—to become an agent of dramatic urban change. Following the University of Chicago's example, many institutions would choose—or be expected—to do the same.

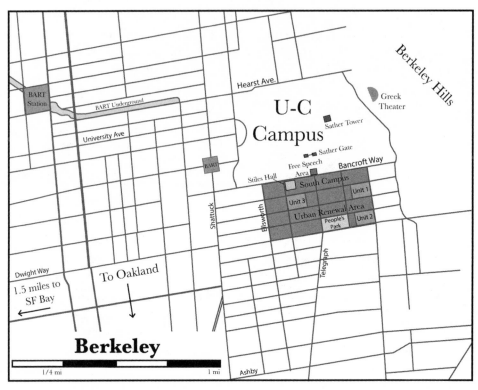

Figure 34. Berkeley, California. Map created by the author.

4 | Radical Politics and Conservative Landscapes

Mario Savio approached the podium in the Greek Theater at the University of California at Berkeley (UCB). Two university officers pounced on the leader of the Free Speech Movement (FSM), grabbing his arms and wrestling him to the ground. They dragged him from the stage before a row of Doric columns meant to invoke the ideals of ancient Greek democracy. More than ten thousand students seated in the hillside theater watched in horror, then shouted in outrage as their fellow student was violently removed from the assembly. UCB president Clark Kerr, had just said the school would discipline FSM demonstrators, but students did not expect it to be enacted so violently and instantly.[1]

The December 7, 1964, assembly had been called to announce a set of campus disciplinary and policy decisions, and administrators held it in the outdoor theater for a reason. Like ancient Greek theaters, the UC Berkeley Greek Theater was a large assembly space that could accommodate the members of a community who came together for debate, entertainment, and civic duty. The whole campus was a set of sites, forms, and symbols about the democratic promise of higher education and the state's commitment to it. Over the preceding century, the university had created Sather Tower, Sather Gate, the Greek Theater, and numerous campus buildings as neoclassical symbols of the principles of democracy, good governance, and citizenship. The colonnaded Greek Theater, nestled in the Berkeley hills, looked out over the city and San Francisco Bay's Golden Gate Bridge, just as theaters throughout the ancient world had looked out on the sea. Berkeley was Athens on the West Coast, a maker of democratic citizens and a beacon of learning to the world (Figure 35).

The University of California at Berkeley and the surrounding community became a key location in the unraveling of the postwar liberal order

Figure 35. Greek Theater, University of California, Berkeley. The theater was one of the improvements fulfilling the Beaux-Arts campus vision selected in the 1898 competition financed by patron Phoebe Hearst. Campus development at the turn of the century often employed neoclassical forms (like the theater) to build an architectural association with the classical world. Free Speech Movement Photographs, courtesy of the Bancroft Library, University of California, Berkeley.

during the 1960s. The forcible removal of Savio from the Greek Theater at the assembly was one of a series of episodes in which students, administrators, and politicians clashed over the meaning of political freedom and the limits of activism while they battled over control of urban and campus space. The creation of a statewide system of higher education in California bound all of these strands together, which snapped apart in a series of episodes including the Free Speech Movement, the People's Park protest, and the leftist April coalition in city politics.

UC Berkeley became the model for elite public universities and a bellwether for institutions around the country. The story of the UC system is well documented, but many institutions like UCB took on new, global responsibilities that required more planning, more development, and revitalization of surrounding areas to accommodate growing enrollment and ambitions. In New York, the state legislature created the State University of New York system in 1948 and expanded it dramatically in the 1950s and 1960s, incorporating university, college, and community colleges under its umbrella, which now includes sixty-four campuses. North Carolina, Wisconsin, Missouri, and Texas established state systems, in some cases modeling them on the California system. Wisconsin established twenty-six campuses, with Madison as the flagship. North Carolina built seventeen university campuses, led by the campus at Chapel Hill; Missouri founded four institutions and Texas, eight. The shared goal was to democratically provide higher education in order to promote economic development. The means was the creation of large, bureaucratically integrated public organizations to do so. This institutional growth, especially at UCB, put universities in tension with local values and began to undermine the community they had helped create.

In Berkeley, radical politics had spatial origins within the academy. The Bay Area was one of the nation's most prominent stages for leftist protest—against racial oppression, against university control of student action and urban space, against the Vietnam War—and experimentation with alternative lifestyles. The university drew from the wealth of the state and the nation to provide an elite education that brought students from around the world, but the stage upon which the drama played out was concrete and local. Urban space in Berkeley became a catalyst for action, a symbolic site of opposition, and a generative source of new ideas about community. As postwar prosperity and liberal ideals came together in the 1950s, 1960s, and 1970s, modern urban planning and design could not prevent cracks from forming in the educational edifice when state and local political forces shifted in the underlying foundation.

Postwar Development

Berkeley had changed quite a bit from the sleepy suburb it had been before World War II. The opening of the San Francisco–Oakland Bay Bridge in 1936 connected San Francisco to Oakland and Berkeley in the East Bay, making regional transportation more fluid and promoting development in outlying areas. East Bay communities like Berkeley, backed against the foothills of the Pacific Coast Range, also saw significant growth. Industrial workers flooded the East Bay during World War II for jobs in the Oakland shipyards and on construction crews in one of the arsenals of democracy, joining university students in Berkeley next door, where university enrollment nearly doubled from 1930 to 1950.[2] The American West, long identified with open spaces and low population density, had become one of the fastest-growing regions in the country by 1950.[3]

After the war's close, the Bay Area became a center for scientific and engineering research and a leading economic region in the state.[4] In the 1950s, California surpassed New York as the country's leading state for military contracts. Metropolitan regions that had been both industrial and scientific leaders like Philadelphia, Detroit, and Chicago fell by the wayside. Santa Clara County, at the south end of San Francisco Bay and just south of Alameda County, was home to the engineering centers San Jose and Palo Alto. The county was the state's number-three recipient of defense funding by the late 1950s, accepting $570 million a year in contracts and services, putting thousands to work all over the Bay Area.[5] In Berkeley, the Atomic Energy Commission took over the Radiation Laboratory near campus and established a classified atomic research center in nearby Livermore, across the Berkeley Hills. New communities sprang up along the undeveloped edges of the bay from Oakland to the south, taking over agricultural land in places like Fremont and Sunnyvale. Tech and science workers' homes supplanted fruit orchards; new roads and highways plowed through agricultural fields.

Postwar growth was a mixed blessing for Berkeley. The city lacked the open land of suburbs farther south and so had to accommodate more residents at greater density. Individual investors converted houses to apartments or added accessory dwellings. These practices put stress on the existing infrastructure and, when done badly, led to the deterioration of blocks and neighborhoods. Population increased by one-third in the 1940s, adding 28,258 new residents—the largest growth in the city's history.[6] The African American population in Berkeley increased even more dramatically in the 1940s, from 3,395 to 13,289, as new residents arrived for jobs in the surrounding industrial communities.[7] Restrictive covenants covered up to 80 percent of Berkeley, and the black population was confined to the city's southwestern neighborhoods, where they faced poor conditions and limited access to capital.[8] Housing starts could not quite keep up with population growth, meaning the city was more crowded and dilapidated in 1950 than it had been in 1940, when more than a tenth of the city's housing needed major repairs.[9]

Two groups found Berkeley's one- and two-story form of shabby postwar urbanism desirable—students and beatniks. Students largely lived within walking distance of the campus, and the area south of campus was the most popular neighborhood for student residence.[10] Beat writers moved to the region in the 1950s. Bay Area bohemianism was created, in part, by the intervention of the federal government. Wartime investments brought jobs, and in the postwar years, areas around the naval bases and shipyards made San Francisco and the Bay Area an attractive area for alternative lifestyles. Aspiring poets, playwrights, and poseurs congregated first in San Francisco, then spread throughout the region, including into Berkeley. Jack Kerouac's novel *The Dharma Bums* begins in Berkeley, where small, cheap cottages in the city's backyards provided writers, poets, and translators low-cost housing and the freedom to pursue their craft as well as access to the professors, libraries, and other intellectual resources of the university.[11] Affluent Berkeleyans built higher into the hills and sought apartments in modern midrises. Berkeley boosters claimed the suburb would become "a major city in its own right." However, decades of disinvestment and a market slow to respond to this new growth meant most working- and middle-class Berkeleyans had to endure crowded urban conditions and growing signs of blight until developers could compensate and make broad investments in housing.[12]

Anti-Communism

On campus, postwar California's changing political winds agitated university administrators. The state turned virulently anti-Communist in the late 1940s as demobilization from World War II turned into fear mongering for the Cold War. Suburban growth and anti-Communism were mutually reinforcing efforts as businessmen linked politics and profit, especially housing developers, who argued home ownership was key to capitalistic freedoms.[13] The defense industry put economic muscle behind Cold War ideology. California politicians like Los Angeles County congressman Richard Nixon, made their careers on anti-Communist rhetoric.[14] The House Un-American Activities Committee (popularly known as HUAC) investigated Communist influence in the Bay Area and Berkeley and produced a critical documentary called *Operation Abolition*. Condemnation of Communism came from all corners.[15] Regents on the left and the right shared a commitment to anti-Communism. Edward Heller, a Democratic Regent, proclaimed, "I yield to no one in my detestation of communism and communists. . . . There is no question that they have no place in the University, and I will enthusiastically vote to remove any found on our faculty."[16] The Regents imposed a loyalty oath on its faculty. In 1949, the Regents dismissed thirty-one faculty members for refusing to take the oath, creating a firestorm over academic freedom.[17] The university was not a remote center of isolation and irrelevant inquiry. It was part of a full frontal assault on Communism, developing cogs for the wheels of democratic capitalism and directing scientific knowledge for Cold War opposition.

Cold War anti-Communism changed the spatial dynamics between the campus and city. The university campus was off-limits for political discussions. At the University of California at Los Angeles in 1949, the Graduate Students Association held a discussion with Communist historian Herbert Phillips, who had been dismissed from the University of Washington. They were forced to move the discussion off the campus grounds, which resonated throughout the university.[18] Cal faculty and students alike turned to the off-campus community for intellectual and political space. Student groups began collaborating with local institutions to host political activities and discussions in an area adjoining the edge of campus. Stiles Hall, a branch of the YMCA on Bancroft Way, was a key forum for these activities and events. It was located a block south of Sather Gate, where students entered the university grounds each day. Stiles Hall was part of the private development that arose in the university district of retail shops, apartment houses, and restaurants across Bancroft that came to be known as the Telegraph Avenue district.[19] It became a key site of interaction between town and gown at Berkeley—a safe haven for the expression of political speech and discussion.[20]

Isolating higher education from politics put it in tension with the humanistic goals of exploration. Critics who rejected the idea of a postwar consensus would point out the university's myriad political faces. UC Berkeley, like the University of Chicago, had supplied physicists such as Ernest O. Lawrence to the nuclear war-making effort in World War II and continued to receive millions of dollars in grants and contracts to conduct defense and nuclear research.[21] The Regents were distinguished men and women from around the state—many of them business leaders with political and ideological affiliations. Administrators served on the Berkeley City Council, and Cal faculty had a long tradition of serving in city government.[22] The city council included planning professor T. J. Kent Jr., who had been planning director for San Francisco and founded the city planning department at the university.[23] When Kent won election as a Democrat, he recalled one of the key issues was "containing and stopping the territorial expansion of the university while respecting and nourishing its life."[24] Despite this nourishment, students could not invite leftist speakers to campus and could not organize against racial segregation under the umbrella of a student organization. Students' education in Western, liberal values emphasized inquiry, but the university set limits on its practice on school grounds.

Planning for Growth

Clark Kerr emerged from this tense environment to become the Berkeley chancellor in 1952 to give direction and form to the midcentury education impetus. Kerr was an economist and labor negotiator who was brought up as a Quaker pacifist. He had done graduate work with agricultural economist Paul Taylor, documenting Depression-era conditions in California with Taylor's wife, photographer Dorothea Lange.[25] Kerr had risen to prominence during the oath controversy and was renowned for keeping his head and his values in a crisis. Bald and bespectacled, the Berkeley chancellor bore a striking resemblance to Milton Muffley, the managerial U.S. president in Stanley Kubrick's 1964 film *Dr. Strangelove*.[26]

Kerr's most lasting legacy as chancellor was a pair of plans. The 1956 Long Range Development Plan (LRDP) for UC Berkeley, followed in 1957 by its academic counterpart, the Statement of Educational Policy and Programs, laid out recommendations for the future of the university.[27] The LRDP gave physical expression to the values and priorities stated in earlier postwar planning documents. They set the university's chief responsibilities as "basic research, graduate and undergraduate instruction, high-level professional training, and expert public service."[28]

Kerr excelled at orderly management, and the plans reflected this. The LRDP called for doubling developed campus space over ten years while limiting ground coverage to 25 percent of the low-density, traditionally planned main campus.[29] The two goals seemed to be in diametric opposition—more developed space but limited development on the existing campus. The university would have to expand beyond its established borders into the city. The LRDP illustrated a land acquisition plan with a several-year horizon, offering state legislators a sense of priority for appropriations and giving local landowners the ability to make economic decisions around the efforts of the university.

Eminent domain gave the plan the aura and power of inevitability. A 1918 amendment to the state constitution gave the Regents the power to acquire land. It was later construed as power to condemn property. In 1957, the university's legal counsel wrote a new bill affirming these powers explicitly in the law. Education advocates in the legislature took up the cause and ushered the bill through to passage.[30] Landowners in Berkeley and across the state who were unwilling to sell their property to the university were powerless to stop the institution's expansion plans. They could barely prolong negotiations. Haggling over a few thousand dollars or stalling in negotiations prompted a swift response, in which the Regents filed to condemn the property.[31]

The planning process made clear the ambitions of the university's leaders. Kerr made a special appearance before the city of Berkeley's Planning Commission in March 1957 to explain the development plan and how it would help the city and the region. He sat before an audience of 250 concerned city residents in a jam-packed public session. Kerr laid out the economic rationale for university growth, calling higher education a new industry that was pollution free, "the largest single employing unit in Northern California," and "depression-proof."[32] The chancellor promised that the university would abide by the city of Berkeley's master plan, but gestured expansively at the reasons for new development. "Some individuals will have to be disturbed. But could we in good conscience not go ahead with a reasonable expansion program? . . . The University has a responsibility to mankind. . . . The last ten elements on the chemical table were discovered here on the Berkeley campus."[33] After the launch of *Sputnik* in the autumn of 1957, discourse on education emphasized the importance of science to national pride and global leadership. Kerr faced Berkeley residents and planning commissioners months before the launch of the Soviet satellite would shock the nation. He presciently asserted scientific discovery and a broader goal of human progress as overriding concerns about local homeownership or urban character.

Midcentury liberals like Kerr were concerned with systems that would modernize and provide broad benefits to community and nation, and less so with the specific concerns of individual private property owners in the neighborhood. Urban space and research productivity were linked. Global institutions such as UCB had a moral and intellectual responsibility to reshape cities to help create knowledge.[34] Kerr was just the man to spread these efforts. In 1958, the Regents named him to succeed Robert Sproul as president of the UC system.

A System of Mass Education

When Clark Kerr assumed the presidency of the University of California, the system was facing epochal change. Waves of state and national investment were surpassing the local flows of capital and natural resources that had been essential to the development of universities in the nineteenth and early twentieth centuries as they had been for Ball State, the University of Texas, and the University of Chicago. Where Ball State had the Ball family and Chicago had the Swifts and the Fields, the Hearst family in Berkeley had been prominent supporters of the University of California. The Hearsts had been a mining family rooted in California. After the deaths of George and Phoebe Hearst, subsequent generations, led by their son, William Randolph Hearst, turned their attention to national ventures. Growing fiscal capacity in the public sector at the state and federal levels, especially after World War II, outstripped the ability of local business leaders to make meaningful economic and philanthropic investments.[35] Evolution in investment, production processes, and networks yielded an increasingly global basis of economic growth in which corporations became less committed and less responsive to local communities.[36] By the 1950s, the city of Berkeley was more of a staging ground for innovation than the source of economic development and the foundation for intellectual capital formation it had been. Muncie, Indiana, and Chicago saw similar developments as prominent families nationalized their approach to investment.

As if to prove the power of the state, Kerr coordinated an effort that turned a loose mix of competing higher-education institutions into a statewide system. The Berkeley LRDP and Statement of Educational Policy and Programs were the models for the statewide 1960 Master Plan for Higher Education. Throughout California, metropolitan leaders recruited and promoted defense-related industries that required skilled workforces. The master plan invested in university and college campuses in these areas, including in Los Angeles, San Diego, and Orange County. In part, these institutions trained scientists and engineers for the defense contractors who created the weapons and technology deployed in both the hot and cold wars of the 1960s and 1970s. Their higher-value jobs and the development of affluent, segregated suburban communities fueled economic growth. These two related sectors of growth provided the state of California the resources to fund the higher-education system.[37] The California legislature passed the Donahoe Higher Education Act, making the master plan law in April 1960. At the signing ceremony, Governor Pat Brown called it "the most significant step California has ever taken in planning for the education of our youth" (Figure 36).[38]

The master plan provided higher education to every qualified citizen of California and landed Kerr on the cover of *Time*. The question that remained unanswered in the midst of this expansion was, what would that education

Figure 36. Sather Gate, the traditional entrance to the Berkeley campus. Students from the Telegraph Avenue neighborhood followed the street full of bookstores, soda fountains, and barber shops to the gate. Until a post–World War II expansion, the city of Berkeley controlled the area just outside the gate, and it became a popular location for student protests and recruitment for campus organizations. It was control over this spot that sparked the Free Speech Movement. This image depicts a 1940 rally against the military draft. University Archives, courtesy of the Bancroft Library, University of California, Berkeley.

be worth to the students who undertook it? Kerr attempted to answer this question in a lecture he delivered in the spring of 1963 at Harvard University. Kerr explained that since World War II, universities such as the University of California no longer provided the intimate, collegiate experience they once had.[39] Such large institutions constituted a "multiversity," with multiple campuses and many areas of knowledge. Their mission had shifted to the new industry of "knowledge production," which contributed a significant share of the American economy through scientific research, engineering improvements, professional career training, and other knowledge-based means of adding value to products and services.[40] Kerr's contemporaries echoed his rhetoric, later published as *The Uses of the University*. University of Pennsylvania president Gaylord Harnwell, for example, described an intellectual economy in which universities were "exporter[s] of American knowledge."[41]

The democratic provision of mass higher education came with significant drawbacks. In essence, Kerr affirmed that making higher education accessible to an ever-larger share of the American population involved significant trade-offs in the college experience. The change in universities' mission meant that white mice were as important as undergraduates and that students might receive their course lectures via closed-circuit television screens rather than from professors in person. In a telling irony, the Berkeley campus created the Center for Studies in Higher Education in 1956 to promote research on student experience, systems, institutions, and processes in higher education. It acknowledged that in an impersonal university, only institutional social scientific inquiry could allow faculty and administrators to understand the breadth of students and the nature of the university experience.[42]

Key among these new instruments of mass education was the IBM punch card and its accompanying mainframe computers. UCB introduced these technological innovations in 1956 to help count, coordinate, and analyze the activities of nearly twenty thousand students on the Berkeley campus alone. The punch cards carried the warning "Do Not Spindle, Fold, or Mutilate," so that they could be inserted flat into mainframe computers. The beauty and the horror of the punch card was that it reduced the material and human requirements for tracking students. No longer would secretaries and other staff need students to wait in long lines and fill out forms that had to be counted by hand. Once the data was in a computer, the computer could generate a report to tell administrators just how large the student body was, what their majors were, and where they were from. The students felt dehumanized by the process and gave rise to the joke that they, like the punch cards they used, should not be spindled, folded, or mutilated.[43] UCB pioneered closed-circuit television for instruction, another means of disembodying education and negotiating the scarce space of the Berkeley campus. For a brief period, the technological spectacle of being taught via television seemed to administrators to offer a wonderful new promise for higher education. Soon, however, students diagnosed the practice of watching professors on monitors as another symptom in the pathology of postwar universities.[44] Students' lived experience of mass education seemed to leave the postwar promise of individual opportunity unfulfilled.

Building Campus Activism

UC Berkeley had a housing crisis that intensified the challenges of changing character. The university had never had much housing on campus. The growing enrollment put students at the mercy of an unforgiving local market. Regents adopted a dormitory system for Berkeley that would install a university-run housing regime, intended to create the collegiality among students that had long eluded the institution. In 1945, the Regents had set a goal of providing campus housing to 25 percent of the student population. The university's first postwar development plan called for five high-rise complexes, each a block in size comprising four residential wings. The targeted area south of the UCB campus was a densely populated, low-rise neighborhood, meaning the architectural accretions and disorder of many decades of small-scale development would be cleared and replaced with the unified vision of a Corbusian modern architect.[45]

The Regents embraced brutalist design in response to the College Housing Program's requirement of economy and to express the liberal ethos of education. A group of architects led by Le Corbusier and the Congrès International d'Architecture Moderne advanced the discourse of modernism and emphasized the aesthetic rationality of modern architecture. The efficiency of production involving concrete was another important factor in its cultural ascendance and its adoption by corporate and educational clients.[46] Indeed, the need for efficiency so thoroughly pervaded the dormitory designs that the buildings were later characterized as housing boxes made to provide square and cubic footage to undergraduate residents. California architects were developing their own strain of design known colloquially as West Coast Modern. Warnecke and Warnecke, a Bay Area firm, won the competition for the initial dormitory project.[47] By reusing the winning design on additional sites, they won other dormitory commissions at UCB, enacting mass production of interchangeable parts. The university evocatively named the nearly identical residential complexes Unit 1, Unit 2, and Unit 3 (Figure 37).

The federal government provided two key funding streams for UCB dormitories. The first was the College Housing Program, a federal loan fund created by a provision in the 1950 Housing Act to aid construction of dormitories and accommodate postwar growth at universities. It enabled scores

Figure 37. Units 1, 2, and 3. The dormitories of Units 1, 2, and 3 were a triumph of brutalist design that efficiently provided housing for students and a design that could be reproduced multiple times on Berkeley urban blocks. Students rejected the spatial implications and lived experience of mass education in the dormitories and in campus life. 1959 *Blue and Gold* Yearbook.

of projects at universities around the country each year. UCB received a loan of $1.6 million as part of an $18 million application for dormitories across all UC campuses.[48]

Nuclear fission gave UCB its second funding stream, one unavailable to the rest of the country. UCB students lived a college experience that was imbued with the tensions of the Cold War, right down to the walls of their dorm rooms. The university held federal contracts for the maintenance and operation of several federal nuclear research laboratories, including facilities in Los Alamos, New Mexico; nearby Livermore, California; and the Radiation Laboratory on the Berkeley campus. These contracts from the Atomic Energy

Commission paid the university millions of dollars each year, about half of which was captured as overhead costs. Overhead was the percentage of each grant universities withheld for general funds on the logic that externally funded research projects also required campus space, staff time, and other generally available university resources. At one point in 1956, it seemed parsimonious state legislators might delay the development of new dormitories. The Regents responded by allocating the specially held overhead funds from the nuclear research contracts—a $4.4 million loan from the overhead account and $1.8 million loan from a nuclear research account—to finance development of the dormitory complexes.[49] When students protested the connections between federal research and their lived experience at UCB, they may not have appreciated how close the relationship, owing to the complicated budgeting of the mammoth university, actually was.

As the first two dormitory units were under development in 1957, several friends met in a garage and planned the formation of a campus political group called SLATE.[50] Mike Miller was an undergraduate and Fritjof Thygeson a graduate student. They found the social and political order of campus conformist and stultifying, where Greek fraternities dominated the student government and McCarthyism had silenced postwar activism.[51] SLATE adopted student housing as one of their key concerns; it was a pragmatic and broadly shared student issue. When construction delays prevented the opening of Unit 1 and 2 dormitories in September 1959, SLATE blamed the administration for making the UCB housing situation worse. Members wrote in a campus publication that "the plight of students in procuring housing has reached crisis proportions. Psychological effects of the crisis, as well as the actual displacement of 840 students, has brought about an increase in rents and a scarcity of housing throughout the university area."[52] Other members chimed in with criticism of university housing policy that had "a widespread effect in the university" and, as political decisions, required political responses.[53]

Students did not like the dormitories. They were a far cry from the informality and accretions of the private apartment houses of the surrounding area south of campus. The older, ramshackle housing off campus actually served the university's purpose, according to Clark Kerr in *The Uses of the University*. He suggested universities could exploit both inner-city neighborhood deterioration and suburban expansion because "an almost ideal location for a modern university is to be sandwiched between a middle-class district on its way to becoming a slum and an ultramodern industrial park—so that the students may live in the one and the faculty consult in the other."[54]

The Bay Area contained both of these types of communities. Farmland in Palo Alto owned by Stanford University at the southern end of the bay provided the national research park prototype.[55] In Berkeley, crowded neighborhoods and industrial communities provided plentiful cheap housing for students around its campus, but the aesthetic and economic lure of modern design was too much to resist.

Dense, centrally planned modernism failed on university campuses before it failed in urban public housing around the country.[56] Students rejected the buildings in favor of the older housing around campus and eventually began calling Units 1, 2, and 3 "the projects."[57] Dormitory vacancies created a budgetary crisis at Berkeley and other UC campuses: the towers could not cover their income projections and debt payments. UCB architecture professor Sim Van der Ryn stepped in to study students' housing preferences and give a design evaluation of the buildings. Students hated the rigid layout of their rooms; they preferred spaces they could personalize and the character they found in apartments around the city. Studying was difficult because of the dorms' interior layouts, and the spatial arrangements broke students' concentration. The placement of their desks made them face each other while they were studying. Finally, Van der Ryn found that even the dormitories' social spaces suffered from the effects of standardization: barren and cavernous.[58] For UCB sociologist Martin Trow, they had "good provisions for sociability; rather more limited and constricted ones for intimacy, and little or no provision for solitude."[59] Units 1, 2, and 3 perfectly fit the drive toward mass education: plenty of space for large groups, little space or attention for the individual.

Students in other places objected to modernist high-rises and laboratories. Richard Fariña set his counterculture novel *Been Down So Long It Looks Like Up to Me* in a loosely disguised Ithaca, New York. He described the new construction as "tinted aluminum plates, long sheets of weatherproofed glass, dymaxion torsions: the synthetic contents of a collective architectural grab bag. Clean, well lighted, cheap to heat, functional, can be torn down and replaced over a long weekend or transported to Las Vegas by helicopter, demolition incorporated in the structural design."[60] Tom Hayden, one of the leading figures in the emerging New Left movement, was first politicized by housing at the University of Michigan. He described his enormous dormitory, built after World War II and containing more than 1,200 students, as suffering from "a barracks culture, with its twin lacks of privacy and community and its sink-or-swim message."[61] Hayden visited Berkeley while in college to report on SLATE and found in the organization a meaningful model for campus political activism. Hayden was a key author of the Port Huron Statement, which became the clarion call for a generation of student activists. It opens, "We are people of this generation, bred in at least modest comfort, housed now in universities, looking uncomfortably to the world we inherit."[62] Disaffection with the liberal order began, in part, with campus planning.

Back in Berkeley, city leaders began worrying about the concentration of beatniks, burnouts, and freethinkers hanging around campus and the Telegraph Avenue neighborhood. Civic leaders turned to demolition and redevelopment to deal with the community's social and economic problems. In January 1957, a panel of city departments examined the causes of urban blight and "the deterioration of many of the city's neighborhoods," as well as the prospect of bringing urban renewal funds to the city. Promotional and lobbying groups at the national level, including the American Council to Improve Our Neighborhoods (ACTION) and the National Clean Up–Paint Up–Fix Up Bureau, advocated for urban investment and housing redevelopment. A local chapter of ACTION made public presentations and advocated for renewal in Berkeley, aiding city departments in the study effort.[63]

The city administration focused on the university community and student housing at the expense of all other areas of Berkeley. The western neighborhoods in the industrial areas near the bay had long faced problems of crowding, disinvestment, and deterioration. The city's report focused on the South Campus student neighborhood and, using visual surveys, specifically identified properties as student housing in contrast to any other kind of housing. In one example, the authors implied that student housing was especially—if not inherently—susceptible to the spread of blight, asking of a house on College Street, "Student Housing—Why paint the place? Why replace the missing handrail? Only students live there anyway!"[64] (Figure 38) A thorough neighborhood analysis later showed, based on 1950 U.S. Census data, that the student areas north and south of campus were hardly blighted by the city's definitions; the central business district and industrial areas near the bay were far more problematic and urgent priorities.[65]

A decade of real-estate exploitation made ACTION's fears a reality. Seeing that the university would soon swoop in and buy up the neighborhood block by block on a schedule, landlords curtailed their building maintenance. Local opponents of renewal blamed the university, claiming that the administration's slow buying process prompted landlords to cease reinvestments and maintenance in their properties. Analysis of the student neighborhood based on 1960 U.S. Census data asserted that fully one-fifth of the city's

BLIGHT THROUGHOUT BERKELEY

2434 COLLEGE . . . .
STUDENT HOUSING — WHY PAINT THE
PLACE? WHY REPLACE THE MISSING
HANDRAIL? ONLY STUDENTS LIVE THERE
ANYWAY !

2631 CHANNING . . . .
THE STAIRS ARE COLLAPSING & ROT IS
CREEPING UP THE PORCH. SMALL WONDER
THE UNIVERSITY IS ENTERING THE
STUDENT HOUSING FIELD.

2635 CHANNING . . . .
THE REAR A CLAPTRAP OF SUB-
STANDARD ADDITIONS. THE WHOLE A
SERIOUS FIRETRAP. ANOTHER EXAMPLE
OF STUDENT HOUSING IN BERKELEY.

HEINZ STREET . . . .
STRUCTURALLY SOUND, THEREFORE NOT A
BLIGHT? HOW CAN YOU GET PEOPLE TO FIX
UP THEIR HOMES WHEN AN UGLY DILAPIDATED
SIGHT SUCH AS THIS IS RIGHT OUTSIDE THE
FRONT DOOR?

Figure 38. Urban renewal in Berkeley. City leaders promoted the potential for urban renewal in Berkeley by singling out student housing and attributing problems of blight to student rentals. This 1957 report was jointly authored by several city departments including the Fire Department and the Board of Health and Safety. Institute for Governmental Studies, University of California, Berkeley.

dilapidated structures were located in the South Campus area, which included only 4.7 percent of the city's housing units.[66] In just a decade, conditions had deteriorated badly. Built-out neighborhoods, towns, and cities around the country faced similar challenges, as Hyde Parkers in Chicago could attest. Density and disinvestment prompted city administrators to create an urban renewal proposal attacking the blight of the South Campus area. Berkeley's urban renewal plan slowly wended its way through city government over the course of several years. University administrators were fully in support of such a plan as the city and university worked hand in glove on development.[67]

Free Speech and Free Space

The mercurial energy of politics would not wait for the plodding pace of public policy. A student walking to campus in the 1940s and 1950s funneled from the South Campus residential neighborhood onto Telegraph Avenue, passing restaurants, bookshops, barbers, and soda joints. It was a concentration of student-oriented retailers that served as a pedestrian vein, collecting vital eyes, feet, and wallets from the neighborhoods and pushing them toward Sather Gate, the traditional south entrance to the UCB campus, then leading to the heart of the campus.[68] For years, students and community members gathered here just off the edge of campus to give speeches, advocate for a cause, or criticize the administration as students streamed through Sather Gate on their way to classes.[69]

In 1941, the university bought up a block of buildings south of the portal and replaced them with the university's Administration Building (now Sproul Hall). Increased postwar enrollment rendered the old student union too small and outdated, and UCB demolished a block of buildings across from the Administration Building. This extended the edge of campus from Allston Way, where Sather Gate was, to Bancroft Street, a block farther south.[70] The city of Berkeley vacated their rights to all the land, streets, and sidewalks between Allston and Bancroft. Students were no longer able to give speeches at Sather Gate under the freer, general public-access rights to the land because of the university rules that forbade political activity on campus. A wide array of student organizations, including SLATE, complained to the campus and university administration in the fall of 1958. Administrators made a tentative arrangement to return a small portion of land to the city of Berkeley at the edge of campus, at Bancroft and Telegraph. Officials never formally executed this planned transaction, and the issue disappeared in 1960, when

Chancellor Glenn Seaborg left the university to become the chairman of the Atomic Energy Commission.[71] No one realized the transfer was incomplete, and students went back to using the land as if it were owned by the city, free from university regulations. University administrators allowed students to distribute pamphlets in their traditional spot outside Sather Gate.

The fall of 1964 saw a political tinderbox waiting to be ignited. Students were alienated from the campus by its modernist character. Freedom Summer, the voter registration effort in the Deep South, invigorated student activism, and the approaching presidential campaign channeled this political energy into electioneering. In previous years, students in organizations such as the Congress of Racial Equality (CORE) had staged sit-ins at Bay Area car dealerships, restaurants, and hotels to protest the exclusion of African American workers.[72] A number of student groups canvassed and recruited by setting up tables at the entrance to campus, between Bancroft Way and Sather Gate, which had been established as a "Hyde Park," or free-speech zone, in the late 1950s, used by liberals and conservatives alike.[73] Groups favored that specific site because of the large proportion of undergraduate students living to the immediate south of campus in their dense quarters of dormitories and apartment houses. Walking up Telegraph to Sather Gate on their way to classes or the library each day, they streamed past the tables of student organizations. One student remembered, "Students coming on campus each day passed the political groups and could stop to browse but were not stopped by them. Nestled between the city and the campus was 1,000 square feet of political space which nourished the student marketplace of ideas."[74] In mid-September, Dean Katherine Towle announced that the city did not officially own this land and that students on it were subject to rules forbidding political activity on campus.[75] Students and their tables had to go.

The movement soon shifted from a technical dispute over land to a forceful confrontation over politics. Students built a broad coalition to oppose the restrictions, from Students for Goldwater to the Ad Hoc Committee to End Discrimination. Together, organizations in a self-described "United Front" decided to move to a location deeper within the campus, challenging the administration at a location in front of Sproul Hall, the administration building. Jack Weinberg was a UCB alumnus who had remained in Berkeley after graduation and was a member of the Berkeley chapter of CORE.[76] He sat at a table during the event in front of Sproul and refused to identify himself to campus officials. Weinberg began rallying the students around him, and, when a policeman in a cruiser arrived to arrest him, students surrounded the car and refused to let Weinberg be taken away. They made speeches from atop the car and used their bodies as shields in a clash over the university's rules on politics. This thirty-two-hour protest resulted in the suspension of several students and began a semester of organizing, protesting, and negotiating. FSM member Michael Rossman recalled, "People start[ed] talking, bringing in the Greek Philosophers, bringing in the French Revolution, talking about all the ideas, Constitutional liberties, as if they had meaning!"[77] Surrounded by structures built to invoke the highest ideals of Western society—Greek democracy, faithfulness and asceticism, Renaissance inquiry— the messages of the campus and its education came together in the plaza in a way students had never felt (Figure 39).

The South Campus neighborhood became the center of the student political coalition's activities.[78] It was already central to campus dissent as the location of campus-oriented religious institutions, including Stiles Hall. When UCB moved political activities off campus, they found an incubator in the South Campus neighborhood, which nurtured a more serious political challenge than the administration anticipated.[79] Mario Savio emerged as the public face of the FSM, and his apartment on College Avenue in the South Campus area became the movement's headquarters.[80] This location was geographically central to establishing and sustaining a coalition of interested students, ground zero for an experiment in participatory democracy that built consensus among members. The building was located within walking distance of both Sproul Plaza and the meeting places or group headquarters of a wide array of on- and off-campus groups composing the FSM. Savio's apartment in the South Campus area was, like the disputed area at Sather Gate, key to the development of a feeling of community in the movement.[81] Savio hosted long meetings of FSM participants and steering committee members to debate policy; correspondence came from and traveled to Savio's apartment; and it was the movement's nerve center, called FSM Central.[82] Historians have argued that the fellowship of sit-ins helped strengthen and expand the bonds among FSM activists.[83] The fellowship of a neighborhood of choice—a new community that students created themselves—was also key to this effort.

The situation escalated with rallies and occupations throughout the fall of 1964. It came to a head in December when nearly eight hundred students were arrested while occupying the Administration Building just outside Sather Gate.[84] The administration arranged an assembly in the Greek Theater on December 7 to announce an agreement between Kerr and the Council

Figure 39. Free Speech Movement rally. Students surrounded a police car to protest the arrest of Jack Weinberg for canvassing on the Berkeley campus and refusing to show his identification. The protest lasted for thirty-two hours and included speeches and singing. Marcus (Steven) Free Speech Movement Photographs, University of California University Archives, courtesy of the Bancroft Library, University of California, Berkeley.

of Department Chairmen. Department chairs leaned more conservatively and were more administration oriented than some of their younger colleagues, such as historian Carl Schorske and philosopher John Searle, who sided with and counseled FSM leaders.[85] FSM members at the Greek Theater seethed at the compromise plan, and the event culminated in the forcible removal of Mario Savio from the stage of the Greek Theater.[86] The next day, the Academic Senate met to assess their position. Most members sided with the FSM, and the administration backed down on the issue of speech. The Free Speech Movement had won its right to Sather Gate political space, and the university acknowledged space for politics on campus.

Rejecting the Landscape of Modernity

With the FSM land and speech issues settled, the campus and the city administrations turned their attention back to the Telegraph Avenue neighborhood. Roger Heyns, the UC Berkeley chancellor, acknowledged in an oral history the university's role in creating blight. "[Landlords] didn't keep it up," he said. "Sometimes we were slow in tearing down buildings. It was very run down, which means in my view that there was a certain kind of culpability on the part of the University."[87] Student protests and the 1964 Free Speech Movement delayed the plodding renewal effort by distracting university and municipal leaders and diverting staff time and attention.

Urban renewal and the battle over political space were not isolated issues, however. When the campus battle resolved, threats to the comfortable, low-rise character of the Telegraph Avenue neighborhood moved the conflict back off campus. Berkeley was in the midst of the Bay Area's regionwide reorganization and modernization.[88] In late 1965, the city of Berkeley's urban renewal staff finally put forth an $11 million plan that needed only the political imprimatur of the city council to move forward. The city's proposal was based on the Section 112 credits program devised by Julian Levi in Chicago. It would set standards for property rehabilitation, demolish buildings for the construction of a new street parallel to Telegraph Avenue, and create new parking lots.[89] Administrators were sympathetic to urban renewal efforts throughout the university system, and UC Berkeley's leaders cooperated with city of Berkeley renewal advocates. University expenditures of $3.87 million for land acquisition would constitute the lion's share of the $4.02 million local contribution, triggering a two-to-one federal match of $7.05 million under the Section 112 program.[90] The city initially estimated the municipality would end up with more than $300,000 of credits that could be devoted to other renewal projects around Berkeley.[91] The League of Women Voters, who had brought the policy debate to the fore ten years earlier, led a set of supportive civic groups, but the city's liberals found fractures in their traditional coalition of supporters.[92]

The politics of space was key to the disintegration of the liberal political order. By the mid-1960s, opposition to urban renewal had gained a foothold in political and architectural discourse and in cities around the country. Architectural critics like Jane Jacobs and antistatist business scholars such as Martin Anderson objected to the heavy hand of government in real estate, while social scientists like Herbert Gans exposed the vibrant culture and community amid neighborhoods deemed slums. Postmodernist critics questioned fundamental notions of progress that had seemed settled in postwar liberalism.[93] "Less is a bore," architect Robert Venturi wrote, playing off the ornamentally stripped, corporate-friendly "less is more" modernism of

Ludwig Mies van der Rohe.[94] Citizens began to revolt against massive interventions in the urban landscape, such as interstate highways and urban renewal in cities from San Francisco to New York, and protested against the destruction and segregation such projects left in their wake.[95]

Berkeley's counterculture and small business interests formed an unusual phalanx against the urban renewal plan.[96] One had a distaste for modernism, the other for laissez-faire ideology; left and right wrapped around the political spectrum to battle redevelopment.[97] Berkeley's local business owners, including realtors and the prominent Sather Gate Merchants Association, were fearful of relocation, worried about the costs of seismic retrofitting, and concerned over the parking prescriptions of the plan. They turned out in force against the project and lobbied their councilmen to defeat urban renewal.[98]

The city's daily newspaper, the conservative *Berkeley Gazette,* concurred with the businessmen's concerns. The paper heavily quoted critics who lashed out at both urban renewal and the counterculture. The city was "aghast at the intrusion of the nationwide Beatnik element in their part of town." Businessmen, the newspaper claimed, generally felt "urban renewal is good in principle but we resent having it forced on us."[99] The beatniks joined a new constituency of students and recent graduates to oppose the renewal plan. These residents of what was popularly called the town's Left Bank echoed student assessment of UCB dormitories, claiming urban renewal would destroy the "casualness" and "variety" of the South Campus neighborhood.[100] One vehement critic recruited Berkeley's working class, alleging that the Section 112 credits created would be devoted to Oceanview, an industrial neighborhood in West Berkeley with a predominantly working class, minority population was the real object of renewal.[101] The city administration faced the public criticism with crime statistics. They justified their program by citing a growing drug trade near the university and drawing on the chief of police for support.[102] Support for urban renewal was support for law and order.

In July 1966, the key proposal in the South Campus plan made its way before the Berkeley City Council amid a wave of negative press and public accusations. Conservative councilman John DeBonis led the objectors by noting that his constituency—businessmen and conservatives—strongly opposed the plan.[103] The council voted the plan down, six to two, which took university leaders by surprise. Despite a strong statement of support early on in the process and cooperation throughout, university administrators failed to lobby on behalf of the plan, expecting that the overall benefits to the city would win the day without direct university politicking. The university administration, like the city administration, was slow to come to terms with the changes in the political order. Efforts like urban renewal, which had been thought of as good government policy promoting urban growth, were increasingly toxic to the electorate. Regents were dumbfounded at the "vehement," "violent," and "vociferous" public response in opposition to the plan.[104]

In the wake of the defeat, the Regents considered several options. The university could try to restart the renewal process, help the neighborhood develop its own plan, or assist a private developer. The democratic process had failed from their perspective: a vocal minority had vetoed a set of benefits accruing to all of Berkeley. The Regents settled upon the least democratic but most straightforward option, one Heyns suggested in a memo: "Redevelop the area unilaterally through greatly increased land acquisition. This we must do."[105] The university's next steps were clear.

Over the same ten years as the urban renewal debate, the city fought for a specific vision of regional rail that minimized redevelopment and disruption of Berkeley's urban form. The creation of the Bay Area Rapid Transit District (BARTD, now BART) connected Berkeley to San Francisco and the rest of the East Bay by rail. Berkeley civic leaders and faculty like T. J. Kent saw problems with an aboveground rail system. They fought BART administrators on the design, insisting on an underground path through the city to limit demolition. In Oakland, BART lines reshaped the city's geography, drawing capital away from black business districts and bringing noise and crime to areas along the line.[106] Berkeley citizens overwhelmingly voted for a bond plan in 1966 to finance the underground construction from near the city's southern boundary to its northern border. Citizens voted 83 percent in favor, so Berkeley could pay up to $20 million in additional costs for running the line underground.[107] Residents felt the city's special character and property values were worth the tax bill.

People's Park

The state's conservatives struck back at Berkeley's radicalism and tax-and-spend liberalism, as the city and campus came to stand in across California for all the excesses of the postwar regime—taxes, disorder, and upheaval. Republicans tied together pieces of the fraying Democratic coalition with conservatives who condemned the Bay Area counterculture and the growing welfare state. At campaign rallies in 1966, gubernatorial candidate Ronald Reagan described psychedelic parties with voyeuristic distaste; his policy agenda included reducing the property taxes that funded the university.[108] Alex Sherriffs, a UCB vice chancellor and critic of campus activists, "was worried about the Communists taking over," according to a colleague, and argued that a permissive society was at the root of the FSM protests.[109] Reagan heard one of Sherriffs's talks in 1966 and incorporated his ideas as he campaigned against the excesses of Berkeleyans. When Reagan won the governorship in 1966, he made Sherriffs his top education adviser and then a vice chancellor for the California State University system. Reagan condemned Clark Kerr's handling of Berkeley protestors and arranged for his termination as UC president. When Kerr emerged from the meeting where the Regents removed him, he joked he left the job as he took it, "fired with enthusiasm," going on to serve on the Carnegie Commission on Higher Education and Carnegie Foundation for Policy Studies.[110] Reagan had the support of California conservatives as he began to roll back the state's commitment to higher education, which had held at the high-water mark for less than a decade.

All of the disparate threads leading through the local politics of space and the state's education efforts were slowly burning fuses leading to an explosive block off Telegraph Avenue in Berkeley's South Campus area. By the late 1960s, growing university enrollment had solved the housing problems of Units 1, 2, and 3, filling the buildings, and the UCB administration wanted even more dormitories. The university assembled a group of parcels on a block bounded by Haste, Dwight Way, and Bowditch Streets in anticipation of a new high-rise student housing complex to match and augment Units 1, 2, and 3. Roger Heyns had asserted the university's responsibility to lead development south of campus rather than waiting for local initiatives. He abandoned Kerr's idea that the LRDP and housing redevelopment in the South Campus area were necessary forms of support for the university's academic mission. Heyns instead framed demolition and redevelopment as a means to reduce crime and alleviate social problems in the student neighborhoods.[111]

The demolition of houses and apartment buildings in the area took over a year, from November 1967 to December 1968. In the midst of a campus housing crisis, the seemingly slow pace of development attracted the ire of university critics.[112] The Regents had expected state funds for the new dormitory, but legislators did not provide them, as the booming economy and flush budgets of the late 1950s and early 1960s had come to an end. After they had already completed demolition of a whole block of houses and apartments, UCB administrators planned to use the block for recreational facilities until the university could secure construction funds.

In the dense and creative neighborhood near campus, the vacuum of activity at Haste and Telegraph could not last. A local resident and activist, Mike Delacour, envisioned the vacant lot as a park, a site for community gatherings, and students began to use it that way in early 1969. In April, a group of residents began organizing work parties on weekends to improve the grounds.[113] The *Berkeley Barb*, a leftist newspaper, promoted these uses. With the first notice, hundreds of volunteers turned out to plant trees and grass and furnish benches and play equipment. Frank Bardacke, a former UCB graduate student in political science, advocated the doctrine of users' rights to the leaders of the park improvement group.

University leaders realized they would soon face another contest over campus property.[114] Heyns ordered a fence erected around the block when community members began calling it "a people's park." The loosely affiliated groups who had been using and working on the park came together into an opposition coalition, set on maintaining control of the landscape they had labored over and to hold an outpost against state imposition and university growth.

The park coalition was wide ranging. Sim Van der Ryn offered to mediate between the university administration and the park advocates. He proposed a community design project that would empower the park advocates and offer an orderly and less confrontational development process for the university land. Locals like Delacour simply wanted a return to a more constructive form of activism and community building after the violence of many recent Vietnam protests. Van der Ryn asserted that the park issue had to be understood in the context of the overall development and education landscape at UCB and in the Bay Area, writing, "For the first time, hundreds of young people felt the sense of performing meaningful work towards creating a place of their own. Many students told me that the park represented their first real involvement in learning at Berkeley, a sense of participating in something significant and important. Many felt the joy of creating beauty in a city increasingly dedicated to ticky-tacky and asphalt."[115] Van der Ryn's use of the phrase "ticky-tacky" from the Malvina Reynolds song "Little Boxes," later popularized by Pete Seeger, illustrated the fusion of culture and politics in the New Left.[116] The coalition of students and local leftists critiqued the modern suburban development regime on multiple axes. University leadership rejected the community design proposal on logistical grounds: it would not be practical when so much planning had already gone into the site. In so doing, leadership also rejected an emerging ideal of distributive problem solving and participatory democracy in favor of centralized institutional authority.

Mario Savio had graduated and moved to the United Kingdom after college, but he later returned to the Bay Area and attended People's Park events, lending a legitimacy to the cause and a connection to earlier radical battles. He said about the park effort, "The great hope implicit in the People's Park is that in our leisure time, so to speak, we will make the social revolution. Property is not a thing to keep men apart and at war, but rather a medium by which men can come together to play—a people's park."[117] Neither the demolished houses at Haste and Telegraph nor the proposed dormitories seemed so important anymore: the battle was over something bigger, over what the site represented.

The confrontation over People's Park was the culmination of an increasingly violent conflict between student radicals and the state's political establishment. The university leadership, no longer headed by Kerr, stood in as the instrument of the Reagan administration. Students who had organized sit-ins, teach-ins, and demonstrations on Telegraph Avenue continued to occupy buildings at UCB after the conclusion of the FSM. State political leaders had deployed the California National Guard as the protests persisted, and the Guard used tear gas on campus. Students sitting in lecture halls or walking across campus where protesters congregated felt the effects of seared lungs and burning eyes as surely as the protesters. One activist leader of the People's Park effort described his hope that the confrontation over the park would "suck Reagan into a fight."[118]

Violent battle would indeed disrupt the movement. On May 15, nearly a month after the first work party on university land, contractors began to erect a fence around the property to keep people out. People's Park organizers held a rally at Sproul Plaza and marched to the park site, chanting "Take the Park!" There a small contingent of armed police officers confronted the protesters. The crowd of more than a thousand pelted law enforcement with bottles and rocks. The county sheriff's department and the California Highway Patrol came to their aid, but they could not impose order. Police shot tear-gas canisters at protestors, who hurled them back at the police. People threw rocks from neighboring roofs. The protest turned deadly when sheriff's forces restocked with shotguns and ammunition. The deputies began firing on the crowd, at men and women on rooftops, and at reporters on the street (Figure 40).[119]

Figure 40. People's Park. The erection of a fence around People's Park—the block at Haste, Bowditch, Telegraph, and Dwight Way—prompted a group of students and locals to march from campus to "take back the park." There, sheriff's deputies confronted the marchers and protestors with riot gear, tear gas, and firearms. Janine Weidel Photography.

One bystander was killed, another blinded, and scores of protesters were wounded along with several police officers who were pelted by objects. Governor Reagan instituted a curfew, and the California National Guard occupied the city for three weeks. Berkeley seemed out of control to the rest of the state and country, as national media coverage blamed the violence on "radicals . . . spoiling for a fight."[120]

Campus to City Politics

The tanks in the streets and occupation by an armed military force while the California National Guard occupied the city made it seem that the Vietnam War had come home to Berkeley. The conflict around People's Park could have been the end of student radicalism. But a number of local leaders saw it as the start of a broader political movement. People's Park veterans began organizing a group that would become the Berkeley Tenants Union in the fall of 1969, capitalizing on the momentum of the park clashes. Delacour claimed the two efforts were part of the same mission. It was "taking us one step further toward controlling the institutions that dominate our lives," he argued.[121] The action struck at real estate, the most traditional form of wealth. More generally, it attacked the American property rights regime. The tenants union aimed to build an alliance of radical organizations and to oppose private developers and investors. The union provided an organized front to negotiate with and promote housing code compliance by the city's landlords.[122] Union organizers canvassed and won modest gains, forcing landlords who had long neglected their property to keep up their rentals. Union members inserted themselves into a broader Bay Area coalition of housing activism, helping Palo Alto create a tenants union.[123] The Palo Alto Tenants Union moved into legal activism, striking against their city's zoning regime.[124] The Berkeley rent strike's concrete effects were short-lived but held enduring political consequences for the city. Out of the crucible of these dramatic events—civil rights organizing, the Free Speech Movement, Vietnam protests, opposition to urban renewal, the People's Park, and the rent strike—Berkeleyans forged a new left-liberal political coalition.[125]

The western flatlands and the East Bay corridor were fertile ground for alternative politics.[126] Segregation and disinvestment had thrown together a tightly knit community that rejected typical strategies for community problems. The growth of the graduate student population and older students at UCB augmented an active and left-leaning segment of voters in Berkeley. This joined with an increasingly organized African American community.[127] The new political coalition began to bear fruit in the rise of Ronald Dellums, who won a Berkeley City Council seat in 1967. He then defeated incumbent liberal Jeffrey Cohelan in the 1970 Democratic U.S. congressional primary and went on to take a seat in Congress. Dellums ran on an antiwar platform, supported the rent strike and the continuing People's Park movement, and took up a Black Panther proposal for community control of police, whose excesses and brutality in preceding years shocked Berkeley and Oakland residents.[128] Berkeley's coalition of leftist organizations, with Dellums as the "titular head," captured three seats on the city council in the April 1971 municipal elections and helped Warren Widener win a four-year term as the city's first black mayor.[129]

After five years of organizing, the city's radicals had become the mainstream rather than a political insurgency, and the Berkeley political left came to be known as the April Coalition.[130] Following closely on the heels of the election was ratification of the Twenty-Sixth Amendment. It lowered the federal voting age from twenty-one to eighteen and enfranchised the majority of college students. Across the country, cities with large, politically active, college-age populations such as Ann Arbor, Michigan; Madison, Wisconsin; and Cambridge, Massachusetts, elected students or more left-leaning representatives in its wake and adopted more progressive policy. For a time, student political power was a force to reckon with. The newly ascendant April Coalition established a program of New Left housing and planning policy as they asserted power in the early 1970s.[131] Since the early 1960s, concerns about rising property values and gentrification had worried working- and middle-class constituencies in Berkeley's western flatlands.[132] The decline of the city's traditional political power centers and the rise of alternative political ideologies allowed several groups to question long-held precepts of land economics and urban growth. Neighborhoods in western and northern Berkeley formed associations to lobby their city council and to counteract the clout of large property owners and the region's pro-growth coalition. These flatland residents feared they were under attack by housing economics, public policy, and architectural design. Rising rents, taxes, and housing prices would force them out of their neighborhoods, or their neighborhoods would no longer be worth living in as speculators and developers demolished human-scale shingle-style homes, constructing multistory apartment buildings in their place.

Progressive urbanism, protecting the interests of the residents who already lived in Berkeley, became a key political and planning framework for the entire decade.[133] It meant controlling the built environment through downzoning and passing a neighborhood preservation ordinance that limited development. It also meant establishing rent control to keep housing affordable for counterculture and working-class residents who already lived in the city. Berkeley's left pursued a forceful alternative to the creative destruction of real-estate investment that, without a strong guiding regulatory hand, promised to replace the city's Craftsman bungalows and Victorian mansions with modern boxes and Machine Age facades to create profitable investment returns. The Nixon price freeze of August 1971 reinvigorated tenant advocates. They proposed a rent control charter amendment for the July 1972 municipal election. The measure passed, 52 percent to 48 percent, rolling rents back to August 1971 levels and creating an elected rent control board to manage rent increases.[134]

Neighborhood activists and members of the April Coalition had established a beachhead against the pro-growth coalition. They made another assault on the East Bay development regime with a neighborhood preservation ordinance. Martha Nicoloff, a veteran of Berkeley neighborhood politics, and Ken Hughes, a recent economics grad from UCB, formed the Berkeley Housing Council, a group of historic preservationists, tenants rights advocates, and rent control promoters pursuing user-oriented public policy. Downzoning in affluent North Berkeley neighborhoods and an increasing impetus for growth control in Berkeley placed limits on new development and provided the leftist coalition with policy precedents and the intellectual foundation for their neighborhood preservation agenda. The preservation coalition held "People's Housing Conferences" to incorporate public input and lobbied to build broad-based support for an ordinance. Nicoloff included students in their agenda, calling them "an integral force" in North Berkeley, a place where "there are very few student neighborhood problems" because of the policy controls that mitigated exploitation of property.[135]

Over the objections of the Chamber of Commerce and city council moderates, 77 percent of Berkeley voters approved the preservation measure in 1973. The Neighborhood Protection Ordinance established a moratorium on new development and demolition while the city rewrote its master plan to incorporate neighborhood goals and environmental mandates for new development.[136]

The upheaval was over. The radicalism of the Free Speech Movement and the People's Park conflict had found a new home in antidevelopment activism and protection of the familiar Berkeley built environment. On January 29, 1973, a BART train filled with local dignitaries rolled into the two Berkeley stations for ribbon-cutting ceremonies. At the Central Berkeley stop, Mayor Warren Widener lauded the city's willingness to spend additional money to put the train lines underground, keeping them from becoming "a physical barrier between different racial sectors and geographical parts of the city." Politically liberal ideals required conservative urban design ideals. A few minutes later, at the second stop, Ashby Station, he spoke again, joking, "Since we spent $10 million to underground BART, we thought we should have at least two ceremonies."[137] Berkeley's main newspaper credited former mayor Wallace Johnson for what was "perhaps the last major act of civic unity in contemporary times here."[138] A journalist noted, "Most of the excitement was already over by the time the trains pulled into Berkeley" for the ceremonies.[139]

That was not an anticlimax, however; it was the point. Berkeley's civic leadership had promoted the underground construction for BART in order to minimize community disruption, especially to residential neighborhoods. The ceremonies were shows of community stability and continuity among the political disruptions of the preceding decade. The campus landscape had helped catalyze student activism in the late 1950s and early 1960s, becoming a flash point for radical politics and protest. The built environment in the early 1970s became the foundation for collaborative politics in which a new coalition rejected modern aesthetics and imposed a set of conservative aesthetics and regulations on the urban landscape.

Berkeley was the site of a dramatic rejection of midcentury planning and liberal ideology, in both cultural and concrete terms. The University of California was the classic Cold War multiversity, and its flagship campus was the proving ground for mass education and Cold War planning. Racial segregation, centralized planning, community participation, and alternative lifestyles were all grounds for debate as students abandoned the mid-century liberal coalition and the center proved unable to hold. The debate over campus expansion and Units 1, 2, and 3; the convulsions of the Free Speech Movement; the conflict over People's Park; and the rise of the April Coalition in electoral politics all centrally featured battles over the design, use, and control of campus and urban space—"the right to the city."

In the underground BART line and the neighborhood preservation efforts, the city's traditionalists and radicals found their initiatives in alignment. They maintained the spatial status quo, opposing and mitigating the effects of a regional development and pro-growth coalition to preserve the city's established form. By planning for the people who were already there, maintaining a traditional landscape, and winning battles for community participation, radical political actors from the university community found common cause with local residents—an alliance between students and working- and middle-class residents. Together, they developed policies that created a new model for political action and urban life, what came to be called the "Progressive City," but included a conservative ideology of traditional urban form as a fundamental premise.

5 The Working Class Versus the Creative Class

Alfred Vellucci glowered. The Cambridge, Massachusetts, mayor was putting the scientists in their place. Mark Ptashne, a Harvard University biochemist, and Maxine Singer, a National Institutes of Health (NIH) biochemist, were testifying in a municipal hearing about DNA and the scientific process. Vellucci nearly bludgeoned them with the sound of his voice. "Is there zero risk of danger? . . . Do scientists ever exercise poor judgment? Do they ever have accidents?"[1] They were in the city council chambers, and cameras were rolling for the public record as the scientists and politicians discussed a proposal by researchers at Harvard to build a new laboratory to clone DNA. A handful of scientists had warned the NIH that the public-health risks of such research were not clear. Ptashne and Singer were both advocates of recombinant DNA (rDNA) research. The mayor had called the 1976 hearings on rDNA at City Hall on Massachusetts Avenue, poking and digging at the uncertainties of doing research with man-made DNA.[2] Cambridge was experiencing a set of transformative changes from an industrial economy to a high-tech economy. The industrial city had endured factory closures and disinvestment and faced a new emphasis on white-collar, scientific, and financial work.

The hearings were a show of working-class political strength to counter the growing prominence of Harvard University and the Massachusetts Institute of Technology (MIT) in Cambridge. The distance from Harvard Square to MIT's Building 7 was just over a mile and a half, and Cambridge city government was nearly equidistant between the two. Both universities were private and pursued national and global priorities distinct from the interests of local residents, but lacked the public oversight and governance of institutions such as the University of Texas and UC Berkeley. City hall was also a fulcrum between industrial East Cambridge and the white-collar

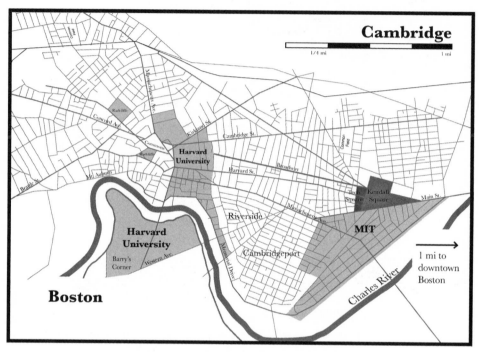

Figure 41. Cambridge, Massachusetts. Map created by the author.

neighborhoods of central and western Cambridge. All of these forces played on city politics. The universities' shift toward scientific and biotech research offered dramatic economic growth opportunities and potential partnerships with industry. This line of research would be key to a generation of health and biomedical advances. However, scientific questions about DNA research presented longtime residents—known as Cantabrigians—like Vellucci an opportunity to squeeze a university pressure point and assert residents' power. The controversy represented a struggle between two poles of power in Cambridge, the largely white ethnic working-class residents and the elites of the academic institutions.

The industrial identity and development future of Cambridge were at stake. Central cities and industrial suburbs across the country that had ridden generation-long waves of prosperity struggled through the economic transformation of the 1970s. Capital fled from central cities to far-flung suburbs and from the Rust Belt to the Sun Belt and beyond. Economic powerhouses and industrial cities of the postwar era including Camden, New Jersey; Flint and Detroit, Michigan; St. Louis, Missouri; and Oakland, California, saw their industrial might sapped, a factory at a time, as jobs shifted from the city to the suburbs, to other regions, and other countries.[3] Cambridge faced these same pressures, but a new and growing source of intellectual and entrepreneurial capital, anchored by the presence of Harvard, Radcliffe College, and MIT, provided a stabilizing counterbalance to industrial capital.[4]

This stability, in part, enabled a political contest where the working class could participate in a debate about the city's future. Other industrial communities suffered disinvestment almost without recourse—when the economic substrate of a community shifted, the field of political battle simply crumbled. Cambridge was in a position to consider and choose its future like almost no other city: in the other industrial cities discussed in this book, Muncie and Chicago, the universities were proportionally too small to counter the massive loss of manufacturing jobs in the second half of the twentieth century. Thus, Cambridge served as a unique political ring where working-class residents and university leaders slugged it out over competing visions of metropolitan America—between industrial continuity and a new high-tech future. The industrial and academic visions for the city's future were highly divergent; the local and regional politics were messy and overlapping. This contest in the late 1960s and the 1970s revealed the interdependence among the city's political constituencies: whatever their position, they relied upon the success and stability of the universities. Similar political battles spanned the next forty years, including urban renewal, rent control, campus expansion, and economic development.

MIT's and Harvard's economic visions for Cambridge and metropolitan Boston brought two differing *spatial* visions for growth. MIT worked to re-develop the area around its own campus in East Cambridge, exploiting the city's deteriorating industrial neighborhoods. MIT supported urban renewal at Kendall Square, a neighborhood on the northeastern edge of its campus, in order to create space for biotech spinoffs, corporate partnerships, and leisure opportunities near its campus, faculty, and research labs. Harvard, surrounded by affluent neighbors and a vibrant commercial district in cen-tral Cambridge, avoided political battles with the local community after they rejected the Kennedy Presidential Library. Harvard shifted its attention to Allston, a working-class Boston neighborhood just across the Charles River. The university sought to expand some of its existing land holdings and put its prodigious financial resources to use in a long-term development plan that would make Harvard, in the words of Boston mayor Thomas Menino, "the future of Boston."[5]

The two institutions faced their own political and economic crises in the 1970s. Student strikes and sit-ins at both universities over the Vietnam War and military partnerships undermined confidence in a shared vision of the institutions' missions. Inflation and energy crises put MIT in a budgetary bind, while the university's entrepreneurial spirit pushed it into closer rela-tionships with corporate partners. MIT president Jerome Weisner wrote in his 1973 annual report that the importance of new funding streams was so great that it was pushing the institution "to the development of new research and academic programs which will generate additional operating revenues."[6]

Harvard in the 1970s and 1980s also put a new emphasis on philanthropy, finance, and applied scientific research, increasing the nation's largest uni-versity endowment and transforming the university to look more like MIT in the sciences. These actions reflected the universities' new roles in the economy—entrepreneurial, financially risky, and philanthropically oriented—and demanded new visions of the role of a campus and its influence on the city surrounding it.

The battle continued for more than a decade. By the end of the 1980s, it was clear that the future of Cambridge depended on the universities: even Boston's fate would rely on the success of MIT's and Harvard's new visions for higher education. By the 2000s, the battle was over, and the white-collar vision for Cambridge and Boston had won out. The two institutions had dramatically changed their own campuses and were altering the spatial logic of metropolitan Boston to boot. The new knowledge and financial economy, however, came with its own characteristic set of pitfalls and crises. When investment and speculation was made concrete on the ground, the structures of education and knowledge creation could prove as shimmering and compelling as any work of art—or as ethereal and unreal as any set of paper profits.

The Origins of Harvard and MIT

Cambridge, Harvard, and MIT had grown up together. The seventeenth-century settlement of Cambridge, then called Newtowne, preceded the 1636 founding of Harvard by a handful of years. Harvard, however, gave Cambridge, located across the Charles River from Boston, its identity. Several settlers, including minister John Harvard, had been educated at Cambridge University in England. When the Massachusetts Bay Colony chartered Newe College, which became Harvard, residents changed the name of the town to Cambridge. The college was first a seminary for New England preachers, the only professionals who required a college education.[7]

Infrastructure connecting Cambridge to Boston helped make the city more than a rural academic community. The West Boston Bridge spanning the Charles River was constructed in 1793, and railroad development in the nineteenth century created high-volume links between the two cities. Affluent residents and burgeoning industrialists, including educator William Bradbury and textile scion Samuel Rindge, built grand Italianate, Greek Revival, and Second Empire homes along Harvard Street on Dana Hill, high ground between central and East Cambridge. Streetcars enabled the lower-density suburban growth of central and western Cambridge. By the end of the Civil War, passenger lines ran on Main Street and Broadway, crossing the Charles River over the West Boston Bridge and carrying commuters past East Cambridge's canals and the Boston City Jail into the heart of downtown Boston.

The eastern part of Cambridge, meanwhile, was well situated for industrial development. Canals and docks gave the city working access to the Charles River, Boston Harbor, and the Atlantic Ocean. Freight lines led the industrial development of the eastern part of the city by connecting to Boston and other industrial cities.[8] Cambridge was close to Boston in that, at the turn of the nineteenth century, it teemed with European immigrants.[9] Industrial enterprises in East Cambridge built factories and warehouses, while developers raised tenements to house the workers who sought to live near their jobs.[10] The socioeconomic divergence of eastern and western Cambridge was concrete and palpable.

In 1911, the Cambridge City Council invited MIT to move from Boston, where it had been founded, to Cambridge. In 1916, MIT relocated to the southeastern part of Cambridge, on infill that had been low-lying, swampy ground on the banks of the Charles, near a working-class settlement known as Cambridgeport. In 1920, Cambridge bustled with a population of nearly 110,000 souls packed in houses and apartments in the city's six-and-a-half square miles. It was vital, flowing with all the chaos, energy, and potential of Atlantic Coast industrial cities in the first part of the twentieth century. MIT's new campus backed up against Vassar Street and a set of rail lines. The railway served the cookie makers National Biscuit Company (Nabisco), the candy kings New England Confection Company (Necco), and the Ward Baking Company (Hostess cakes and Wonder Bread), all of which were arrayed in a row just on the other side of the Boston and Albany freight tracks. Boiler works, box companies, car makers, and more crowded up and down the streets of East Cambridge, providing work for the urban population. By 1930, there were more than 18,500 manufacturing jobs in Cambridge, greater than a third of the workforce.[11]

Industrial Cambridge and Urban Renewal

At midcentury, the departure of manufacturing anchors prompted a crisis within the city. Manufacturing jobs across the United States dropped from 13 million in 1945 to 12.7 million in 1999, despite the doubling of the American population, and the decrease was more severe in the Northeast and Midwest.[12] Older industrial cities like Cambridge suffered most acutely from the movement of manufacturing to Southern states and international locales. Chicago and Muncie had felt the same forces. In Cook County, Illinois, home to Chicago, manufacturing jobs declined from 393,000 in 1940 to 328,000 in 1980 and continued to drop from there.[13] Industrial growth in Muncie stagnated a bit later. The Ball Corporation began acquiring technology innovators located in other states rather than expanding their production of glass in Indiana. Muncie's population peaked in the 1980 census and dwindled in the following decades.[14] In 1998, the Ball Corporation spun off its glass division and moved its corporate headquarters to Broomfield, Colorado.

Cambridge, like Chicago and Muncie, would rely more heavily on universities for economic viability than ever before.

Lever Brothers, the soap maker, moved its headquarters from Cambridge to New York in 1949 and closed its factory in East Cambridge a decade later.[15] This move left about fifteen acres of land vacant at Broadway and Portland Streets near MIT. Simplex Wire and Cable, an electric wire manufacturer, closed its factory just north of the MIT campus in 1969 and moved operations to newer facilities in Maine. Across Cambridge, the factories of turn-of-the-century industrial innovators became dark, rambling, antiquated hulks with shuttered doors. Tax revenue, industrial employment, and the very stability of the community seemed in jeopardy.

Urban renewal promised to impose order on chaotic parts of the city in Cambridge as in Chicago, as they navigated through these economic disruptions. Urban redevelopment allowed civic leaders to address what at first seemed to be the temporary failures of the industrial economy—moments of deterioration, pockets of blight, and periods of disinvestment. Eventually, federally financed redevelopment in East Cambridge physically removed the remainders of the industrial economy and paved the way for a new, university-centered economy. The first wave, slum clearance, represented efforts to eliminate blight through large-scale demolition. The next wave, urban renewal, sought to build on neighborhood assets like churches, schools, and universities by clearing unwanted pockets of poverty and deterioration around them. Selective clearance would strengthen the community that remained.

Cambridge residents welcomed the city's first urban redevelopment project in 1957. "Half of Cambridge Homes Facing Blight" a civic organization claimed in a pamphlet to build support for slum clearance in the city.[16] The Rogers Block was a four-and-a-half-acre parcel of tenements sandwiched between the MIT campus and the Lever Brothers factory property, crowded with more than 140 families.[17] Community leaders were so unified in support of the Rogers Block demolition that they threw an all-day party to celebrate the first swing of the wrecking ball and push of the bulldozer. A drum and bugle corps played on "Demolition Day" while three thousand spectators cheered. The next day, NBC's *Today* show carried film of the demolition.[18] This area was the city's first beachhead in a battle against blight, according to the city manager. It was not clear which side the universities were on. The mayor echoed a refrain heard from Berkeley to Boston and warned landlords not to '"[jam] students in slums at high rentals' in the vicinity of the universities."[19] MIT and Harvard students were thought part of the cause of blight, because slumlords exploited their housing needs and low incomes. Thus, the universities were seen to be in a loose alliance with the forces of deterioration.

MIT may have contributed to residential deterioration, but it was the heart of the city's industrial redevelopment strategy. Leaders renamed the Rogers Block as Technology Square. They expected its proximity to MIT would make it suitable for commercial enterprises and light industrial uses key to the new knowledge economy.[20] Cabot, Cabot and Forbes, a development company, helped build Technology Square at the same time they were helping create a set of suburban research parks on Route 128, the outer highway that ran through the suburbs around Boston and Cambridge. MIT alumni and faculty who founded tech companies often located them along Route 128, "America's Technology Highway." Tech Square would counter the process of urban deterioration and maintain the city's vitality. MIT would help keep the inner-ring suburbs in balance with outer suburban communities, including Lincoln and Lexington, which saw new jobs and growth supported by federal subsidies and defense contracts.[21]

The glow of Demolition Day had hardly faded when, in May 1961, President John Kennedy raised the stakes of the space race and announced the goal of putting a man on the moon. The National Aeronautics and Space Administration (NASA) had only been created in 1958 under President Dwight Eisenhower. His science adviser, former MIT president James Killian, had promoted the idea of the agency.[22] Kennedy, who was on the Astronomy Committee of the Harvard Board of Overseers while president, put major resources into the agency and identified the industrial neighborhood around Kendall Square as the site for mission control. Hundreds of NASA engineers working next to one of the nation's great engineering schools and a scientific powerhouse was an attractive prospect. The city began condemning property and clearing hurdles for redevelopment. Before NASA could plan the site, however, Vice President Lyndon Johnson successfully lobbied for mission control to be located in Houston, Texas, instead.

NASA left a crater at Kendall Square that MIT stepped in to fill. It was not a traditional rectilinear town square but a crossing of several oblique streets in the eastern part of Cambridge. MIT administrators wanted more land for their growing student body and research facilities, but found the campus surrounded by the legacy of the city's industrial history: warehouses, older factories, and dilapidated buildings. It was "a desolate place" without evening activity, according to Howard Johnson, MIT president from 1966 to 1971.[23] Planning scholars Kevin Lynch and Donald Appleyard helped MIT assess its needs and make the case that Kendall Square should serve the institution.[24] The city wanted urban renewal and Section 112 credits. Cambridge civic leaders and city boosters supported collaboration with MIT, just as politicians and administrators in Chicago and Berkeley had done to enact urban renewal. MIT invited Julian Levi from Chicago to coach their planners on how to use the Section 112 program he had created.[25] Any money MIT spent acquiring or demolishing property around the Kendall Square redevelopment area would create the federal urban renewal credits that could be used anywhere in the city. MIT spent $6.1 million acquiring land, demolishing buildings, and constructing buildings to expand its campus, including the vacant Simplex Wire property.[26] As a result, the city was set to receive more than $10 million in Section 112 urban renewal funds from the federal government. The Cambridge Redevelopment Authority (CRA) created a new plan, featuring a smaller NASA electronics research center. The Massachusetts Urban Renewal Administration approved the Kendall Square plan in 1965, and the CRA set about acquiring land for NASA.[27] The promise of this development settled East Cambridge building plans for a time, but this orderly process was not long-lived. Just five years after approval of the Kendall Square plan, federal budget cuts threw the city's redevelopment plans into disarray again. In 1970, the Nixon administration scaled back NASA plans and ordered closure of the research center.[28] Massachusetts politicians began scrambling to fill the site with something besides surface parking and arranged for a research center for the state's Department of Transportation. Most of the renewal site was left undeveloped for several years while the city and the CRA debated new plans. After the taking of land by eminent domain, the city had lost jobs, industrial firms, and hundreds of thousands of dollars of tax revenue.[29] The policy discussions were not amicable.

Cambridge Politics

Control of local public policy in the 1970s was up for grabs. In Cambridge, a handful of liberal politicians allied with working-class populists and brought the weight of a new coalition to bear on city policy—including development. Johnson-era federal antipoverty legislation had empowered local actors by mandating "maximum feasible participation" in community development programs. University students allied with Cambridge residents in the 1969 Harvard Strike and events afterward to bring working-class and neighborhood issues to the forefront of political debate.[30] Meanwhile, the rise of residential politics and local organizing in "the decade of the neighborhood" created political space for populist government reform. This localism, demanded by some communities and mandated by the participatory call in Great Society legislation, extended the promise of midcentury liberalism to the least powerful in the community.[31]

University leaders organized around a vision for a white-collar Cambridge and an entrepreneurial higher-education sector, but the city's residents had other plans. Cambridge had been predominantly industrial for decades, and the city's working class and immigrants had slowly accumulated political clout in the course of the twentieth-century industrial boom. Civic leaders and council members were as likely to be longtime natives from a working-class background as they were to be professional class or faculty members. Working-class leaders saw the administrators of Harvard, MIT, and the CRA trying to close the door on the world they had known; they thrust their foot in its way. University alumni and student radicals forging a coalition of leftist intellectuals and labor unionists joined them in several efforts, including rent control. Thus the economic transformation of Cambridge played out in local politics. Natives and residents like Alfred Velucci had enough influence to balance the power of Harvard Brahmins and MIT technocrats in city hall.

Opposition to Harvard and MIT made strange bedfellows. Saundra Graham, an African American community activist and single mother who first made a name opposing Harvard's real estate expansion in the 1960s, allied with Alfred Velucci. She and a group of residents from Riverside, the neighborhood south of Harvard, disrupted the university's 1970 commencement in protest.[32] Graham won election to city council in 1971, representing Cambridgeport, the neighborhood abutting MIT. When tenants in Cambridge began to organize in favor of rent control, Velucci and Graham sided with rent payers and pointed the finger at Harvard. "Technicians come to Cambridge on Federal grants for research and must find a place to live," Velucci said. "The universities accept grants without making provisions for those who have come to study. . . . The technicians have a far greater income than residents. Then the vultures arrive."[33] University growth drove up rents by attracting students, faculty, and staff from outside the city and by constraining residential development. By the middle of the 1970s, only one-third of the city's six-and-a-half square miles were residential.[34]

In the meantime, the universities' role in the economy grew more important. Scientific research employment grew while the manufacturing economic base continued to crumble. On average, Cambridge lost nearly a dozen industrial firms a year during the 1960s.[35] As a populist politician, Vellucci used Harvard as a convenient foil, once threatening to pave Harvard Yard. As the city's mayor, he relied upon Harvard and MIT as economic anchors: Cambridge needed jobs, and Harvard and MIT could provide them.[36]

A handful of liberal activists bridged the divide between blue-collar and white-collar Cambridge. Barbara Ackermann and Frank Duehay of the Cambridge Civic Association, in particular, allied with stalwarts like Vellucci and Graham on the city council. Ackermann had begun her political life on the Cambridge School Committee and won election to city council in 1967. The wife of a Boston University professor, she had been a housewife and part-time writer and journalist before entering the political ring. Duehay was another local with elite credentials. He had grown up in Cambridge, graduated from Harvard, and become a schoolteacher. He grew up politically along with Ackermann on the Cambridge School Committee and ran for city council in 1971. His key motivation was dismissing the Cambridge school superintendent, Frank Frisoli, and Duehay narrowly won the last spot on the council by thirty-six votes.[37] He put Frisoli out of a job in short order.

Ackermann and Duehay joined Vellucci and Graham in promoting populist leftist causes. They supported rent control, increased mental health support, and opposed the Inner Belt proposal, which would have run a highway through Cambridge.[38] Vellucci and Ackermann, in particular, opposed Cambridge city manager John Corcoran, who ran the city like a suburban corporate executive, counting dollars and cents and refusing to hew to the demands of the city's working-class population.[39]

The Cambridge Housing Convention brought together neighborhood groups to deal with the city's housing problems.[40] Housing costs prompted students and working-class residents to ally and organize against corporate development of the city. Cambridge was expensive: the median rent was 20 percent higher than in Boston and 10 percent higher than the metropolitan area as a whole, which included exclusive suburbs such as Newton and Needham.[41] Stories of Cambridge old-timers being tossed out of their homes prompted longtime residents to line up against developers and landlords.[42] In several cities across the country, rent control helped student radicals realize the goal of a student-proletariat alliance since both groups suffered under high rents and an anticompetitive housing regime. Rent strikes and pressure for rent control had led to passage of measures in Ann Arbor, Michigan; Madison, Wisconsin; and Berkeley, California. In 1969 and 1970, Cambridge Housing Convention activists demonstrated and lobbied for a rent control measure, including vigils on the steps of City Hall. The city council passed a rent control measure that froze rents and established a city administrator and board to manage increases.[43] It gave a win to "the little people of Cambridge," in the words of one advocate, rather than the "rent gougers, speculators, banks and Harvard and MIT."[44]

Students' battles with landlords were kin to their battle against urban development policy centered on Cold War science. MIT students and faculty abandoned research work in March 1969 for a day of reflection, scrutinizing and discussing the institution's role in the military-industrial-academic complex. Harvard students went further and seized the campus in May 1969. The renowned protest, known as the "Harvard Strike," condemned the university's complicity in the Vietnam War, challenged the institution's authority, and demanded less exploitative actions in their development policies for local neighborhoods.[45] In shared actions across the country from Berkeley to Boston, Students for a Democratic Society and other, locally based groups rejected university authority and critiqued faculty research that was complicit in making war. In Cambridge, students extended their opposition to corporate development policies that demolished, isolated, and segregated the residents of the city.

The assassination and memorialization of Cambridge's favorite son could not quell residents' opposition to big projects imposed from the outside. Before his death, John F. Kennedy had chosen a spot near Harvard, his alma mater, for his presidential library. After his death, the Kennedy foundation began planning for the library, with the support of key Cambridge leaders.[46] The politics shifted after architect I. M. Pei's firm released his design featuring an eighty-five-foot pyramid and residents heard estimates that there would be one million visitors a year. Cambridgeport residents came out against the library in full force. Saundra Graham, their representative on city council, opposed its location near Harvard. Brattle Street residents near Harvard Square joined her, in part because of a fear it would bring foot traffic and auto congestion. A group filed a lawsuit in federal court, and in 1975, the Kennedy library corporation agreed to withdraw their proposal, choosing to develop in Boston at the University of Massachusetts–Boston campus instead.[47]

Decades of growing white ethnic prominence and an increasingly powerful labor movement had invigorated and empowered working-class politics all across metropolitan Boston. Racial segregation and court-ordered busing in the city of Boston was the most contentious set of issues in the era.[48] Cambridge, as a separate city and school district, had its own working-class political battles including rent control, the Kennedy library, the Inner Belt, and Kendall Square—battles over housing and the built environment that were key to the shifting terrain of Cambridge politics. During the 1970s, populist Cambridge, and especially blue-collar Cambridge, won more than it lost.

Kendall Square

Back in the industrial neighborhoods, Cambridge struggled to recover from Nixon's cancellation of the NASA research center. By 1970, urban renewal had both lost its constituency of civic elites and faced opposition from working-class residents, crippling the program's ability to bring about large-scale development changes. In 1959, Harvard and MIT had formed a policy alliance in the Joint Center for Urban Studies (now the Joint Center for Housing Studies). Business professor Martin Anderson published a renowned attack on urban renewal in 1964, *The Federal Bulldozer*. Political scientist James Q. Wilson had followed suit with his own tract, "Urban Renewal Does Not Always Renew."[49] Faculty in business and government at the nation's leading universities were dissenting from urban liberalism and lining up against urban renewal. They had captive audiences as well and were training the nation's future developers and planners in opposition to urban renewal.[50] Projects were increasingly vulnerable to populist attack when local community members anticipated the demolition of their homes, factories, or neighborhoods for the benefit of big business. The legacy of urban renewal was visible from Cambridgeport. In Boston's West End, just across the Longfellow Bridge from MIT, the Italian American community had stridently opposed a slum clearance project in the 1950s.[51] The Boston Redevelopment Authority evicted people from their homes, demolished their neighborhood, and scattered the residents, creating a legacy of bitterness. More than a decade later, the wounds of urban renewal were still raw. Increasingly, groups targeted by urban renewal would not go quietly. This was part of an assertive political populism that was, in part, catalyzed by opposition to urban redevelopment. It did not give CRA officials much guidance to go forward.

Residents of East Cambridge worked together with student critics to oppose Kendall Square redevelopment that would prioritize MIT rather than new industrial development. Together, they slow-walked any municipal action for nearly ten years. Hard Times, an organization that embodied a student and working-class alliance, advocated for the Cambridge working class. Community-oriented Harvard and MIT alumni worked in an organization called Urban Planning Aid to provide technical expertise to community groups and neighborhoods with funding from the federal Office of Economic Opportunity.[52]

In 1973, the CRA released a new Kendall Square proposal that sparked a planning rivalry among city interests. Neighborhood groups were largely against it, and institutions were for it. The city's head planner said, "It all comes down to a question of whether you are trying to maximize the tax base and revenue in the City or jobs for Cambridge residents—they're not compatible in every instance." The new CRA proposal emphasized tax base rather than industrial jobs.[53] Richard Brescia, one of the leaders of the local opposition, summarized his objections to the new Kendall Square proposal, saying, "It isn't providing low and moderate-income housing. We're against the high-rise concept. We want to bring back more blue collar jobs."[54] Hard Times illustrated the stark choices in MIT-oriented development: 2,750 industrial jobs versus 3,600 commuter cars. The factories bulldozed in Kendall Square had employed nearly 3,000 workers. The MIT-oriented plan would bring in white-collar jobs and thousands of workers who commuted into the city, filling the streets at rush hour and requiring parking spaces during the day. Flyers from Hard Times and the Cambridge Tenants Organizing Committee urged the public to stop the Kendall Square urban renewal project, proposing "build only low-rise, low-rent housing for poor & working people."[55]

Local opposition led the city council to vote down the MIT proposal, pitting the two sides and their plans against each other. Cambridge residents realized they would have to develop their own vision for the site because the redevelopment authority was representing MIT's vision. Residents, through a group called the East Cambridge Planning Team, created a community plan in direct competition with the interests of MIT.[56] Locals often used the language of anti-imperialism to describe and criticize MIT's efforts to build in and influence East Cambridge. There were plainspoken critics, too. At one public meeting, a woman complained, "Colleges, like MIT and Harvard, are slowly taking over Cambridge properties. I don't give a hoot about colleges. I only care about my neighborhood."[57]

MIT leaders responded by creating their own guidelines to shape urban renewal. Their plan emphasized mixed-use development and a hotel that would serve the university community: there was little room for old-line industrial employment in MIT's vision and in their Kendall Square urban renewal proposal. MIT had a trump card, just as Julian Levi had intended—the Section 112 credits. At one city council meeting, Frank Duehay called MIT's actions "divisive . . . power politics" and reported "it was made clear by MIT that, if housing was not included, MIT would not certify Section 112 credits."[58] Another round of debate led the city council to pass the MIT "neighborhood plan" in 1974 and reject the vision of industrial employment for the site.[59]

By late 1975, the city of Cambridge was running out of time. Kendall Square could not be held up any longer; for two reasons, it had to either move forward to redevelopment or return to private development. First, the city had already lost millions of dollars of tax revenue by leaving the ground vacant and fallow. Second, and perhaps even more pressing, the Section 112 credits were set to expire because university expenditures could only qualify for a finite amount of time: the program was created to allow up to seven years of backdating. The loss of federal funds would postpone the project indefinitely. City officials also nervously approached MIT and asked its planners to certify more expenditures for Section 112 credits—in effect, to goose their numbers so that the city of Cambridge did not have to pay any more local match, even though the overall project had grown more expensive.[60] Senator Edward Brooke, a Republican, came to the rescue and wrote a Senate bill that limited Cambridge's local match to the contributions MIT had made. The city had to contribute nothing. This amounted to a gift of about $6 million to Cambridge and knocked the legs out from under working-class opposition to the project. Congress passed the bill in the waning days of 1975, and President Gerald Ford signed it in early 1976.[61] Mayor Vellucci later struck a far more conciliatory tone. "Kendall Square has been held up long enough," he stated flatly. When millions of dollars were on the line, Vellucci could play the pragmatist. In 1977, he asked the Cambridge City Council to approve new plan amendments and throw its weight behind the MIT vision. Harvard and MIT contributed tens of millions to the Cambridge economy just through payroll: more community debate would not roll back deindustrialization in Cambridge or bring back the old manufacturing jobs.[62]

Some of the old jobs had been gone for twenty years by then, and the city's future had been murky for the better part of a decade; but the picture was finally becoming clearer. The city council approved the plan in February and moved forward with a plan emphasizing tech and retail. An environmental impact statement awaited.

Recombinant DNA

MIT had won the battle over Kendall Square, but working-class Cambridge was not beaten. They stepped up for another battle when scientific research initiatives at Harvard and MIT came under public scrutiny. In the 1970s, the Nixon administration declared a "War on Cancer" and supported new types of genetic research to help find causes and cures for the disease.[63] A key research technique in developing gene therapies for cancer was cloning of recombinant DNA (rDNA). In the laboratory, researchers would chemically break apart existing DNA strands and put them back together, or recombine them, in ways that never existed in nature. Once an rDNA strand proved of interest, labs would clone them by letting cells with the new DNA divide again and again. Some scientists expressed concern that if a microbe with synthetic DNA escaped from its laboratory environment, it might pose a danger to humans. Leading genetic researchers recommended a voluntary moratorium on rDNA research in 1974. The NIH undertook a two-year process to solicit comment and create guidelines for such federally funded research.[64]

In 1974, Harvard University proposed a moderate-security genetic research facility in Cambridge that would perform rDNA research, and Alfred Vellucci brought the scientific debate to the public. The Cambridge mayor called a hearing to assess the safety of DNA cloning, to which he invited several scientists to testify. Vellucci maintained his resentment against all things Harvard; he saw his opportunity to put faculty through a public wringer and score political points. His inquisition at the July 1976 hearing made the Harvard research scientists squirm for the cameras.

Faculty opponents suggested that the issue was a political matter rather a scientific one. MIT biologist Jonathan King supported a moratorium and questioned the safety of rDNA work. The council approved a three-month moratorium and created an exploratory committee to investigate rDNA research, the Cambridge Experimentation Review Board.[65] The board agreed that the question whether to permit Harvard to build the lab was a political one. Thus, it was one for nonscientists to decide. Elite Cambridge would have to convince working-class Cambridge that the city faced no hazard and that their scientific inquiry was worth pursuing.

The moratorium shut down the Center for Cancer Research, which MIT had established in 1974, two years before the hearings. The cancer research lab was considered moderate risk but fell within the net of the municipal moratorium. Salvatore Luria, a Nobel laureate in physiology or medicine, directed the center. David Baltimore, who won the Nobel Prize in 1975, served as one of the faculty affiliates. Baltimore later recalled, "It became very clear early on that it was totally an MIT problem, because Harvard didn't have a facility in which they could do anything, and that we were the ones who were going to suffer from a moratorium."[66] Harvard couldn't *open* its lab; MIT had to *close* its lab that had already been operating. The Cambridge Experimentation Review Board investigated the matter for seven months, learning about the science and visiting labs. It eventually declared that moderate-risk facilities that followed NIH guidelines, including handwashing by staff researchers and controlled access to the research laboratory, should be allowed.

In February 1977, the Cambridge City Council decided it would permit rDNA research in the city so long as a Cambridge citizens' committee oversaw the facility.[67] Vellucci counted citizen oversight as a triumph for Cantabrigians, despite an assessment of the risk as basically safe. "You can see . . . that the little people did triumph over the big scientists or the big universities of the big United States of America," he said, striking a familiar political note.[68] The cancer laboratory resumed operations in the spring of 1977. Eight other cities across the country conducted reviews of microbiology safety in these years. In affluent communities including Princeton, New Jersey, and Berkeley, California, highly educated citizens considered ethical questions and public safety measures.[69] In Ann Arbor, Michigan, Mayor Albert Wheeler had earned a Ph.D. in public health and was a University of Michigan faculty member sensitive to the institution's research ambition—a scientist deciding science policy. In few other cities considering rDNA policy were the class dynamics so clear as they were in Cambridge. The battle was explicitly over microorganisms, but the real tension, as in Kendall Square, was over what kind of city Cambridge was to become.

The Entrepreneurial University

The battle over DNA waged against Harvard and MIT ended in a truce, but it was nearly the last gasp for industrial Cambridge. In the 1970s, both institutions were pioneering dramatic internal changes that altered the emphasis and form of university growth, making them far more formidable foes to industrial and working-class advocates. MIT helped change patent law to bring the institution, and higher education more generally, closer to industry—ideologically, financially, and geographically.[70] Harvard shifted its endowment strategy and led a movement among universities to raise more funds from private donors and invest in riskier ventures. The new economy emerged first on university campuses in Cambridge.

MIT researchers and administrators began complaining that they had trouble bringing products of federally funded research to market. Discoveries made with all of the federal grant money available since World War II were in the public domain and could not be patented. Corporate partners who wanted to create a new medication based on a scientific discovery might spend millions of dollars in development and would face open competition once it received approval from the Food and Drug Administration. Funding agencies also created different structures and licensing allowances, many of which were in conflict with one another. It was difficult to commercialize and market an invention without clear patent protection to shield industry partners. A 1968 study of federal patent policy indicated that no medication had ever been brought to market in which the federal government had funded the scientific research and held the intellectual property.[71]

Seven universities, including MIT, stepped into the breach. They created a private lobbying association called the Society of University Patent Administrators. The organization began advising lawmakers and businessmen to create a bill that would allow universities and researchers to commercialize their discoveries.[72] In 1978, the society found its advocate. Purdue University was having trouble getting licensing rights to an alternative fuel process that the Department of Energy had funded. A university administrator contacted the office of Indiana's Senator Birch Bayh, a Democrat, and asked him to intervene.[73] Bayh took to the cause and sought a cosponsor. A University of Arizona psychologist on the staff of Senator Bob Dole, a Republican from Kansas, as a science policy fellow convinced Dole to put his support behind the bill as well.[74]

The pair of senators held a press conference in 1978 detailing the horrors of federal patent policy, alleging that cancer treatments and hepatitis medications were waiting to be brought to market but federal agencies were holding the paperwork behind a web of red tape. "Rarely have we witnessed a more hideous example of overmanagement by the bureaucracy," Dole said.[75] Major players, including MIT, Harvard, and the University of California, lobbied on behalf of the bill as it moved through Congress.[76] The Bayh–Dole Patent and Trademark Law Amendments Act passed in 1980, during the lame duck session on the last day of the Ninety-Sixth Congress. The act received President Jimmy Carter's signature before he left the White House.[77]

The Bayh–Dole Act institutionalized a set of commercially oriented practices; the resulting changes were human and concrete, not just bureaucratic.[78] Universities around the country accelerated their patenting and pursued licensing with industry partners. The typical number of patents the federal government issued each year quadrupled in the first ten years following the bill's passage, to a thousand.[79] Research universities such as UC Berkeley, UCLA, MIT, and Yale University hired dozens of staff to facilitate technology transfer and chase the potential windfall from a major discovery. Universities responded to these demands by moving in the direction of marketable scientific discoveries, just as Jerome Weisner had suggested for MIT in 1973. By the 2000s, the largest holder of technology licenses was the University of California (all campuses), followed by the University of Washington, Stanford University, and MIT, which held 818 licenses. MIT ranked first or second in the nation for funding from industrial partners among institutions without a medical school.[80]

Farther down Massachusetts Avenue, the oldest and wealthiest university in the country could not keep up. What Harvard may have lacked in entrepreneurialism it had made up for in wealth and tradition. Harvard's endowment led the nation in the 1950s and 1960s, reaching $1 billion in 1964.[81] By the early 1970s, Harvard's conservative investment managers could not keep pace with the university's expenses, and the institution ran deficits each year.[82] In response, the Harvard Corporation, the governing body for the university, established a central endowment fund to bring together investments from all of its colleges. It created the Harvard Management Company (HMC) in 1974 to invest more strategically and aggressively.[83]

The management company's growth strategy joined financial innovation with traditional patron support. A new investing strategy sought large gains and exploited short-term market inefficiencies, sending a tremor through Boston financial circles. Speaking of Harvard Management Company's investment advisers in Boston, the university treasurer told a *New York Times* reporter, "We originally thought we would pick their brains. It has turned out they're picking ours."[84] Harvard's endowment grew to $1.4 billion by the end of the 1970s, twice that of Yale, the next largest in the country.[85] Then, in 1979, Harvard launched the largest capital campaign in university history. Conceived in the lean middle years of the decade, the campaign to raise $259 million would ultimately consolidate the university's position atop the higher-education hierarchy.

In 1981, the administration of the newly inaugurated Ronald Reagan announced dramatic education cuts, and Harvard responded with even greater reliance on its endowment.[86] Harvard investors calculated they needed to increase the university endowment by another $20 million in order to compensate for the cuts Reagan had proposed. To make up for the shortfall, in 1982, Harvard leaders boosted the capital campaign goal to $350 million. In 1985, the campaign reached the new goal and capped a half-decade of financial accumulation.[87] The capital campaign ended with a flourish, and Harvard's president, Derek Bok, was awash in money.[88]

The election of 1980 was seen as a watershed of conservative ideology, but the foundations of neoliberalism had already arrived on campuses in Cambridge. Harvard and MIT had changed their governance to anticipate and incorporate the logic of the marketplace and economic deregulation. They focused on commercially valuable patents, conducted finance-oriented investing, and pursued a renewed commitment to philanthropic support.

It was no coincidence that the controversy over Kendall Square resolved when it did. MIT had moved aggressively into rDNA research, and, as it had done with the Radiation Lab and Media Lab, the school's faculty moved to the forefront of a research area with practical application that involved collaboration with private industry. The Center for Cancer Research at the edge of the MIT campus became an important research site, and the Kendall Square area around it held the potential for housing other new science and technology initiatives.

New science needed new lab and office spaces, and the embattled area came to the fore again. Technology Square had not been enough to counter the centrifugal force of Route 128. The outer ring of suburban research parks continued to draw high-earning jobs and investment from the region's interior, more than the urban redevelopment plans had delivered to Cambridge. The new plans for Kendall Square intended to bring high-earning jobs, high-value research buildings, and alumni back to East Cambridge. That centralizing vision helped transform Cambridge into a new kind of urban entrepreneurial community. In the late 1970s, however, the surface

Figure 42. Aerial image of Kendall Square parking lots. After demolition of numerous buildings in Kendall Square, sites sat empty or as surface parking lots during civic debate about the future of the urban renewal area and the city. This image from the early 1970s looks east toward downtown Boston. The Volpe Transportation Center on the site of the proposed NASA center is just under construction in the left middleground. Cambridge Redevelopment Authority, Cambridge, Massachusetts.

parking lots on the sites of old factories in and around Kendall Square did not look much like a site of regeneration (Figure 42).

In 1978, the U.S. Department of Housing and Urban Development had approved the Kendall Square environmental impact statement, clearing the way for redevelopment. The CRA contracted with Boston Properties, a regional real-estate developer, to build out the renewal area, which would be called Cambridge Center.[89] By 1980, the land had been cleared, and construction soon followed. Lotus Development Corporation, creator of the popular software programs Lotus 1-2-3 and Lotus Notes, was a key early tenant in Cambridge Center.[90] A new biomedical research center, endowed by financier Edwin "Jack" Whitehead and loosely affiliated with MIT, opened in Cambridge Center in 1984. David Baltimore directed the Whitehead Institute in its early years, and the sponsor's $35 million gift led to development of the institute's building on Main Street. Researchers would help map the human genome and anchor the new scientific neighborhood, providing outreach to pharmaceutical and biotech firms including Biogen, a global biotech company founded by MIT professor Phillip Sharp and Harvard's Walter Gilbert, along with Novartis, which located offices and labs nearby in Kendall Square. After more than two decades of waiting, MIT and the CRA finally had the developments they wanted in the heart of East Cambridge.

Politics

The left-liberal political alliance in Cambridge did not last amid these epochal changes for universities and cities. Federal politicians led by Reagan promised trickle-down economic growth, but the changing American political economy had the most direct effect on local politics in Cambridge. Demographic succession in Cambridge led to political succession, and the discourse of economic development shifted. As science and tech companies moved into Cambridge, they replaced the industrial firms whose workers had made up a large proportion of the electorate in the 1960s and 1970s. The political support that white ethnic working-class communities had built up over generations drained away, in numbers and strength.[91] Other key members of the left-liberal coalition aged or moved on, without meaningful heirs. Barbara Ackermann, the city's mayor in 1972 and 1973, held her city council seat until 1977, when she campaigned for the 1978 governor's election, losing in the Democratic primary. Saundra Graham left city government when she won a seat in the state house in 1977 and held it until 1988. Alfred Vellucci retired from city council in 1989.

The terms of rhetoric in Cambridge changed from promoting industrial work to celebrating corporate research and even a new entrepreneurial society. In the 1960s, urbanist Jane Jacobs had promoted the ideal of working-class labor and neighborhood diversity for cities in the era of urban renewal.[92] Later, scholars including Daniel Bell, William Mitchell, and Richard Florida advanced the ideology of national deindustrialization, but their works, shaped by their positions in Cambridge, had local consequences. These researchers and theorists promoted the value of white-collar workers and the influence of nontraditional knowledge labor in city making. Bell, a Harvard sociologist, predicted a growth in white-collar work and a simultaneous decline of manufacturing in his 1973 book *The Coming of Post-Industrial Society*. A generation later, Mitchell, an MIT professor, elaborated on those changes for city planning, arguing that the old rules for urbanism were ready for revision. A new information society needed cities not shaped by traditional forms of industrial work, economic organization, and information flows. In short, the telecommuter and the mobile employee should dominate plans for city growth and design. After publishing *City of Bits* in 1995 and *E-topia* in 1999, Mitchell became the dean of the MIT's School of Architecture and Planning, leading the country's top program in urban planning and teaching the planners of the next generation.

Richard Florida, a Carnegie Mellon University economic development researcher, became more influential than Bell or Mitchell. Florida spent a year as a visiting scholar at Harvard in the mid-1990s and began researching the relationship between diversity, social tolerance, and economic growth. In 2001, he published a popular article in *Washington Monthly* arguing that fundamentally postindustrial conditions—creative enterprise and tolerant behaviors—were the keys to economic growth. A new generation of young men and women "share[d] a common ethos that values creativity, individuality, difference, and merit." Back in Pittsburgh, he told the story of a tattooed, pierced Carnegie Mellon student he had met on campus who had just signed with an Austin technology company. The student asked of the steel city, "'How would I fit in here?' This young man and his lifestyle represent a profound new force in the economy and life of America."[93] By implication, the conservative moral values of Catholic communities and the established work patterns of industrial unionism—for example, patriarchal, heteronormative values and a seniority system—were hindrances to economic dynamism and creative thinking. Florida wrote the working class out of economic and urban development discourse; he placed Boston among the cities with the greatest economic potential.

The next year, Florida's book *The Rise of the Creative Class* launched to popular acclaim and policy approbation. Economic development officials in Rust Belt cities, foundering on the shoals of postindustrial urban transformation, eagerly grasped for the lifeline this rhetoric offered. Older cities had the assets to create a new template for economic growth and cultural revitalization. In 2005, Florida's *Cities and the Creative Class* elaborated the theme.

The two books came to dominate popular discourse on urban revitalization and economic development.[94]

Frank Duehay was mayor when these economic development ideas began to rise to prominence in Cambridge. His tenure included two terms during the 1980s and a term at the end of the 1990s. In 1999, he presided over the groundbreaking of a new Cambridge Center building for Biogen. Duehay called Biogen "a model corporate citizen" for its community investments. Senator Edward Kennedy heralded the jobs to come because of the project and noted the millions of research dollars that would be spent on site.[95] Kennedy was a liberal lion in the Senate but was a leader of the left who no longer guaranteed services and demanded equity.

Massachusetts, emerging as a liberal bastion, led the national change toward market rhetoric, and this spelled the death knell for rent control. The economic growth of the Bay State, driven in part by computer makers along Route 128, was moving back toward Boston in the 1990s and the cities around it—especially Cambridge, which retained a strong rent control law. The differential between controlled rental rates and market rents grew with the economy, meaning property owners lost more revenue each month and year. Throughout the 1980s, local real-estate interests pushed to roll back rent control in cities around the state, but public support and the regulatory regime remained strong in Cambridge until the 1990s. In 1994, real-estate groups promoted a statewide ballot issue to repeal rent control in the last three cities: Boston, Brookline, and Cambridge. Rent control was highly popular in those cities, but real-estate managers sought to dilute supportive community ballots with outstate votes. Over acrimonious legal challenges, the landlords narrowly prevailed, 51 to 49 percent, as Brookline, Boston, and Cambridge were the only three cities where rent control won.[96] The market had struck back, and there was no more lid on Cambridge rents.

The White-Collar Future

Harvard turned its gaze toward Boston in the early 1970s, the same era where MIT found such opposition in Kendall Square. Centuries of development hemmed in Harvard's main campus, and there was little opportunity for growth in central Cambridge. In 1972, Harvard's planning office began a long-range evaluation of campus lands and infrastructure in Cambridge and the Allston neighborhood across the river. The planning office released a new development plan in 1975, and it was a ready tool for President Bok and the

Harvard Corporation.[97] The capital campaign of the early 1980s called for expanding the facilities across the Charles and provided all the financial resources necessary to do it.

By 1985, the financial engorgement of the university required profitable ways to invest money. Campus expansion provided a spatial fix. Harvard learned in the 1980s it could not be complacent as it had been a decade earlier: modest investments and returns would not maintain its top position in higher education. The protracted negotiations over Kendall Square and the aborted plans for the Kennedy library had illustrated the political battles administrators could expect to face in Cambridge. Harvard found an alternative at a bend in the Charles River. Boston's Allston-Brighton neighborhood had long housed the university's business school and athletic fields, but the area had an underutilized set of parcels and plenty more open space. The university had the resources to begin enacting the plan and the patience to do it right.

In 1984, the university's real-estate office had secretly contracted for a developer, Beal Brothers, to buy parcels in the Allston neighborhood. Beal purchased the land and buildings without disclosing its client's identity. Over the course of six years, from 1988 to 1994, Beal bought fifty-two acres for $88 million, including strip malls, auto body shops, and a railroad warehouse. In June 1997, Harvard was about to release a new university master plan, and the institution went public with its purchases.[98]

Bostonians were not happy. Politicians and residents complained in dismay that the university paid rock-bottom prices and would bulldoze the community. Boston mayor Thomas Menino criticized Harvard's stinginess, emphasizing that nearby Simmons and Bentley Colleges gave more scholarships to Bostonians than Harvard did. "Our people should be of as much interest to you as our property," Menino said, and called the plan "the highest level of arrogance seen in our city in many years."[99] A state senator joked, "They're buying so many auto body shops, I thought they might want to start a vocational school at Harvard."[100] The *Boston Globe* featured hard-luck stories of locals who had unwittingly sold to the nation's wealthiest and most prestigious university. An asphalt contractor was on the verge of bankruptcy when he sold the industrial building where he operated but continued to rent the space. Three years later, rent increases from his new landlord forced him out.[101] Elizabeth Hanlon, a septuagenarian who lived in a duplex bought for Harvard, pledged, "They'd have a job to get me out. They'd have to pull me out by the feet."[102]

Harvard was turning from Cambridge and reemphasizing its longtime affiliation with Boston. Harvard was as much a Boston institution as it was a Cambridge university, in geography as well as regional identification. The lion's share of its employees lived outside of Cambridge, and by the late 1990s, the Boston campuses of Harvard University—in the neighborhood of Jamaica Plain as well as Allston—cumulatively covered more land than Harvard Yard. Even before the expansion plans, the developed indoor space in Boston— including Harvard Business School, the medical school, the university press, and the athletic complexes—were approaching half the total of the university's buildings in Cambridge.[103] A member of the Cambridge town-and-gown committee welcomed the school's pivot to Boston, commenting in the *Boston Globe,* "Instead of visiting expansion on us, we suggest they visit it on Allston."[104] Menino met with Harvard's president Neil Rudenstine, and the mayor's criticism turned into support for the project.[105]

University officials responded to neighborhood protest with assurances and optimism. They stressed that the university had no pending plans for the area around their business school except to revitalize the neighborhood.[106] Two years later, Harvard administrators began publicly discussing the possibility of moving some graduate schools across the river to Allston.[107] Lawrence Summers, a former Harvard professor and secretary of the U.S. Treasury, assumed the Harvard presidency in 2001 and made the Allston project a top priority. "This is a huge moment of opportunity for Harvard, and it's very important that we take advantage of it," he said.[108] His administration accumulated more land and developed a new campus vision for Boston. It would feature a mix of instructional, laboratory, cultural, and retail space—an interdisciplinary high-tech, high-culture, high-intellect community that would wipe away the industrial, working-class landscape of Barry's Corner, a small neighborhood in Allston. The project had such momentum that even Summers's troubles with the faculty and subsequent resignation in 2006 could not stop the expansion initiative he helped advance.

Cambridge Center

Back in Cambridge, there was a feedback loop between rhetoric and redevelopment. Kendall Square exemplified it. The Cambridge City Council approved a revision in the urban renewal plan in 1993 that allowed biotech firms to move into the neighborhood.[109] By the end of the decade, biotech companies had crowded into the MIT neighborhood, cheek by jowl with computer software companies. The California firm Amgen joined Biogen in Cambridge Center, along with Microsoft, Google, and pharmaceutical company Pfizer. Massachu-

Figure 43. Building 20. The plain design allowed users to make alterations and reconfigure space as they desired, winning the building a reputation as a favorite among researchers. Courtesy MIT Museum.

setts was home to the greatest concentration of biotech firms and employees in the country. The largest proportion of them was in Kendall Square.

Developments in the middle of the 2000s—one in Cambridge, the other in Boston—illustrated the shift in metro Boston and the role of universities in fostering them. In 1997, MIT announced the demise of its famed Building 20 on Vassar Street, across from Kendall Square, and unveiled its planned replacement, the Stata Center. Building 20 at MIT—where most buildings had numbers instead of names—was a simple wood-frame three-story structure built during World War II. It had housed numerous research laboratories, including the famed Radiation Lab, where radar was developed and put to military use; the MIT Research Lab of Electronics; and the Cambridge office of the Atomic Energy Commission. It was an unimpressive structure that could be modified, customized, or beaten up to suit a research group's needs: this feature made it an MIT favorite and is often credited for a stream of discoveries by MIT scientists (Figure 43).[110]

The Stata Center was a new visual signature for MIT, a radical departure from the school's midcentury utilitarian cream-brick and black-steel aesthetic. The center brought together MIT's artificial intelligence laboratory and its computer science lab into a single home on campus, the Computer Science

Figure 44. Stata Center, MIT. Designed by Frank Gehry, the center replaced the utilitarian and much-loved Building 20 in 2004. The center houses the MIT Computer Science and Artificial Intelligence Laboratory, or CSAIL, bringing high-tech research and innovation to the edge of Kendall Square and giving it a distinctive, idiosyncratic architectural aesthetic. Photograph by the author.

and Artificial Intelligence Laboratory—dubbed CSAIL and pronounced "see-sale." Designed by Frank Gehry, the building would have his iconic look of molded stainless steel, nonparallel lines, and oblique angles. All of this was possible because of Gehry's emphasis on computer-aided and technology-enhanced design, featuring unprecedented architectural forms (Figure 44).[111] The interior's flowing, adaptable spaces would provide collaborative opportunities and exchanges—as Building 20 had done—but with a sculptural, recognizable building that advertised innovation within and without. The building cost $285 million and, owing to Gehry's design, brought MIT's research to the pages of architectural magazines, not merely scientific journals.[112] Research and innovation had become a cultural value deserving a building with Gehry's globally recognized stylistic innovations. Like the new Guggenheim Museum in Bilbao, Spain, MIT was a site of regeneration, creativity, and economic development for an old industrial city. The Stata Center opened in 2004 to critical architectural acclaim.[113] It gave form to the new vision of MIT, Kendall Square, and Cambridge at the edge of campus, next door to the Center for Cancer Research.

In 2007, MIT announced a $100 million gift from billionaire David Koch to turn the Center for Cancer Research into the Koch Institute for Integrative Cancer Research. Koch was a crusader for low taxes and reduced government regulation. He exemplified the transition from government-funded medical research to philanthropy and corporate partnership, following in the steps of MIT patrons like Jack Whitehead. Koch's gift would fund the construction of a new building at the edge of the MIT campus and would pay for lab space, equipment, and new interdisciplinary faculty. The Koch Institute remade MIT's campus edge and created a seamless transition to the glossy high-rise buildings of Kendall Square and Cambridge Center, visually, architecturally, organizationally, and commercially (Figure 45).

Harvard made its own transformative announcement in 2007. On January 11, interim president Derek Bok announced plans for the Allston neighborhood—a multibillion-dollar mixed-use campus of more than two hundred acres featuring science, museums, and the arts.[114] Bok was showing his commitment to the vision of his predecessor, Larry Summers, in which life sciences and a stem-cell institute would be the centerpiece of the university's expansion.[115] Thomas Menino had come around on the project in Allston and welcomed the new development. "The implications for the well-being of humanity are staggering, and the potential economic spinoff enormous," Menino told the *Boston Globe*.[116] He reaffirmed the importance for Boston and Allston in particular, claiming, "The community will benefit with the job creation efforts and new amenities."[117]

The central feature of the plan was a new square to organize Allston public space around a bourgeois identity. Barry's Corner, the intersection at the center of Harvard's land, was the public heart of the working-class community. It would become a "'major urban space' similar to Harvard Square in Cambridge." The *Boston Globe* quoted the plan, which promised, "It will be urban, active, and . . . a bustling scene." Harvard's school of education would move across the Charles River, flanked by new science labs, expanded athletic fields, retail, museums, and the school of public health.

There was no groundbreaking ceremony to commemorate the start of work clearing the Allston site in December 2007, but it was a triumphant moment. Harvard seemed at the top of the education world, and few people lamented the businesses and residents it had displaced in Allston. Boston was

Figure 45. Aerial view of Kendall Square. New development at Kendall Square and MIT filled what had been vacant parcels and surface parking lots with high-rise buildings. Kendall Square, by 2005, was more intensely developed than the MIT campus. The Stata Center is visible at the lower right. Cambridge Redevelopment Authority, Cambridge, Massachusetts.

one of the centers of the new economy and one of the rhetorical centers of the creative class. Researchers, graduates, and entrepreneurs from MIT and Harvard were the new drivers of the regional and national economy. They provided the American public with greater health through biotech research and products at Biogen and Boston Scientific, more wealth through their financial institutions and investment companies like Fidelity Investments, and more connectivity through digital communication institutions such as social media giant Facebook, which had been founded at Harvard.

Figure 46. Barry's Corner. Harvard University bought parcels in the working-class commercial district known as Barry's Corner through a real-estate firm in order to expand its campus in the Allston section of Boston. In 2007, the university released a major plan for mixed-use development featuring science, retail, and cultural institutions. Hit hard by the 2008 financial crisis, Harvard stopped work in 2009. Most of the Harvard holdings are along the Charles River, including Soldier's Field and the Harvard Business School. In the middle of this 2011 aerial photo, the parcel with white buildings and piles of building material is the location cleared beginning in 2007 and where construction stopped in 2009. City of Boston GIS.

Moments of ascendance like this in the new economy did not last. Bust followed boom, and fortunes could be lost as quickly as they were won. When Harvard president Drew Gilpin Faust sent her letter to university deans, she announced the university had lost nearly a third of its endowment, would freeze faculty hiring, and halt construction of the life sciences center in Allston (Figure 46). Harvard's science and art complex in Allston represented the volatile potential of the new system of growth in higher education. Philanthropy and high-yield investments paid off handsomely in boom times. Harvard could buy more land, conduct more research, enroll more students, and provide more financial aid than ever for students at the nation's leading university.[118] The stellar returns of high-risk investing, however, left universities at the mercy of the financial markets during economic busts. The economic crisis had come about as a result of banks overleveraging, investing in mortgage-backed securities, and using increasingly complicated financial instruments, such as credit default swaps to backstop losses.

Leverage hurt Harvard Management Corporation as well. It had long had a negative 5 percent cash position, meaning it had borrowed 5 percent more than its cash reserves.[119] It was a bet made in expectation of a rising market and profitable investments. Harvard had outperformed the Standard and Poor's index by a wide margin over the preceding fifteen years, but suffered large losses and fire-sale discounts of its stakes in private equity firms during the crash.[120] MIT, which had a $10 billion endowment in 2008, the sixth largest in the nation, saw a decline of 20 percent in the crisis, resulting in budget cuts of $150 million over two years.[121] All over the country, institutions with similar policies suffered such losses. The University of Chicago endowment declined 23 percent, resulting in millions in cuts. The University of Texas, which had briefly eclipsed Harvard's endowment in the 1980s on the strength of oil prices, faced an endowment loss of 18 percent, from $13.5 billion to $11 billion.[122]

The construction outlook in Cambridge was somewhat rosier than that in Allston in 2009, where the site was essentially a gaping hole. Buildings in Technology Square and Kendall Square had been completed long ago. The massive Draper Laboratories building dominated Technology Square, while biotech companies populated Kendall Square, some of which had been spun off from or licensed research from MIT. Biogen, makers of therapies for multiple sclerosis, leukemia, and hemophilia, was now headquartered in a glassy building in Kendall Square near Google and Microsoft. Incomes were high, culture was plentiful and accessible, and business was humming.

Working-class Cambridge had won several battles but lost the war for an industrial community. The development and the design of the city followed the new economic opportunity, especially Kendall Square, which grew from empty parking lots into the glass skyscrapers of Cambridge Center. The city's manufacturing was in the past, no longer a living legacy but consigned to blue oval historical markers around East Cambridge, giving character to neighborhoods dotted with art galleries and brew pubs patronized by the new tech class of metro Boston.

Epilogue
The New Contested City

On March 25, 1911, a Saturday afternoon, fire broke out on the eighth floor of the Triangle Shirtwaist Factory in the Washington Square neighborhood of Manhattan. On the three upper floors of the ten-story Asch Building at the corner of Greene Street and Washington Place, less than a block from Washington Square Park, workers made fashionable shirtwaist blouses. The fire spread quickly as fabric remnants, cloth scraps, and uncut material ignited throughout the factory. Exit doors had been locked to keep workers at their stations, and now the women who did the garment work found themselves trapped. Faced with the prospect of burning to death, dozens of workers leapt from the building's upper floors to the street below. Even more died in the blaze, especially workers on the ninth floor, where no one was told of the fire as it began to spread. By the time firefighters extinguished the blaze in the high rise, 146 people, mostly women, had died in one of the nation's worst industrial disasters. The Asch Building in the Greenwich Village garment district was a charred and bloody tombstone for workers and strikers who had agitated for better industrial working conditions. The Triangle Shirtwaist fire came to stand in for the excesses and costs of capitalistic production in the heart of one of America's manufacturing centers, reigniting labor organizing and a workers' safety movement in the Progressive Era.[1]

Looking back to the beginning of the twentieth century, we can see in this deadly industrial disaster the start of an epochal shift that took place over the next one hundred years. The labor landscape began to change dramatically after the Triangle fire, as activists grew more vigorous and policy makers in the Progressive Era and later, workers empowered by the New Deal institutionalized their rights. At the same time, New York University led changes in the physical and economic landscape of Greenwich Village. After the Triangle Shirtwaist fire, a real-estate investor bought the building and, in 1929, donated it to New York University (NYU). NYU renamed it the Brown Building after its donor and used the structure for its growing activities in Greenwich Village. During World War II, NYU used the eighth floor, where the fire had broken out, training nurses for the war effort. In the decades after the war, the NYU campus grew to dominate the Washington Square neighborhood, pursuing Title I slum clearance projects and urban renewal efforts, and taking over real estate in the area.[2] NYU established the Center for Developmental Genetics on the top floors of the Brown Building, where scientists and medical researchers study the *Drosophila* fly and find models for understanding genetic development. The collaborations between geneticists, molecular biologists, and the NYU medical school put the research at the Brown Building at the center of basic life-sciences research, a key area of inquiry with relevance to aging, biotech, and pharmaceuticals. Led by NYU, the Washington Square neighborhood, once an immigrant district and later lauded by Jane Jacobs as a diverse middle- and working-class area, became what is now an upper-class neighborhood and home to Yeshiva University's law school and the art schools of the New School for Social Research, among other higher-education institutions that have followed NYU's lead. As the university expanded its mission and its footprint in Greenwich Village to feature scientific research, the neighborhood around Washington Square has shifted from industrial production in a bohemian immigrant district to scientific and high-tech research in an exclusive area populated by economic elites. NYU students from the law school next door helped save tenth-floor workers from the Triangle fire in 1911; the whole institution provided Greenwich Village a means of escape from the urban crisis and industrial stagnation in the second half of the twentieth century.

Throughout the twentieth century, higher-education institutions helped create a new type of urban community in cities across the country. Italian Village in Columbus, Ohio, and the University District in Seattle, Washington—well educated, affluent, young, and economically robust—are examples of university communities that became key sources of employment, locales of desirable residence and of consumption, creative sites of cultural and intellectual production, and vigorous markets for development and real-estate investment. As a result, these communities were also areas of gentrification, exclusivity, and contentious neighborhood politics.

Scholars have written of the death of the city and the triumph and transformation of the suburbs, but neither of these explains the increased vitality of cities in the twenty-first century *and* the continuing growth of the metropolitan edge.[3] The American landscape is now dotted with multinode metropolitan regions, from major to midsized cities. Universities are a key reason for this growing set of interlocking communities expanding at the periphery and densifying at the center. They are neither inherently urban nor suburban. In many cases, the institutions were founded before these distinctions were meaningful, and metro areas have grown to envelope them. A single university, such as Rutgers University, might have multiple campuses in one region, where liberal arts, engineering, and medical education are spatially distinct. The University of Chicago has both a main campus in Hyde Park and a business campus near the Loop. And Harvard has more than a dozen outposts in the Boston region—research labs, housing sites, and support spaces—besides the main campus in Cambridge. Regardless of their location, universities are agents of growth and development—vital centers of economic activity and knowledge creation.

This new type of education community typically emerged in the wake of the urban crisis but was certainly not "post"–urban crisis; it did not develop independently of the urban crisis. The legacy of twentieth century urban disinvestment and discrimination endures in different ways. Many of these new developments arose, as in Chicago, in the same areas that saw abandonment or that were marked for demolition and renewal decades before: the crisis created opportunity. Universities took the increased resources of the new era of philanthropy and plowed them into neighborhoods once troubled by crime, unemployment, and dilapidation. In North Philadelphia, Temple University has bought ever-larger numbers of buildings and blocks in the impoverished neighborhood. The campus is now surrounded on multiple sides by corporate retailers aiming for student, faculty, and staff wallets. This new investment may be seen as a victory for higher education and even for cities as a whole, desperate for tax revenue and new investment. These neighborhoods, however, have histories that still shape their trajectory and political grievances about measures, such as tax increment finance districts, that starve the community of the benefits of development. They have residents who do not welcome the unsettling of community relations and encroachment of new campus development in favor of national or global ambitions. In short, the expanding city of knowledge remains a highly contested form, bringing conflict and creative destruction to the communities that must negotiate the new cultural, social, and economic opportunities of higher education and the information society.

Abbreviations

BAP	Beadle Administration Papers, University of Chicago
BRC	Balcones Research Center
BSU	Ball State University
BSUASC	Ball State University Archives and Special Collections
BTC	Ball Teachers College
CAHUT	Center for American History, University of Texas
CEDL	College of Environmental Design Library, University of California
CORE	Congress of Racial Equality
CPI	consumer price index
CRA	Cambridge Redevelopment Authority
EINU	Eastern Indiana Normal University
EINUA	Eastern Indiana Normal University Association
FHA	Federal Housing Administration
FLL	Francis Loeb Library
FSM	Free Speech Movement
HEA	Higher Education Act
HHFA	Housing and Home Finance Agency
HPKCC	Hyde Park–Kenwood Community Conference
IAF	Industrial Areas Foundation
IIT	Illinois Institute of Technology
KAP	Kimpton Administration Papers, University of Chicago
LAP	Levi Administration Papers, University of Chicago
LBJPL	Lyndon Baines Johnson Presidential Library
LCRA	Lower Colorado River Authority
LRDP	Long Range Development Plan
MIT	Massachusetts Institute of Technology
NAACP	National Association for the Advancement of Colored People
NARA	National Archives and Records Administration
NASA	National Aeronautics and Space Administration
NDEA	National Defense Education Act
NIH	National Institutes of Health

NYA	National Youth Administration
NYU	New York University
PPP	Lyndon B. Johnson Pre-Presidential Papers
PWA	Public Works Administration
RG	Record Group
ROHO	Regional Oral History Office, University of California, Berkeley
SECC	South East Chicago Commission
SWHPR	South West Hyde Park Redevelopment Corporation
TWO	Temporary Woodlawn Organization
UABL	University of California Archives, Bancroft Library
UC	University of California
UCB	University of California, Berkeley
UCLA	University of California, Los Angeles
UCSC	University of Chicago Special Collections
UT	University of Texas
WPA	Works Progress Administration

Notes

Introduction

1. Donovan Slack, "Harvard Unveils Its Vision of Campus Across Charles: A Public Square Seen for Allston," *Boston Globe*, January 12, 2007, A1.

2. Katie Zezima, "Harvard Outlines Plans to Expand Campus Across the Charles River," *New York Times,* January 12, 2007, A18.

3. Richard Chacon, "Menino Softens Stance on Harvard Cites Panel Planned on Development," *Boston Globe,* June 19, 1997, B8.

4. Andreae Downs, "Trust in Harvard Is Eroding: Construction Goes Too Late for Some," *Boston Globe,* February 10, 2008, 7.

5. An increasing number of universities, especially elite institutions, offer full scholarships to poor, working-class, and middle-class students. Harvard was one of the first to announce such an initiative, offering full scholarships to students in families making $65,000 or less beginning in 2004. Stanford, Princeton, and Yale followed, among others.

6. For recent trends in university-led urban development, see David C. Perry and Wim Wiewel, *The University as Urban Developer: Case Studies and Analysis* (Cambridge, MA: Lincoln Institute of Land Policy, 2005).

7. In the key work on the subject, Paul Turner asserts a flat break from urban settings in America, noting "the placing of colleges in the countryside or even in the wilderness, an unprecedented break with European tradition." Paul V. Turner, *Campus: An American Planning Tradition* (Cambridge, MA: MIT Press, 1984), 4. Historian Neil Harris, for example, calls the University of Chicago "in the city, but not of it." Neil Harris, "Foreword," in Jean Block, *The Uses of Gothic: Planning and Building the University of Chicago, 1892–1932* (Chicago: University of Chicago Press, 1983). Thomas Bender's work does the most to bring these two realms together but still promotes an idea of separation and difference. Thomas Bender, ed. *The University and the City: From Medieval Origins to the Present* (New York: Oxford University Press, 1988). Thomas Bender, *New York Intellect: A History of Intellectual Life in New York City from 1750 to the Beginnings of Our Own Time* (Baltimore: Johns Hopkins University Press, 1988).

8. Frederick Rudolph, *The American College and University: A History* (New York: Knopf, 1962).

9. See, for example, Robert Fogelson, *Downtown: Its Rise and Fall, 1880–1950* (New Haven, CT: Yale University Press, 2001). Thomas Sugrue, *The Origins of the Urban Crisis: Race and Inequality in Postwar Detroit* (Princeton, NJ: Princeton University Press, 1996). In two notable exceptions, Margaret O'Mara introduced universities and research parks into the postwar narrative of suburbanization and metropolitan development, and Robin Bachin illustrated the changing role of university experts in Progressive Era urban contexts. Margaret Pugh O'Mara, *Cities of Knowledge: Cold War Science and the Search for the Next Silicon Valley* (Princeton, NJ: Princeton University Press, 2005). Robin Bachin, *Building the South Side: Urban Space and Civic Culture in Chicago, 1890–1919* (Chicago: University of Chicago Press, 2004).

10. This was not the first aid to higher education, but it bears recognition as a dramatic increase that catalyzed economic growth and initiated an ongoing stream of increasing aid. John R. Thelin, *A History of American Higher Education* (Baltimore: Johns Hopkins University Press, 2004), 74–76.

11. For a classic account of this boosterism, land speculation, and politicking in the foundation of the University of Illinois, see Allan Nevins, *Illinois* (New York: Oxford University Press, 1917), 30–40. The story of the University of Michigan's founding is told in Howard Peckham, *The Making of the University of Michigan, 1817–1992* (Ann Arbor: University of Michigan Press, 1997), 20–21.

12. For example, both the University of Chicago and Northwestern University operated settlement houses in Chicago. The University of California created the Institute for Public Administration in 1919.

13. On the University of Chicago, see Thomas W. Goodspeed, *The Story of the University of Chicago* (Chicago: University of Chicago Press, 1925). Rudolph, *American College and University*, 348–54.

14. Duke University became a member of the Association of American Universities in 1938, one of the key signs of overall institutional excellence in higher education.

15. A classic liberal interpretation of the Roosevelt administration is Arthur M. Schlesinger's multivolume *The Age of Roosevelt* (New York: Houghton Mifflin, 1959). Alan Brinkley illustrates the limits of New Deal reform in *The End of Reform: New Deal Liberalism in Recession and War* (New York: Knopf, 1995). A recent effort to rehabilitate the reputation of the New Deal is found in Ira Katznelson, *Fear Itself: The New Deal and the Origins of Our Time* (New York: W. W. Norton, 2013).

16. Kenneth Jackson, *Crabgrass Frontier: The Suburbanization of the United States* (New York: Oxford University Press, 1985). Thomas Sugrue, *The Origins of the Urban Crisis: Race and Inequality in Postwar Detroit.* (Princeton, NJ: Princeton University Press, 1996). N. D. B. Connolly, *A World More Concrete: Real Estate and the Remaking of Jim Crow South Florida* (Chicago: University of Chicago Press, 2014).

17. Data tabulated from federal sources, chiefly "PWA Non-Federal Allotments for Colleges and Universities," 1938, Box 13 Publications, RG 135 Public Works Administration, National Archives and Records Administration (NARA) II, College Park, MD. Aid of $112 million in 1939 dollars inflates to $1.9 billion in 2016 dollars, while $747 million of construction activity inflates to $12.9 billion in 2016 dollars. Consumer Price Index Inflation Calculator, http://data.bls.gov/cgi-bin/cpicalc.pl (accessed March 6, 2017).

18. Franklin D. Roosevelt, "Address at Temple University, Philadelphia, on Receiving an Honorary Degree," February 22, 1936. Online in Gerhard Peters and John T. Woolley, *The American Presidency Project*, http://www.presidency.ucsb.edu/ws/?pid=15240. Temple University was one of only three private universities in the United States to receive a PWA allotment.

19. "PWA Non-Federal Allotments," NARA II.

20. Christopher Loss, *Between Citizens and the State: The Politics of American Higher Education in the 20th Century* (Princeton, NJ: Princeton University Press, 2011).

21. See, for example, Jason Hackworth, *The Neoliberal City: Governance, Ideology and Development in American Urbanism* (Ithaca, NY: Cornell University Press, 2006), and Elizabeth Popp Berman, *Creating the Market University: How Academic Science Became an Economic Engine* (Princeton, NJ: Princeton University Press, 2012).

22. Richard Florida, *The Rise of the Creative Class: And How It's Transforming Work, Leisure, Community, and Everyday Life* (New York: Basic, 2002), and *Cities and the Creative Class* (New York: Routledge, 2004).

23. Jon Peterson, *The Birth of City Planning in the United States, 1840–1917* (Baltimore: Johns Hopkins University Press, 2003). Abraham Flexner, *Medical Education in the United States and Canada: A Report to the Carnegie Foundation for the Advancement of Teaching* (New York: Carnegie Foundation for the Advancement of Teaching, 1910). Paul Starr, *The Social Transformation of American Medicine: The Rise of a Sovereign Profession and the Making of a Vast Industry* (New York: Basic, 1984).

24. United States Census, *Fourteenth Census of United States* (Washington, DC: GPO, 1924). Fifteenth Census of United States (Washington, DC: GPO, 1932).

25. George Norris Green, *The Establishment in Texas Politics: The Primitive Years, 1938–1957* (Westport, CT: Greenwood, 1979). Ricky Dobbs, *Yellow Dogs and Republicans: Allan Shivers and Texas Two-Party Politics* (College Station: Texas A&M University Press, 2005). This political transformation was a particular flavor of a nationwide political shift. Steve Fraser and Gary Gerstle, eds., *The Rise and Fall of the New Deal Order, 1930–1980* (Princeton, NJ: Princeton University Press, 1989).

26. Dietrich Rueschemeyer and Peter Evans, "The State and Economic Transformation: Toward an Analysis of the Conditions Underlying Effective Intervention," in *Bringing the State Back In* (Cambridge: Cambridge University Press, 1985).

27. Kenneth Ragsdale, *Austin, Cleared for Takeoff: Aviators, Businessmen, and the Growth of an American City* (Austin: University of Texas Press, 2004).

28. Jacquelyn Dowd Hall, "The Long Civil Rights Movement and the Political Uses of the Past," *Journal of American History* 91, no. 4 (March 2005): 1233–63.

29. James Grossman, *Land of Hope: Chicago, Black Southerners, and the Great Migration* (Chicago: University of Chicago Press, 1989). Nicholas Lemann, *The Promised Land: The Great Black Migration and How It Changed America* (New York: Vintage, 1991).

30. Arnold R. Hirsch, *Making the Second Ghetto: Race and Housing in Chicago, 1940–1960*, 2nd ed. (Chicago: University of Chicago Press, 1998). Sugrue, *Origins of the Urban Crisis*.

31. John Aubrey Douglass, *The California Idea and American Higher Education, 1850 to the 1960 Master Plan* (Stanford, CA: Stanford University Press, 2000). This type of

study investigating state higher-education policy stands in stark contrast to dominant examinations of postwar higher education emphasizing research growth and achievements, such as Roger L. Geiger, *Research and Relevant Knowledge* (New York: Oxford University Press, 1993).

32. In this characterization, I am informed by Marshall Berman's discussion of traditions of modernism and a cultural desire for development, both of which universities represented and pursued as key goals in the last century. Marshall Berman, *All That Is Solid Melts into Air: The Experience of Modernity* (New York: Simon and Schuster, 1982).

Chapter 1

1. This amount translates into $650,200 in 2016 dollars. Consumer Price Index (CPI) Inflation Calculator, http://data.bls.gov/cgi-bin/cpicalc.pl (accessed April 1, 2016).

2. Charles Van Cleve, "Beneficence: A History of Ball State Teachers College," mss. (Muncie, IN: Ball State University Archives, 1961), 42–43, quoted in Anthony Edmonds and E. Bruce Geelhoed, *Ball State University: An Interpretive History* (Bloomington: Indiana University Press, 2001), 60.

3. Edmonds and Geelhoed, *Ball State University*, 57–66.

4. A key exception is found in Robin Bachin, *Building the South Side: Urban Space and Civic Culture in Chicago, 1890–1919* (Chicago: University of Chicago Press, 2004).

5. Christine Ogren, *The American State Normal School: An Instrument of Great Good* (New York: Palgrave Macmillan, 2005), 58.

6. 1880 U.S. Census of Population (Washington, DC: GPO, 1884). 1900 U.S. Census (Washington, DC: GPO, 1904), vol. 2, Table 5, p. 136. PDFs available at https://www.census.gov/prod/www/decennial.html (accessed February 22, 2017).

7. 1881–82 Emerson's Muncie Business Directory, Muncie City Directories Collection, Ball State University, University Libraries, Archives and Special Collections (BSUASC) (http://libx.bsu.edu).

8. Frank C. Ball, *Memoirs of Frank Clayton Ball* (Muncie, IN: Privately printed, 1937). Edmonds and Geelhoed, *Ball State University*, 48.

9. Edmonds and Geelhoed, *Ball State University*, 49.

10. For discussion of the walking city and the transformation of urban form, see Sam Bass Warner, *Streetcar Suburbs: The Process of Growth in Boston, 1870–1900* (Cambridge, MA: Harvard University Press, 1962).

11. 1899–1900 Emerson's Muncie Directory, Muncie City Directories Collection, BSUASC, http://libx.bsu.edu/cdm/landingpage/collection/MunCityDirs.

12. Emily Kimbrough, *How Dear to My Heart* (New York: Dodd, Mead, 1944), 8–13.

13. Andrew Carnegie, "The Gospel of Wealth," *North American Review* 148, no. 391 (June 1889), http://www.swarthmore.edu/SocSci/rbannis1/AIH19th/Carnegie.html (accessed November 1, 2013). Andrew Carnegie, "The Best Fields for Philanthropy," *North American Review* 149, no. 397 (December 1889), 682–98, http://www.jstor.org/stable/25101907 (accessed May 19, 2015).

14. Bachin, *Building the South Side*, 34, 42. Field made an eightfold profit on the land he sold in Hyde Park.

15. See also the founding of the University of Michigan, where local business leaders donated fifty acres of undeveloped land, and the University of California, Berkeley, the creation of which entailed several land schemes. Howard Peckham, *The Making of the University of Michigan, 1817–1992* (Ann Arbor: University of Michigan Press, 1997). Verne Stadtman, *The University of California 1868–1968* (New York: McGraw-Hill, 1970), 19–34.

16. Edmonds and Geelhoed, *Ball State University*, 56.

17. Ibid., 53.

18. Ibid., 51–54. For classic studies detailing the importance of rail transit in the expansion of urban and suburban development, see Sam Bass Warner's *Streetcar Suburbs* on metropolitan Boston; Ann Durkin Keating's *Building Chicago: Suburban Developers and the Creation of a Divided Metropolis* (Columbus: Ohio State University Press, 1988) on metro Chicago; Robert Fishman's *Bourgeois Utopias: The Rise and Fall of Suburbia* (New York: Basic, 1987), including chapters on Philadelphia and Los Angeles; and, more generally, Kenneth Jackson's *Crabgrass Frontier: The Suburbanization of the United States* (New York: Oxford University Press, 1985). In each of these cases, real-estate developers served as driving forces behind the expansion of rail transit and urban development.

19. Edmonds and Geelhoed, *Ball State University*, 52.

20. Ibid., 56.

21. Glenn White, *The Ball State Story: From Normal Institute to University* (Muncie, IN: Ball State University, 1967), 33–34.

22. Edmonds and Geelhoed, *Ball State University*, 57, 60–61. This translates to $7.4 million dollars in 2016 dollars (CPI Inflation Calculator, http://data.bls.gov/cgi-bin/cpicalc.pl [accessed April 1, 2016]).

23. Ancestry.com. *1920 United States Federal Census* [database on-line]. Provo, UT: Ancestry.com, 2010. Images reproduced by FamilySearch. Original data: Fourteenth Census of the United States, 1920 (National Archives and Records Administration microfilm publication T625, 2076 rolls). Records of the Bureau of the Census, Record Group (RG) 29. National Archives, Washington, D.C.

24. The Balls had bought the land in the 1890s. "Bertha Crosley Ball Art Center Ball State University," pamphlet, University Archives, Folder "Buildings," Folder 1, Box 1, p. 33, BSUASC.

25. Earl Conn, *Beneficence: Stories About the Ball Families of Muncie* (Muncie, IN: Minnetrista Cultural Foundation, 2003), 47.

26. See, for example, Fishman, *Bourgeois Utopias*.

27. Edmund B. Ball, "A Lifetime Investment," quoted in Edmonds and Geelhoed, *Ball State University*, 60.

28. Lloyd Lieurance, "The History of the Organization, Administration, and Control of the Normal School at Muncie, Indiana" (MS thesis, Indiana State Normal School, 1926), 172–74, BSUASC.

29. The stated aim of the legislation was to improve state park resources. Lieurance, "History," BSUASC. The Muncie transactions sparked interest around the state in public acquisition of private education institutions. Horace Ellis to James Goodrich, December 26, 1918, Box 137, Goodrich Papers, Indiana State Archives.

30. Pamphlet, List of Members of the Muncie Rotary Club, 1932, "Membership Lists 1932–1957," Folder 7, Box 5, Muncie Rotary Collection, MSS 125, Stoeckel Archives, BSUASC. For a broad history of organizations such as the Rotary, see Jeffrey Charles, *Service Clubs in American Society: Rotary, Kiwanis, and Lions* (Urbana: University of Illinois Press, 1993). Two significant early studies of such clubs include Charles F. Marden, *Rotary and Its Brothers: An Analysis and Interpretation of the Men's Service Clubs* (Princeton, NJ: Princeton University Press, 1935), and the University of Chicago Social Science Survey Committee, *Rotary? A University Group Looks at the Rotary Club of Chicago* (Chicago: University of Chicago, 1934). *Middletown*, however, remains the classic small-city study of the influence of such an organization. R. S. Lynd and H. M. Lynd, *Middletown: A Study in Modern American Culture* (New York: Harcourt, Brace, 1929).

31. Charles Van Cleve, "Beneficence," 44, quoted in Edmonds and Geelhoed, *Ball State University*, 58.

32. Dane Starbuck, *The Goodriches: An American Family* (Indianapolis: Liberty Fund, 2001). Herbert Hoover note to George Ball, November 30, 1932, Folder 7, Box 14, George A. Ball Papers, Minnetrista Cultural Center, Muncie, Indiana.

33. Lieurance, "History," 179.

34. The Balls had to offer a small additional gift to the state to provide for any losses the state would incur. Edmonds and Geelhoed, *Ball State University*, 63. "State Can Take Balls' Gift," *Muncie Morning Star*, March 1, 1918.

35. Thomas Buchanan, "The Life of Rollin 'Doc' Bunch, the Boss of Middletown" (PhD dissertation, Ball State University, 1992), 65. Industry was the location of one of two African American neighborhoods in Muncie before World War I and, at midcentury, became the site of the Munsyana Homes, a federal low-income housing project.

36. Buchanan, "Life of Rollin 'Doc' Bunch," 62–65.

37. "Bunch and Annexation, Etc.," *Muncie Evening Press*, October 28, 1917.

38. Obituary, Miami *Daily News-Record*, July 15, 1948, 12.

39. "Dr. Bunch Runs on His Record," *Muncie Morning Star*, October 29, 1917.

40. Buchanan, "Life of Rollin 'Doc' Bunch," 64.

41. Indiana law did not require a majority affirmative vote of residents within areas proposed for annexation. The northwestern side of Muncie voted more heavily Republican and the southern side more heavily Democratic: thus, Grafton was alienating his potential base in favor of good government and metropolitan equity in hopes of creating a wedge issue to attract members of the Bunch coalition. This changing political geography would continue to roil city elections, particularly during the politically populist rise of the Ku Klux Klan in the 1920s. Carollyle Frank, "Who Governed Middletown? Community Power in Muncie, Indiana, in the 1930s," *Indiana Magazine of History* (1979), 320–43. Leonard Moore, *Citizen Klansmen: The Ku Klux Klan in Indiana, 1921–1928* (Chapel Hill: University of North Carolina, 1991).

42. Margaret Bourke-White, "Muncie, Ind. Is the Great U.S. 'Middletown,'" *Life* 2, no. 19, May 10, 1937.

43. Anonymous interviewee (Black Middletown Oral History Collection—S125), audio oral history and transcript, p. 15, http://libx.bsu.edu/cdm/ref/collection/MidOrHis /id/259.

44. Ibid.

45. 1917–18 Emerson's Muncie Directory, Muncie City Directories Collection, BSUASC, http://libx.bsu.edu/cdm/ref/collection/MidOrHis. See Luke Eric Lassiter and Hurley Goodall, *Other Side of Middle Town: Exploring Muncie's African American Community* (Walnut Creek, CA: AltaMira, 2004).

46. The normal school system was adapted from the *école normale* in France. Anne Quartararo, *Women Teachers and Popular Education in Nineteenth-Century France: Social Values and Corporate Identity at the Normal School Institution* (Newark: University of Delaware Press, 1995), 23–24. Jurgen Herbst, *And Sadly Teach: Teacher Education and Professionalization in American Culture* (Madison: University of Wisconsin Press, 1989). Ogren, *American State Normal School.*

47. As Lynn Gordon illustrates, a woman's pursuit of higher education in the postbellum era had been a politically radical act, but by the early twentieth century, women had been integrated into the mainstream of higher-education institutions—virtually segregated within them—and attendance per se had largely been stripped of its political meaning, limiting the turbulence of a formerly self-consciously political force. Staffing at *The Easterner* was dominated by neither sex, whether in the editorial positions or the reporting positions, as indicated by the paper's masthead. Mary McComb locates a confluence of business ideology and middle-class conservatism in higher education in the 1930s, but these elements already constituted a formidable presence in the vocational school by the 1920s. Lynn Gordon, *Gender and Higher Education in the Progressive Era* (New Haven, CT: Yale University Press, 1990). Mary McComb, *Great Depression and the Middle Class: Experts, Collegiate Youth and Business Ideology, 1929–1941* (New York: Routledge, 2012). For comparison, particularly an examination of collegians, see Robert Cohen, *When the Old Left Was Young* (New York: Oxford University Press, 1993).

48. Noyer to Pittenger, August 23, 1940, RG 3, President's Papers, BSUASC.

49. From sample of student residences, 1928–29 B Book, BSUASC.

50. *Muncie Evening Press,* September 29, 1917, 5, quoted in Buchanan, "Life of Rollin 'Doc' Bunch," 62.

51. At a point prior to prohibition, Muncie was home to more than forty saloons for a population of roughly 11,000. Lynd and Lynd, *Middletown,* 258n. See also the Muncie City Directory for 1917–1918, which indicates the location of thirty-three saloons.

52. Lynn Gordon, "The Gibson Girl Goes to College: Popular Culture and Women's Higher Education in the Progressive Era, 1890–1920," *American Quarterly* 39, no. 2 (1987): 211–30.

53. Alyson King, "Centres of 'Home-Like Influence': Residences for Women at the University of Toronto," *Material History Review* 49 (Spring 1999): 39–59.

54. Edmonds and Geelhoed, *Ball State University,* 81.

55. DeHority to Frank Bales, April 21, 1925, Folder 31, Box 25, RG 3, President's Papers, BSUASC.

56. The transgression was for "illicit relationships on two separate occasions." Memo from Executive Committee to L. A. Pittenger, May 5, 1932, Folder 32, Box 25, RG 3, President's Papers, Lemuel A. Pittenger, BSUASC. The female partner appears to have been allowed to graduate. *The Orient,* 1932, BSUASC.

57. Jesse Nixon, from Muncie, was the first African American to graduate from the public institution, in 1925. Hurley Goodall and Elizabeth Campbell, "A City Apart," in *The Other Side of Middletown: Exploring Muncie's African American Community*, edited by Luke Eric Lassiter (Walnut Creek, CA: Altamira Press, 2004), 60.

58. "Vacant Rooms for Fall Quarter," Folder "Dean of Women 1924–1937," Box 13, President's Papers, BSUASC.

59. Claudia Goldin, "Enrollment in Institutions of Higher Education, by Sex, Enrollment Status, and Type of Institution: 1869–1995," Table Bc524, in *Historical Statistics of the United States, Earliest Times to the Present: Millennial Edition,* edited by Susan B. Carter, Scott Sigmund Gartner, Michael R. Haines, Alan L. Olmstead, Richard Sutch, and Gavin Wright (New York: Cambridge University Press, 2006).

60. A 33.3 percent sample of students from 1928 indicates approximately 4.1 percent of BTC students (14 of 344) lived on the south side of the city. BTC Student Directory, 1928–29, BSUASC.

61. The Lynds contrast the education planning of the business class, where preparation for college—including family saving and consideration of high school coursework—was nearly universal, to the working class, where preparation for college was rare and, when it did occur, was vague and aspirational rather than concrete and operational. Lynd and Lynd, *Middletown*, 185–87.

62. Enrollment Table, "Statistics—Enrollment School," Folder 14, Box 25, RG 3, President's Papers, BSUASC.

63. National enrollment grew at about a 10 percent rate per year from 1917 to 1925, from 441,000 to 941,000. Table Bc523. Carter et al., eds., *Historical Statistics of the United States.*

64. The institution formally remained a branch of the Indiana State Normal School but was granted informal recognition as Ball Teachers College until 1929, when it became budgetarily independent.

65. Edmonds and Geelhoed, *Ball State University*, 78–79.

66. Jon Peterson, *The Birth of City Planning in the United States, 1840–1917* (Baltimore: Johns Hopkins University Press, 2003).

67. Jena Noll, *The Residential Architecture of Cuno Kibele in Muncie, Indiana, 1905–1927* (MS thesis, Ball State University, 1999), 14–15.

68. Peterson, *Birth of City Planning*, 60–61, 88.

69. McKim went to the École; Gilbert went to MIT. Peterson, *Birth of City Planning*, 61–73.

70. Edmonds and Geelhoed, *Ball State University*, 82–83.

71. White, *Ball State Story*, 27.

72. The Lynds quote a local who called Pittenger a small-time politician who was given the BTC presidency to prevent him from running for U.S. Congress. However, Pittenger held a long association with the Balls and after leaving BTC became president of the George and Frances Ball Foundation when Ball purchased and resold the 23,000-mile Van Sweringen railroad network in 1936. Lynd and Lynd, *Middletown in Transition*, 216–17. Nelson Polsby, "Power in Middletown: Fact and Value in

Community Research," *Canadian Journal of Economics and Political Science* 26, no. 4 (1960): 597.

73. Edmonds and Geelhoed, *Ball State University*, 81.

74. Ball, *Memoirs*, 137. Recent BSU publications indicate the donation and cost were only $150,000.

75. Memo from W. W. Wagoner to Benjamin Burris, December 7, 1925, "Statistics—General," Folder 17, Box 25, RG 3, President's Papers, BSUASC. While historians of higher education have identified the early twentieth century as a period of the return of collegiate life, emphasizing on-campus living and clubby associations, smaller institutions such as Ball Teachers College diverged from the trend. Until 1936, there were no men's accommodations on campus, indicating dramatically different attitudes among administrators toward men and women. Frederick Rudolph, *The American College and University: A History* (New York: Alfred A. Knopf, 1962), 449–61. The number of women increased from about 60 to 143, or about 20 percent of the college's approximately 700 women. The dean of women's records in the Pittenger Papers attest to regular disciplinary action over curfews and correspondence to women's families about their moral character and personal relationships. See President's Papers for Pittenger Administration, BSUASC.

76. Edmonds and Geelhoed, *Ball State University*, 116–18.

77. Ibid., 117.

78. Ibid.

79. Lynd and Lynd, *Middletown in Transition*, 81.

80. Ibid., 82.

81. Frederick Graham and Dawn Lee Patrick, *Westwood: A 75 Year History* (Muncie, IN: Minnetrista Cultural Foundation, 2000).

82. Plat of Westwood, Delaware County Plat Book, p. 68, County Recorder, Muncie, IN.

83. Plat of Westwood, Delaware County Plat Book, pp. 65–68, County Recorder, Muncie, IN.

84. Advertisement, "Westwood—A Residential Park," *Muncie Sunday Star*, October 19, 1924.

85. See, for example, the discussion of the development and disharmony of the "student ghetto" in Ithaca, New York, and the animosity between university affiliates and nonstudents in Newark, Delaware, in Blake Gumprecht, *The American College Town* (Amherst: University of Massachusetts Press, 2008), 71–107, 296–334.

86. Plat of Westwood Park. Delaware County Plat Book, County Recorder, Muncie, IN.

87. Leonard Moore, *Citizen Klansmen: The Ku Klux Klan in Indiana, 1921–1928* (Chapel Hill: University of North Carolina Press, 1991).

88. Goodall and Campbell, "A City Apart," 61.

89. Martin Schwartz interview, Middletown Jewish Oral History Project, R 14, 33. Sherman Zeigler interview, Middletown Jewish Oral History Project, R 14, 6, 9. Both in BSUASC.

90. Zeigler admitted an accommodationist position, noting at the time, "I certainly don't want to live where I'm not wanted." Zeigler's wife, a gentile, worked for a law firm that enforced such restrictive covenants. Zeigler interview, Middletown Jewish Oral History Project, R 14: 3, 9, BSUASC.

91. Recent scholarship has turned a critical eye on the relationship between Progressivism and city planning. See, for example, David Freund, *Colored Property: State Policy and White Racial Politics in Suburban America* (Chicago: University of Chicago Press, 2007).

92. For an analysis of the relationship between zoning and exclusion in this period, see Freund, *Colored Property*, 45–98.

93. On the history of suburbanization in the United States, see Jackson, *Crabgrass Frontier*. Robert Fishman, *Bourgeois Utopias*. On Olmsted in particular, see Witold Rybczynski, *A Clearing in the Distance: Frederick Law Olmsted and America in the Nineteenth Century* (New York: Scribner, 1999). On the role of real-estate developers in creating suburban communities, see Marc Weiss, *The Rise of the Community Builders: The American Real Estate Industry and Urban Land Planning* (New York: Columbia University Press, 1987). On Nichols in particular, see William Worley, *J. C. Nichols and the Shaping of Kansas City: Innovation in Planned Residential Communities* (Columbia: University of Missouri Press, 1990). The Lynds indicate that another wealthy Muncie family, independent minded, developed its own compound on the White River in the southeastern part of the city but did not shift the overall pattern of business-class residence. Lynd and Lynd, *Middletown in Transition*, 82n.

94. The Westwood development had a minimum lot allocation per family of 7,500 square feet, the highest in the city along with the Minnetrista development. By contrast, much of the working-class south side bore minimum lots of 2,400 square feet, with some areas ranging up to 4,800 and, in a few instances, down to 600. "Zoning Ordinance for Muncie Indiana—As Amended December 17, 1929," BSU Stoeckel Archives.

95. The Lynds devote a great deal of attention to social and civic clubs in Muncie and their role in community organization. Lynd and Lynd, *Middletown*, 285–306.

96. Abraham Flexner, *Medical Education in the United States and Canada: A Report to the Carnegie Foundation for the Advancement of Teaching* (New York: Carnegie Foundation for the Advancement of Teaching, 1910). Paul Starr, *The Social Transformation of American Medicine* (New York: Basic, 1982).

97. Ball, *Memoirs*, 138.

98. Edmonds and Geelhoed, *Ball State University*, 87–88.

99. Wiley, *Ball Memorial Hospital*, 45.

100. Ball, *Memoirs*, 138.

101. Frank Ball could arrange for hospital groundskeepers to mow college land next door because the hospital had a larger, more efficient lawnmower. Letter from Ball to Pittenger, May 1, 1937, Folder "Buildings 1936–1938," Box 6, RG 3, President's Papers, BSUASC.

102. Ball, *Memoirs*, 139. The amount of $2,010,000 in 1929 dollars is equivalent to $27.9 million in 2016 dollars. CPI Inflation Calculator, http://data.bls.gov/cgi-bin/cpicalc .pl (accessed April 9, 2016).

103. In the first years of the Westwood development, industrialists predominated. However, throughout the twentieth century, the number and proportion of the industrialist class declined, while the number of physicians and educators dramatically increased, together far outnumbering industrialists by the end of the century. Graham and Patrick, *Westwood*.

104. Graham and Patrick, *Westwood*, 78.

105. On the resonance between the Lynds' and Capra's work, see Eric Smoodin, *Regarding Frank Capra: Audience, Celebrity, and American Film Studies, 1930–1960* (Durham, NC: Duke University Press, 2004). Richard Maltby, "It Happened One Night: Recreation of the Patriarch," in *Frank Capra: Authorship and the Studio System*, edited by Robert Sklar and Vito Zagarrio (Philadelphia: Temple University Press, 1998), 130–63.

106. Lynd and Lynd, *Middletown in Transition*, 76–77.

107. Ibid., 74.

108. Pullman's control over his company town likewise extended to the built environment. See Margaret Crawford, *Building the Workingman's Paradise: The Design of American Company Towns* (New York: Verso, 1995).

109. "Muncie, Ind. Is the Great U.S. 'Middletown,'" *Life*, May 10, 1937, 16–25.

110. Michael Richman, *Daniel Chester French, an American Sculptor* (New York: Metropolitan Museum of Art, 1976).

111. Robert Henry Myers, *Beneficence: The Statue on the Campus of Ball State University, Muncie, Indiana* (Muncie, IN: Ball State University, 1972), 15.

112. Lynd and Lynd, *Middletown in Transition*, 82.

113. Myers, *Beneficence*, 18.

Chapter 2

1. Julia Cauble Smith, "Santa Rita Oil Well," *Handbook of Texas Online*, http://www.tshaonline.org/handbook/online/articles/dos01 (accessed May 13, 2015), published by the Texas State Historical Association.

2. When crude oil is refined, 46 percent becomes gasoline. Heating oil and diesel fuel compose 20 percent, and jet fuel, 8 percent. Source: U.S. Energy Information Administration, http://www.eia.gov/tools/faqs/faq.cfm?id=41&t=6 (accessed May 14, 2015).

3. See, for example, Peter Wallenstein, ed., *Higher Education and the Civil Rights Movement: White Supremacy, Black Southerners, and College Campuses* (Gainesville: University of Florida Press, 2007).

4. Ronald Bayor, *Race and the Shaping of Twentieth-Century Atlanta* (Chapel Hill: University of North Carolina Press, 1996). Thomas Sugrue, *The Origins of the Urban Crisis: Race and Inequality in Postwar Detroit* (Princeton, NJ: Princeton University Press, 1996).

5. Margaret Pugh O'Mara, *Cities of Knowledge: Cold War Science and the Search for the Next Silicon Valley* (Princeton, NJ: Princeton University Press, 2005).

6. Constitution of the State of Texas (1876), https://tarltonapps.law.utexas.edu/constitutions/texas1876 (accessed February 24, 2016).

7. Carol McMichael, *Paul Cret at Texas: Architectural Drawing and the Image of the University in the 1930s* (Austin: University of Texas Huntington Art Gallery, 1983), 18.

8. Margaret C. Berry, *Brick by Golden Brick: A History of Campus Buildings at the University of Texas at Austin, 1883–1993* (Austin, TX: LBCo., 1993), 10.

9. W. J. Battle, "A Concise History of the University of Texas, 1883–1950," *Southwestern Historical Quarterly* 54, no. 4 (April 1951): 397.

10. Susan Richardson, "Oil, Power, and Universities: Political Struggle and Academic Advancement at the University of Texas and Texas A&M, 1876–1965" (PhD dissertation, Pennsylvania State University, 2005), 119.

11. Battle, "Concise History of the University of Texas," 395–96.

12. The Confederacy blockaded the export of cotton to Great Britain to try to force British diplomatic recognition of the Confederacy. Sven Beckert, *Empire of Cotton: A Global History* (New York: Vintage, 2014), 246.

13. "Served Family 94 Years—Former Texas Slave Who Went to War with Master Dies at 105," *New York Times,* February 3, 1936, 19.

14. Frank Erwin Jr., "Review of the History of the Brackenridge Tract," July 10, 1973, UT Board of Regents Minutes. Margaret Berry Papers, Briscoe Center for American History, University of Texas (CAHUT).

15. Peter H. Hassrick, "Alexander Phimister Proctor in Texas," *Southwestern Historical Quarterly* 107, no. 2 (October 1, 2003): 218–37; Walter L. Buenger, *The Path to a Modern South: Northeast Texas Between Reconstruction and the Great Depression* (Austin: University of Texas Press, 2001).

16. For the sculptor's account, see Pompeo Coppini, *From Dawn to Sunset* (San Antonio, TX: Naylor, 1949), 250–68.

17. 1930 U.S. Census of Population (Washington, DC: GPO, 1934). Campbell Gibson, "Population of the 100 Largest Cities and Other Urban Places in the United States: 1790 to 1990," Population Division Working Paper No. 27, http://www.census.gov /population/www/documentation/twps0027/tab16.txt (accessed February 13, 2012).

18. Judith Jenkins, "Austin, Texas During the Great Depression, 1929–1936" (MA thesis, University of Texas, 1965), 34–35.

19. As an intellectual and political entrepôt, Austin was a hotbed of ideologies across the political spectrum, and the university drew scholars from around the country. This intellectual life was in many ways opposed to segregation and was part and parcel to the tensions in Austin that would break apart later. Neil Foley, *The White Scourge: Mexicans, Blacks, and Poor Whites in Texas Cotton Culture* (Berkeley: University of California Press, 1998), 1–4.

20. 2300 Lafayette, data tallied from 1930 manuscript census information for Austin, TX (digital file in the possession of the author). Five thousand dollars inflates to $71,300 in 2016 dollars. CPI Inflation Calculator, http://data.bls.gov/cgi-bin/cpicalc.pl (accessed April 15, 2016).

21. In the late nineteenth century, Austin's black population was far more dispersed, often at the periphery of the city, in areas including South Austin across the Colorado River, Wheatsville northwest of the university campus, and Clarksville west of the downtown, in addition to several settlements in East Austin. Michelle Morgan Mears, "African

American Settlement Patterns in Austin, Texas, 1865–1928" (MA thesis, Baylor University, 2001).

22. Data transcribed from manuscript folios of 1930 U.S. Census of Population (digital file in possession of the author).

23. In the early years of the 1900s, developers promoted Hyde Park as "Exclusively for White People." "Austin's Racial Geography in Maps," http://projects.statesman.com /news/racial-geography/ (accessed April 18, 2016).

24. Data show that 2,190 of 2,460 black female workers, by either occupation title or code, fell into this category. Data tallied from manuscript folios of 1930 U.S. Census of Population (digital file in possession of the author).

25. Austin's population included 2,685 adult black men aged 16 or above. Of these, 2,414 were employed. Shown by either title or occupational code, 1,620 worked as laborers, porters, servants, cooks, waiters, chauffeurs, or launderers. Of the total workers, 146 were classified as employers or business owners, and 105 were skilled workers in the building trades. Data transcribed from manuscript folios of 1930 U.S. Census of Population (digital file in possession of the author).

26. Jason McDonald, *Racial Dynamics in Early Twentieth Century Austin, Texas* (Lanham, MD: Lexington, 2012), 109–10.

27. Christopher Silver, "The Racial Origins of Zoning: Southern Cities from 1910 to 1940," in *Urban Planning the African American Community: In the Shadows*, edited by June Manning Thomas and Marsha Ritzdorf (Thousand Oaks, CA: Sage, 1997), 189–205.

28. McDonald, *Racial Dynamics in Early Twentieth Century Austin, Texas,* 110.

29. Austin City Council Meeting Minutes, July 21, 1927, http://www.austintexas.gov /edims/document.cfm?id=89783 (accessed April 18, 2016).

30. Deborah Pollack, *Visual Art and the Urban Evolution of the New South* (Columbia: University of South Carolina Press, 2015), 236. Roxanne Williamson, "Kuehne, Hugo Franz," *Handbook of Texas Online*, http://www.tshaonline.org/handbook/online/articles /fku12 (accessed June 1, 2015), published by the Texas State Historical Association.

31. *Sunday Morning News*, "City Plan Supplement: Being the Report and Recommendations of Koch and Fowler, City Plan Engineers, for the City of Austin," February 12, 1928, p. 14. (CAHUT).

32. McDonald, *Racial Dynamics in Early Twentieth Century Austin, Texas,* 107.

33. *Sunday Morning News*, "City Plan Supplement," February 12, 1928.

34. The key work on race in Austin illustrates there were segregationist policies and tendencies affecting the Hispanic community but less so than the African American community. McDonald, *Racial Dynamics in Early Twentieth Century Austin, Texas.*

35. Data tallied from manuscript folios of 1930 U.S. Census of Population (digital file in possession of the author).

36. John Mason Brewer, *An Historical Outline of the Negro in Travis County*, (Austin: Sam Huston College, 1940), 60.

37. W. Astor Kirk, interview by Anthony Orum, August 29, 1984, oral history transcript, Austin History Center, Austin, TX.

38. Ada Simonds, interview by Anthony Orum, April 19, 1983, p. 44, oral history transcript, Austin History Center, Austin, TX.

39. Jacquelyn Dowd Hall, "The Long Civil Rights Movement and the Political Uses of the Past," *Journal of American History* (March 2005): 1233–63.

40. Lee Lewis Campbell was the dominant African American political figure of the first quarter of the twentieth century. He helped found a series of civic institutions in East Austin. See McDonald, *Racial Dynamics in Early Twentieth Century Austin, Texas.*

41. The 1944 U.S. Supreme Court decision in *Smith v. Allwright* ruled the all-white primary unconstitutional (321 U.S. 649 [1944]). Political scientist V. O. Key details the widespread practice of the white-only primary in *Southern Politics in State and Nation* (New York: Alfred A. Knopf, 1949), 620.

42. Quoted in McDonald, *Racial Dynamics in Early Twentieth Century Austin, Texas*, 287.

43. *Sunday Morning News*, "City Plan Supplement," February 12, 1928.

44. "Austin, TX," 1935, Sanborn Fire Insurance Maps, 1867–1970—Texas, http://sanborn.umi.com.

45. Kirk oral history, Austin History Center, Austin, TX.

46. McDonald, *Racial Dynamics in Early Twentieth Century Austin, Texas*, 287.

47. Ibid., 285–86.

48. Ibid., 102.

49. Ibid., 288–93.

50. Investors bid upon bonds in an auction, and Austin's bonds were judged comparable or superior to other Southern municipalities issuing bonds at the same time, including Shreveport, Louisiana, and Winston-Salem, North Carolina. Austin was more generally on par with Northern cities such as Lowell, Massachusetts; Elizabeth, New Jersey; and Bronxville, New York. "Other Municipal Loans: Bond Issues to Be Offered to Investment Bankers—One Award Announced," *New York Times*, November 23, 1929, 33. "Municipal Loans: New Bond Issues Announced for Offering to Investment Bankers and the Public: Province of Ontario. Winston-Salem, N.C. Elizabeth, N.J. Austin, Texas. Dallas County, Texas. Lowell, Mass. Buncombe County, N.C.," *New York Times*, May 3, 1929, 41.

51. See, for example, Scott Ellsworth, *Death in a Promised Land: The Tulsa Race Riot of 1921* (Baton Rouge: Louisiana State University Press, 1982); and Kevin Boyle, *Arc of Justice: A Saga of Race, Civil Rights, and Murder in the Jazz Age* (New York: Henry Holt, 2004).

52. "All Bond Issues Got Substantial Victories," *Austin American*. May 19, 1928, 1.

53. Simonds oral history, p. 44, Austin History Center, Austin, TX.

54. 1940 U.S. Census, Minnesota Population Center, *National Historical Geographic Information System: Version 2.0* (Minneapolis: University of Minnesota, 2011), http://www.nhgis.org.

55. The state constitution of 1876 precluded African Americans from attending the University of Texas. Instead, Texas had created Prairie View Normal School in a neighboring county and forbade black students from attending UT, a policy reinforced by the 1896 decision *Plessy v. Ferguson.*

56. Richardson, "Oil, Power, and Universities," 124.

57. W. J. Battle, *Town and Gown Club: Memories of Past Days* (Austin, TX: Town and Gown Club, 1952).

58. Ibid.

59. Jenkins, "Austin, Texas, During the Great Depression," 41–42. Long was also a prominent advocate for passage of the municipal bond election in 1928.

60. Floylee Hemphill, "Mayor Tom Miller and the First Year of the New Deal in Austin, Texas." (M.A. Thesis, University of Texas, 1976), 29.

61. Richardson, "Oil, Power, and Universities," 117.

62. The architect's name is pronounced "cray."

63. The relationship would allow the architect to continue Cass Gilbert's Beaux-Arts campus planning and design efforts from the 1910s, but would provide Cret with the resources for a much more ambitious set of developments. Battle, "Concise History of the University of Texas," 397. Cret's imprimatur from the Eastern cultural and financial establishment included commissions for the Folger Shakespeare Library in Washington, D.C., and the Detroit Institute of Arts; his later works included the Federal Reserve headquarters in Washington, D.C., and the Federal Reserve branch in Philadelphia. The most robust discussion of Cret's career is found in Elizabeth Grossman, *The Civic Architecture of Paul Cret* (New York: Cambridge University Press, 1996). The key examination of Cret's work at the University of Texas is in McMichael, *Paul Cret at Texas*, 22–24.

64. See the Paul Phillipe Cret Drawings in the Alexander Architectural Archives at the University of Texas, Austin.

65. The nearby Wheatsville neighborhood, once one of the city's main black settlements, saw a declining minority population in 1940 and was largely drained of its African American and Hispanic residents by 1950 as a result of the city's development plans. From 1940 and 1950 U.S. Census data, Minnesota Population Center, *National Historical Geographic Information System: Version 2.0* (Minneapolis: University of Minnesota, 2011).

66. Charles Z. Klauder and Herbert Wise, *College Architecture in America and Its Part in the Development of the Campus* (New York: Scribner's, 1929), 148–50.

67. Taylor lived at 301 W. 21st Street, now demolished. The Scottish Rite Dormitory was renowned as the most desirable residence for women at UT in the 1920s and 1930s. Jan Jarboe Russell, *Lady Bird: A Biography of Mrs. Johnson* (New York: Taylor, 2004), 76. Michael Gillette, *Lady Bird Johnson: An Oral History* (New York: Oxford University Press, 2012), 34–35.

68. Letter from C. L. Stone, assistant attorney general, to C. W. Goddard, University Health Service, January 23, 1924, advising of attorney general's opinion about university's legal authority to regulate student housing, VF 18/D.b, University Archives, CAHUT.

69. Linda Gordon, *Gender and Higher Education in the Progressive Era, 1890–1920* (New Haven: Yale University Press, 1990).

70. Paul Cret, "Report Accompanying General Plan of Development," (mss, University of Texas, 1933), 33. CAHUT.

71. Enrollment dropped from more than 1.15 million to 1.05 million students, a loss of 100,000 students. Claudia Goldin, "Enrollment in Institutions of Higher Education, by Sex, Enrollment Status, and Type of Institution: 1869–1995," Table Bc523–536, in *Historical Statistics of the United States, Earliest Times to the Present: Millennial Edition,* edited by Susan B. Carter, Scott Sigmund Gartner, Michael R. Haines, Alan L. Olmstead, Richard Sutch, and Gavin Wright (New York: Cambridge University Press, 2006), http://dx.doi.org/10.1017/ISBN-9780511132971.Bc510-73610.1017/.

72. Unemployment among construction workers was 73.9 percent, according to Robert Margo, "The Microeconomics of Depression Unemployment," *Journal of Economic History* 51, no. 2 (June 1991): 333–41. Construction funds from Table A in Peter Stone, *Construction Expenditures and Employment* (Washington, DC: Works Progress Administration, 1937), 14. Construction expenditures amounted to $153.4 billion and $54.9 billion in 2016 dollars, respectively. CPI Inflation Calculator, http://data.bls.gov/cgi-bin/cpicalc.pl (accessed April 20, 2016).

73. Harold Ickes, *Back to Work: The Story of the P.W.A.* (New York: Macmillan, 1935).

74. Franklin Delano Roosevelt, First Inaugural Address, in *The Public Papers and Addresses of Franklin D. Roosevelt,* edited by Samuel Rosenman (New York: Random House, 1938), 2:11, 13; quoted in Jason Scott Smith, *Building New Deal Liberalism: The Political Economy of Public Works, 1933–1956* (New York: Oxford University Press, 2006), 19–20. Smith's book examines New Deal public works through the lens of political economy.

75. The Public Works Administration supported the construction of approximately 70 percent of the nation's new school construction between 1933 and 1939. William Leuchtenberg, *Franklin D. Roosevelt and the New Deal, 1932–1940* (New York: Harper Perennial, 2009), 133. Proportionally, education buildings were the second best-funded PWA project type in both number of projects and project funds after streets and highways. Streets and highways received 15.7 percent of funds while education buildings received 14.0 percent. Smith, *Building New Deal Liberalism,* 90.

76. Franklin D. Roosevelt: "Address at Temple University, Philadelphia, on Receiving an Honorary Degree," February 22, 1936, online in Gerhard Peters and John T. Woolley, *The American Presidency Project,* http://www.presidency.ucsb.edu/ws/?pid=15240. Temple University was one of only three private universities in the United States to receive a PWA allotment. (Accessed April 20, 2016).

77. Nationally, college enrollment increased from 1.15 million in 1931 to 1.49 million in 1939. Goldin, "Enrollment in Institutions of Higher Education," Table Bc523–536.

78. Christopher Loss, *Between Citizens and the State: The Politics of Higher Education in the 20th Century* (Princeton, NJ: Princeton University Press, 2012).

79. United States Federal Housing Administration, *Underwriting Manual: Underwriting and Valuation Procedure Under Title II of the National Housing Act* (Washington, DC: GPO, 1936), pt. 229.

80. McMichael, *Paul Cret at Texas,* 24. In 2008 dollars, this becomes $9.9 million. CPI Inflation Calculator, http://data.bls.gov/cgi-bin/cpicalc.pl (accessed February 10, 2009). In one month, May 1945, the endowment funds received $173,000 from oil

and gas royalties. "Statement of Income from University Endowment Lands and Oil and Gas Development Thereon for the Month of May 1945," VF 23/D, University Archives, CAHUT.

81. The grant percentage was initially limited to 30 percent of total cost by the 1933 National Industrial Recovery Act. Reauthorization in 1935 raised the grant limit to 45 percent of cost. United States Public Works Administration Division of Information, *America Builds: The Record of PWA* (Washington, DC: GPO, 1939), 37–43.

82. The first was the North Building at Hunter College, located on expensive Park Avenue real estate in Manhattan's Upper East Side. "P.W.A. Non-Federal Allotments for Colleges and Universities," 1938. Box 13 Publications, RG 135 Public Works Administration. NARA II. College Park, MD. This becomes approximately $46 million in 2016 dollars.

83. The skyscraper was a new building type for higher education. Charles Klauder's Cathedral of Learning and the Camden, New Jersey, City Hall both influenced Cret's design. The Cathedral of Learning held its first classes in 1931, though it was not completed until 1934. Klauder was one of the most prominent campus architects of the period, and his reputation and influence were strengthened by publication of the campus guide.

84. Franklin D. Roosevelt, "Excerpts from the Press Conference," December 28, 1943, online in Gerhard Peters and John T. Woolley, *The American Presidency Project*, http://www.presidency.ucsb.edu/ws/?pid=16358 (accessed April 20, 2016).

85. Quoted in James Schneider, *The Navy V-12 Program: Leadership for a Lifetime* (Boston: Houghton Mifflin, 1987), 3. "The Future Development of the University of Texas: A Report to the Board of Regents by the President of the University," July 15, 1944, 12, CAHUT.

86. "Order Establishing the National Defense Research Committee." June 27, 1940, Franklin D. Roosevelt Presidential Library, http://docs.fdrlibrary.marist.edu/psf/box2 /a13v01.html (accessed April 20, 2016).

87. "J. J. Pickle Research Campus" (also known as the War Physics Laboratory), http://www.tshaonline.org/handbook/online/articles/sqjng (accessed February 22, 2016).

88. The War Research Laboratory was renamed the Defense Research Laboratory at the war's end.

89. George Norris Green, *The Establishment in Texas Politics: The Primitive Years, 1938–1957* (Westport, CT: Greenwood, 1979).

90. Richardson, "Oil, Power, and Universities," 196–204.

91. Memo from A. O. Greist to Sam Husbands, October 22, 1945, Folder "War Projects—Austin Magnesium Plant," Box 220, Pre-Presidential Papers (PPP). Lyndon Baines Johnson Presidential Library (LBJPL).

92. Walter Long, *From a Magnesium Plant to a Research Center* (Austin: Austin Chamber of Commerce, 1962), 32.

93. Letter from Johnson to Long, July 12, 1945. and letter from Johnson to Miller, July 13, 1945, Folder "War Projects—Austin Magnesium Plant," Box 220, PPP, LBJPL. Long, *From a Magnesium Plant to a Research Center*, 21.

94. John Adams Jr., *Damming the Colorado: The Rise of the Lower Colorado River Authority, 1933–1939* (College Station: Texas A&M University Press, 1990), 93–108.

95. Plancor 265 had contracted with the LCRA for 30,000 kilowatts of hydroelectric power each year. Long, *From a Magnesium Plant to a Research Center*, 30. Memo from A. O. Greist to Sam Husbands, October 22, 1945, Folder "War Projects—Austin Magnesium Plant," Box 220, PPP, LBJPL.

96. The Surplus Property Administration became the vehicle for transferring extraneous government war material to private hands after its creation in 1944 and handled the transaction with the University of Texas.

97. Telegram from Theophilus Painter to Lyndon Johnson, November 27, 1943, Folder "War Projects Austin Magnesium Plant," Box 220, PPP, LBLPL.

98. Letter from T. S. Painter to J. W. Toelken, June 18, 1946, Folder "War Projects Austin Magnesium Plant #2," Box 220, PPP, LBJPL.

99. Letter from R. G Rhett to T. S. Painter, May 21, 1946, Folder "War Projects Austin Magnesium Plant #2," Box 220, PPP, LBJPL.

100. "UT Offers to Purchase Magnesium Plant Here," *Austin Statesman*, April 4, 1946, 12. Long, *From a Magnesium Plant to a Research Center*, 38. This amount becomes approximately $13.4 million in 2008 dollars. CPI Inflation Calculator, http://data.bls.gov /cgi-bin/cpicalc.pl (accessed December 1, 2008)

101. Long, *From a Magnesium Plant to a Research Center*, 52.

102. "Off Campus UT Research Pursues War Trend," *Austin American-Statesman*, July 29, 1951, quoted in Andrew Busch, "Building a City of Upper-Middle-Class Citizens: Labor Markets, Segregation, and Growth in Austin, Texas, 1950–1973," *Journal of Urban History* 39, no. 5 (2013): 979.

103. Busch, "Building a City of Upper-Middle-Class Citizens": 979. Professors John E. Breen (chair), Charles Alan Wright, L. O. Morgan, Ned H. Burns, and Richard L. Tucker, "In Memoriam: J. Neils Thompson," December 7, 1999, https://www .utexas.edu/faculty/council/1999-2000/memorials/ThompsonJ/thompson.html (accessed April 20, 2016).

104. The economic logic of highway building found advocates within the New Deal who dramatically reconfigured the national transportation network ever afterward. See John Mollenkopf, *The Contested City* (Princeton, NJ: Princeton University Press, 1983), 47–96. Thomas Sugrue, *Origins of the Urban Crisis*, 6. Andrew Highsmith, *Demolition Means Progress: Flint, Michigan, and the Fate of the American Metropolis* (Chicago: University of Chicago Press, 2015), 175.

105. The Federal Aid Highway System Progress Maps (North Central Texas)/1931 U.S. Department of Agriculture, Bureau of Public Roads. Base map from U.S. Geological Survey, 1931, https://www.tsl.texas.gov/cgi-bin/aris/maps/maplookup.php ?mapnum=0903 (accessed April 2, 2016).

106. The campus is now called the J. J. Pickle Research Campus, named for the late U.S. congressman for the Tenth District who was a Johnson protégé. As Margaret O'Mara argues, the availability of large amounts of open space for university and business development was a key feature in the success of the Stanford Research Park, which set a template for the development of other university research parks around the country. O'Mara, *Cities of Knowledge*.

107. "Proposed Plan for State Highways," January 1940, and supporting documentation, in Folder "Travis County Master Plan," Box 2002/101-95, Texas State Highway Department Records, Texas State Library and Archives, Austin, Texas. See also Austin Chamber of Commerce Records, Austin History Center, Austin, TX.

108. Map 12, Austin TX, 1900, Sanborn-Perris Map Company, Perry-Castañeda Library, University of Texas, Austin, http://www.lib.utexas.edu/maps/sanborn/austin_1900_1t.jpg (accessed May 16, 2016).

109. "Voters Okeh 11,739,000 Program," *Austin Statesman*, May 8, 1946, 1.

110. "UT Offers to Purchase Magnesium Plant Here," *Austin Statesman*, April 4, 1946, 12.

111. "All Bonds Believed Passed," *Austin Statesman*. May 9, 1946, 1.

112. "Bond Wagon Rolls Again," *Austin Statesman*. April 29, 1946.

113. "City Bond Crusade Gains New Backing," *Austin Statesman*. April 24, 1946, p. 10.

114. See City of Austin, "The Austin Plan," 1958, University of Texas Architecture and Planning Library, Austin, TX.

115. Amy Finstein, "Lofty Visions: The Architectural Intentions and Contrary Realities of Elevated Urban Highways in America, 1900–1959" (Ph.D. dissertation: University of Virginia, 2009).

116. Homer Thornberry (1909–1995), U.S. Court of Appeals judge, interviews 1188 and 1189, interview by Anthony Orum, February 28, 1984, Austin History Center. Austin, TX.

117. Bruce Schulman, *From Cotton Belt to Sunbelt: Federal Policy, Economic Development, and the Transformation of the South* (New York: Oxford University Press, 1991), David Goldfield, *Cotton Fields and Skyscrapers: Southern City and Region* (Baltimore: Johns Hopkins University Press, 1989).

118. Michael Gillette, "The NAACP in Texas, 1937–1957" (PhD dissertation, University of Texas, Austin, 1984), 40.

119. Dwonna Goldstone, *Integrating the 40 Acres: The Fifty-Year Struggle for Racial Equality at the University of Texas* (Athens: University of Georgia Press, 2006). Gillette, "NAACP in Texas."

120. Gary Lavergne, *Before Brown: Heman Marion Sweatt, Thurgood Marshall, and the Long Road to Justice* (Austin: University of Texas Press, 2010), 100.

121. Howard Ball, *A Defiant Life: Thurgood Marshall and the Persistance of Racism in America* (New York: Crown, 1998), 67–69.

122. Gillette, "NAACP in Texas," 63–64. Everett Givens subsequently filed suit, requesting that the University of Texas establish a separate black dental school so that he could pursue a refresher course in dentistry. "Givens Files Second Suit Against U.T." *Houston Informer*, October 5, 1946.

123. Goldstone, *Integrating the 40 Acres*, 23–24. This amount becomes $982,450 in 2008 dollars. CPI Inflation Calculator, http://data.bls.gov/cgi-bin/cpicalc.pl (accessed September 21, 2008).

124. Gillette, "NAACP in Texas," 65. The court eventually distinguished the *Sweatt* case from a similar case filed in 1946 in Oklahoma, determined in favor of an African

American law applicant, based on the Fourteenth Amendment's equal protection clause: *Sipuel v. Board of Regents,* 332 U. S. 631 (1948). In that case, the university made no attempt to create a parallel law school for black students.

125. In his writing and speeches in this period, Marshall argued that there were economic, political, and moral costs to the American system of segregation. Goldstone, *Integrating the 40 Acres,* 23. Thurgood Marshall, "Segregation and Desegregation" (1954), in *Supreme Justice: Speeches and Writings—Thurgood Marshall,* edited by John Clay Smith (Philadelphia: University of Pennsylvania Press, 2003), 78–88.

126. *Sweatt v. Painter,* 339 U.S. 629 (1950).

127. Committee of Law Teachers Against Segregation in Legal Education, "Segregation and the Equal Protection Clause," 34 *Minn. L. Rev.* 289 1949–1950. Edward Levi, one of the authors, was about to be named the dean of the University of Chicago law school in the fall of 1950, and his brother would be hired as the executive director of the South East Chicago Commission, discussed in Chapter 3.

128. *Sweatt v. Painter,* 210 S.W.2d 442 (1948). This institution is now Texas Southern University. This amount becomes $20.28 million in 2008 dollars. CPI Inflation Calculator, http://data.bls.gov/cgi-bin/cpicalc.pl (accessed March 15, 2010).

129. Lavergne, *Before Brown,* 253.

130. Goldstone, *Integrating the 40 Acres,* 29. Bernie Weberman and Steve Jackson, "Sweatt Paints Dim Past," *Texas Law Forum,* October 3, 1974, quoted in Goldstone, "In the Shadow of the South," 46. Sweatt suffered from health problems and never completed the law degree, eventually leaving Texas and earning a graduate degree in social work from Atlanta University.

131. The house address was 1209 East 12th Street, Austin, TX. Lavergne, *Before Brown,* 286.

132. Busch, "Building a City of Upper-Middle-Class Citizens," 983.

133. The University of Mississippi's opposition to James Meredith's college admission twelve years later illustrated that the process of fulfillment was no easier at the university level than it was in grade schools.

134. Long, *From a Magnesium Plant to a Research Center,* 64.

135. Ibid., 51–52.

136. Karl and Alma Taeuber, *Negroes in Cities: Residential Segregation and Neighborhood Change* (Chicago: Aldine, 1965), 40, quoted in McDonald, *Racial Dynamics in Early Twentieth Century Austin, Texas,* 104.

137. U.S. Department of Commerce, Bureau of the Census, *Eighteenth Decennial Census of the Population,* vol. 1, Characteristics of the Population, Part 45, Texas, Table 5 (Washington, DC: GPO, 1961). PDFs available at https://www.census.gov/prod/www/decennial.html (accessed February 22, 2017).

Chapter 3

1. Arthur Sears Henning, "Atomic Bomb Story! Tell How Deadly Weapon Was Developed," *Chicago Daily Tribune,* August 7, 1945, 1. "Chicago: Scientific Center of the World," *Chicago Daily Tribune,* August 13, 1945, 1.

2. Vannevar Bush, *Science, the Endless Frontier: A Report to the President* (Washington, DC: GPO, 1945).

3. "World War II, Post-War Planning Committee, proposed, 1943–44," Folder 5, Box 245, University of Chicago Office of the President Hutchins Administration Records, 1892–1951.

4. "Morningside Heights," Folder 1, Box 177, Kimpton Administration Papers, University of Chicago Special Collections (UCSC).

5. Hilary Ballon and Kenneth Jackson, eds., *Robert Moses and the Modern City: The Transformation of New York* (New York: W. W. Norton, 2007).

6. J. Mark Souther, *Believing in Cleveland: Managing Decline in "The Best Location in the Nation"* (Philadelphia: Temple University Press, forthcoming).

7. I draw on Gary Gerstle's characterization of the "protean" nature of liberalism and its instantiation in the New Deal, which produced both urban renewal and the mid-century liberal coalition. Gerstle, "The Protean Character of American Liberalism," *American Historical Review* 99, no. 4 (October 1994): 1043–73. Samuel Zipp, *Manhattan Projects: The Rise and Fall of Urban Renewal in Cold War New York* (New York: Oxford University Press, 2010).

8. Ann Durkin Keating, *Building Chicago: Suburban Developers and the Creation of a Divided Metropolis* (Columbus: Ohio State University Press, 1988), 15–16, 24.

9. Thespians like Paul Sills, Mike Nichols, and Elaine May worked in the Compass Theater on East 55th Street before founding the Second City company. Janet Coleman, *The Compass: The Improvisational Theatre That Revolutionized American Comedy* (Chicago: University of Chicago Press, 1991). The Compass Theater was originally housed at 1152 East 55th Street, then was forced by urban renewal to move to 6473 Lake Park Avenue in Woodlawn in 1956, and North Broadway, when it closed in 1957. Jeffrey Sweet, *Something Wonderful Right Away* (New York: Avon, 1978), xxvii.

10. Peter Rossi and Robert Dentler, *The Politics of Urban Renewal: The Chicago Findings* (Glencoe, IL: Free Press of Glencoe, 1961), 17.

11. Julie Richman and Mary Louise Womer, *Chicago's 57th Street Art Fair: The First 50 Years, 1948–1997* (Chicago: The Fair, 1997).

12. Alan Trachtenberg, *Brooklyn Bridge: Fact and Symbol*, 2nd ed. (Chicago: University of Chicago Press, 1979). Robin Bachin, *Building the South Side: Urban Space and Civic Culture in Chicago, 1890–1919* (Chicago: University of Chicago Press, 2004), 1–19.

13. Arnold R. Hirsch, *Making the Second Ghetto: Race and Housing in Chicago, 1940–1960*, 2nd ed. (Chicago: University of Chicago Press, 1998), 17.

14. Hirsch, *Making the Second Ghetto*. Margaret Garb, *City of American Dreams: A History of Home Ownership and Housing Reform in Chicago, 1871–1919* (Chicago: University of Chicago Press, 2005). James Grossman, *Land of Hope: Chicago, Black Southerners, and the Great Migration* (Chicago: University of Chicago Press, 1989), 175.

15. The second, eighth, and tenth highest census tracts in the city by amount of black population increase in the 1940s were on the border of the Washington Park and Woodlawn neighborhoods. Their growth in black population ranged between four thousand and six thousand additional people each over the decade. Minnesota Population

Center, *National Historical Geographic Information System: Version 2.0* (Minneapolis: University of Minnesota, 2011), http://www.nhgis.org.

16. Hirsch, *Making the Second Ghetto.*

17. "Kidnaped Wife Tells Story: Rape Threat During Ordeal in Car Related," *Chicago Daily Tribune*, May 12, 1952, 1.

18. From 1945 to 1961, the university's top officer held the title of chancellor. In all other periods, this office has been designated as the president.

19. Bachin, *Building the South Side,* 58–60; Hirsch, *Making the Second Ghetto*, 144–45. Wendy Plotkin, "Deeds of Mistrust: Race, Housing, and Restrictive Covenants in Chicago, 1900–1953" (PhD dissertation, University of Illinois–Chicago, 1999), 116–38. *Shelley v. Kraemer*, 338 U.S. 1 (1948). On the NAACP fight against restrictive covenants, see Jeffrey Gonda, *Unjust Deeds: The Restrictive Covenant Cases and the Making of the Civil Rights Movement* (Chapel Hill: University of North Carolina Press, 2015).

20. Julian H. Levi, oral history interview by Daniel Meyer, September 21, 22, 23, 1992. Special Collections Research Center, University of Chicago Library, p. 42, UCSC. Muriel Beadle, *Where Has All the Ivy Gone?* (New York: Doubleday, 1972).

21. From the start, citizen participation was guided to align with university interests, as four of the five committee members had ties to the university.

22. For more on the origins and actions of this organization, see Julia Abrahamson, *A Neighborhood Finds Itself.* (New York: Harper & Brothers, 1959), 27–28.

23. "Report of Citizens' Committee on Law Enforcement," p. 4, May 19, 1952, Folder "Urban Renewal, Chicago 1960," Box 278, Kimpton Administration Papers (KAP), UCSC.

24. Ibid., 5.

25. Documents and meetings on role playing and practice exercises, Box 92, Hyde Park Kenwood Community Conference Records, UCSC.

26. Chicago-trained housing economist Richard Muth later asserted that the existence of low-income slums was due to an unfettered market and that Chicago's demand for housing by African Americans, even slum housing, reflected consumer choice rather than the obstruction or shaping of housing markets in a way that discriminated against African Americans. Muth, *Cities and Housing: The Spatial Pattern of Urban Residential Land Use* (Chicago: University of Chicago Press, 1969).

27. Hirsch, *Making the Second Ghetto*, 146.

28. Report from R. W. Harrison for Board of Trustees Agenda, September 13, 1956, Folder 4, Box 238, KAP, UCSC. Memo from Bill Palmer to Margaret Perry, August 4, 1959, "Autumn Quarter Freshman Enrollment from 1928 to 1958," Folder 2, Box 238, KAP, UCSC. The conclusion of the Korean War meant that by 1954 a new, smaller wave of veterans was able to help repopulate the campus, reaching a high-water mark of 612 in the autumn of 1958. Memo from Anita Sandke to Mr. Netherton, October 31, 1958, Folder 2, Box 238, KAP, UCSC.

29. This number, 87, is what would typically be considered "freshmen," first-year students enrolling for the lowest year of college instruction, but because of Chicago's unorthodox structure, it did not quite mean the same thing. These were sixteen- and seventeen-year-olds who had just finished their sophomore years of high school. Total

first-year students in 1953 (first year of college enrollment, even if entering in the first, second, third, or fourth year of instruction) numbered 314, down from 443 in 1952. Applications were also down about a third from the previous year. "Comparative Analysis of College Classes, Autumn, 1953 and 1952," Folder 2, Box 238, KAP, UCSC. A few sources, including John Boyer, the current dean of the college, offer a figure of 275 freshman enrollees in autumn 1953, which includes new first-year, second-year, and third-year students. Boyer offers no citation for the number, but it is consistent with the summing practice under the category "Freshmen" used by the college's dean of students at the time. John W. Boyer, *The University of Chicago: A History* (Chicago: University of Chicago Press, 2015), 325. Memo from John Netherton, March 18, 1957, "A Project of Enrolments, and of Admissions Budget, for Five Years," Folder 2, Box 238, KAP, UCSC. Report on enrollment in November 11, 1953, in Minutes of Board of Trustees, Folder 2, Box 238, KAP, UCSC.

30. Boyer, *University of Chicago*, 200–201.

31. John W. Boyer, "'The Kind of University We Desire to Become': Student Housing and the Educational Mission of the University of Chicago," *Occasional Papers on Higher Education XVIII*, College of the University of Chicago, 74–76, https://college.uchicago .edu/about-college/college-publications (accessed October 1, 2012). Memo from Robert Strozier to R. Wendell Harrison, September 11, 1952, Folder 2, Box 238, KAP, UCSC.

32. Ibid. and Boyer, *University of Chicago*, 327.

33. Ibid., 328.

34. "Interview of Christopher Kimball with George H. Watkins," August 25, 1987, p. 25, Oral History Program, UCSC.

35. Hirsch, *Making the Second Ghetto*, 167–68.

36. The previous South Side institution known as the University of Chicago folded after nearly thirty years of operation owing to financial difficulties. Its board dissolved in 1890, changed its name to the Old University of Chicago, and allowed the new institution to go by the name the University of Chicago. Thomas W. Goodspeed, *A History of the University of Chicago Founded by John D. Rockefeller: The First Quarter-Century* (Chicago: University of Chicago Press, 1916).

37. Though Levi names whites as a concern here, most effort was explicitly focused on black in-migration and what it would do to the desirability of Hyde Park. Confidential memo from Julian Levi to Lawrence Kimpton, November 3, 1954, Folder 1, Box 231, KAP, UCSC.

38. "Memorandum—Planning Objective," n.d., Folder 6, Box 234, KAP, UCSC.

39. See Neil Harris, "Foreword," in Jean Block, *The Uses of Gothic: Planning and Building the University of Chicago, 1892–1932* (Chicago: University of Chicago Press, 1983). Quoted in Bachin, *Building the South Side*, 25. For an account of Chicago machine politics, see Milton Rakove's classics, *Don't Make No Waves, Don't Back No Losers* (Bloomington: University of Indiana Press, 1975) and *We Don't Want Nobody Nobody Sent: An Oral History of the Daley Years* (Bloomington: Indiana University Press, 1979).

40. Levi, for example, regularly lauded the Chicago faculty in public and praised HPKCC members, while in private he lambasted them and was hostile to members of the faculty, community, and student body who attempted to engage the university on

urban renewal activities and issues. Levi to Kimpton, December 7, 1956, Folder 4, Box 231, KAP, UCSC.

41. *The State of the University: A Report by Lawrence A. Kimpton to the Faculties of the University of Chicago*, October 14, 1952, UCSC.

42. Julian Levi quoted in Hirsch, *Making the Second Ghetto*, 154.

43. Julian Levi interview, p. 25, UCSC. Martin Kennelly served as mayor from 1951 to 1955. Richard J. Daley served from 1955 until his death in 1976. See Adam Cohen and Elizabeth Taylor, *American Pharaoh—Mayor Richard J. Daley: His Battle for Chicago and the Nation* (Boston: Little, Brown, 2000); and Mike Royko, *Boss: Richard J. Daley of Chicago* (New York: New American Library, 1971).

44. Roger Biles, *Big City Boss in Depression and War: Edward J. Kelly of Chicago* (DeKalb: Northern Illinois University Press, 1985).

45. Julian Levi interview, p. 25, UCSC.

46. Julian Levi, *The Neighborhood Program of the University of Chicago* (Washington, DC: GPO, 1961), 12; and Rossi and Dentler, *Politics of Urban Renewal*, 158.

47. Julian Levi interview, 46, UCSC. "Agreement Between the University of Chicago . . . ," Folder 2, Box 67, KAP, UCSC.

48. Hirsch, *Making the Second Ghetto*, 15. James Q. Wilson, *Negro Politics: The Search for Leadership* (New York: Free Press, 1965). More recent research offers a more complex view of black politics in this era. Christopher Manning, *William L. Dawson and the Limits of Black Electoral Leadership* (DeKalb: Northern Illinois University Press, 2009). Julian Levi interview, p. 83, UCSC.

49. See, for example, Andrew Shanken, *194X: Architecture, Planning, and Consumer Culture on the American Home Front* (Minneapolis: University of Minnesota Press, 2009).

50. Hermon Dunlop Smith, for example, was a member of the both the University of Chicago Board of Trustees and the Field Foundation. This amount translates to approximately $892,000 in 2016 dollars. CPI Inflation Calculator, http://data.bls.gov/cgi -bin/cpicalc.pl (accessed February 22, 2017).

51. Hirsch, *Making the Second Ghetto*, 115–17. See Michael Carriere, *Between Being and Becoming* (Philadelphia: University of Pennsylvania Press, forthcoming).

52. "Agreement Between the University of Chicago . . . ," Folder 2, Box 67, KAP, UCSC.

53. Hirsch, *Making the Second Ghetto*, 152. Julian Levi interview, p. 96, UCSC.

54. This illustrates that even before the 1954 *Berman v. Parker* decision ratified such logic through a case in Washington, D.C., Chicagoans were pursuing the idea of conservation and blight prevention. Levi, *Neighborhood Program of the University of Chicago*, 12.

55. Rossi and Dentler, *Politics of Urban Renewal*, 169.

56. The four-block site was never housing for married students; it is now the location of the athletic fields, moved from the site of what is now the Regenstein Library in the early 1970s. The university took possession from the SWHPR in the late 1960s. See deed books in Cook County Recorder of Deeds office, Chicago.

57. Memo from Edward Ryerson to Clarence Randall, July 13, 1954, Folder 1, Box 231, KAP, UCSC. Memo from Clarence Randall to Edward Ryerson, July 19, 1954, Folder 1, Box 231, KAP, UCSC.

58. Julian Levi interview, p. 45, UCSC. The $15 million was to be transferred to the city of Chicago, with another $198,000 for additional planning.

59. "Chicago, IL," 1905–1951, Vol. 14, Sanborn Fire Insurance Maps, 1867–1970—Illinois, http://sanborn.umi.com.

60. Housing Act of 1954, Public law 560-Aug. 2, 1954, https://www.gpo.gov/fdsys /pkg/STATUTE-68/pdf/STATUTE-68-Pg590.pdf (accessed May 10, 2016).

61. The SECC opposed the development of public housing in Hyde Park—an express goal of the HPKCC and Hyde Park integrationists—and worked to redirect it to Woodlawn and Kenwood. Levi to Kimpton, Kirkpatrick, Harrell, July 27, 1959, Folder 1, Box 233, KAP, UCSC. Levi to Kirkpatrick. June 4, 1959, Folder 1, Box 233, KAP, UCSC.

62. Jean Block, *Hyde Park Houses: An Informal History, 1856–1910* (Chicago: University of Chicago Press, 1978).

63. Levi argued that the Catholic Church was defending the boundaries of its largely ethnic white parishes in other neighborhoods from integration. Hirsch, *Making the Second Ghetto*, 165, 250.

64. Editorial, "Urban Renewal for Whom?" *Chicago Daily Defender*, May 26, 1958, 11, col. 1.

65. National Opinion Research Center, "NORC Survey: Characteristics of Displaced Families in the Hyde Park Redevelopment Project, Aug, 1954 [dataset]," US-NORC1954-0361, version 2, Cornell University, Ithaca, NY, Roper Center for Public Opinion Research.

66. Julia Abrahamson, *A Neighborhood Finds Itself*, 241. Rossi and Dentler, *Politics of Urban Renewal*, 145.

67. While sociologist Peter Rossi terms the disagreements between the university and the HPKCC over planning efforts "failure to achieve consensus," this interpretation is tinted by the lens of community pluralism, an argument advanced by Robert Dahl. The university and SECC never sought consensus and only engaged the HPKCC when Levi thought it would facilitate the university's plans. Rossi and Dentler, *Politics of Urban Renewal*. Robert Dahl, *Who Governs? Democracy and Power in the American City* (New Haven, CT: Yale University Press, 1961).

68. Editorial, "We Support Leon Despres," *Chicago Defender*, February 10, 1959, 11.

69. For Despres's own accounts, see Leon Despres, *Challenging the Daley Machine: A Chicago Alderman's Memoirs* (Evanston, IL: Northwestern University Press, 2005).

70. Hirsch, *Making the Second Ghetto*, 164. Levi worked to discourage public input during hearings on the urban renewal plan, referring to HPKCC executive director (and former University of Chicago official) James Cunningham as "a damned fool" for trying to increase public participation. James Cunningham to Julian Levi, September 11, 1958, Folder 4, Box 231, KAP, UCSC. Julian Levi to Lawrence Kimpton, September 11, 1958, Folder 4, Box 231, KAP, UCSC.

71. Memo from Rev. Leslie Pennington to Lawrence Kimpton, March 17, 1955, Folder 1, Box 231, KAP, UCSC.

72. Trustee committees on the off-campus area and on campus development sometimes met together explicitly for the purpose of coordinating their campus and urban

renewal activities. Minutes of May 6, 1955, Joint Meeting of Area Committee and Campus Development Committee, Campus Development Committee Meetings, 1955–1967, Folder 5, Box 71, Beadle Administration Papers (BAP), UCSC.

73. See Alan J. Plattus, "Campus Plans," in Eeva-Liisa Pelkonen and Donald Albrecht, *Eero Saarinen: Shaping the Future* (New Haven, CT: Yale University Press, 2006), 308–322. Antonio Roman, *Eero Saarinen: An Architecture of Multiplicity* (New York: Princeton Architectural Press, 2003). Jayne Merkel, *Eero Saarinen* (New York: Phaidon, 2005). Scott Knowles and Stuart Leslie, "'Industrial Versailles': Eero Saarinen's Corporate Campuses for GM, IBM, and AT&T," *Isis* 92, no. 1 (March 2001): 1–33. For the broadest treatment of suburban corporate developments, see Louise Mozingo, *Pastoral Capitalism: A History of Suburban Corporate Landscapes* (Cambridge, MA: MIT Press, 2011).

74. Notes from Committee on Budget meeting, May 16, 1955, Folder 13, Box 59, KAP, UCSC. See also Eero Saarinen, "Campus Planning: The Unique World of the University," *Architectural Record* (November 1960): 123–30.

75. The university trustees had formed a corporation in 1954 to pursue redevelopment of the area south of the Midway, which would become a flash point in 1960. Minutes of Committee on Budget, University Trustees, February 15, 1954, Folder 1, Box 231, KAP, UCSC.

76. Saarinen & Associates, "Campus Development Plan," Folder 11, Box 230, KAP, UCSC. Minutes from May 6, 1955, meeting, Campus Development Committee Meetings, 1955–1967, Folder 5, Box 72, BAP, UCSC.

77. Memo from SSA Dean of Students Margaret Strozier to Ray Brown, October 10, 1963, Folder 7, Box 205, BAP, UCSC.

78. Minutes of April 27, 1956, Campus Development Committee Meetings, 1955–1967, Folder 5, Box 72, BAP, UCSC.

79. The development of Woodward Court was facilitated in no small measure by a $2 million loan from the College Housing Program of the Housing and Home Finance Agency, predecessor to the Department of Housing and Urban Development. The total cost of the complex was $3.2 million, and it housed over five hundred undergraduate women.

80. "Chicago, IL," Sanborn map 1925, vol. 14, http://sanborn.umi.com. Spurred by community and university concerns about taverns and vice, the SECC had identified the area in the 1958 urban renewal plan as a candidate for redevelopment. University of Chicago Planning Unit, *Hyde Park-Kenwood Urban Renewal Area* (Chicago: University of Chicago, 1955). David Spatz, "'Safeguarding Community Values and Standards on Every Front': The Crusade Against Taverns in Hyde Park Urban Renewal" (MSS in possession of author).

81. The original scheme called for two nearly identical towers to be constructed in phases at opposite ends of the block, but the second was never built.

82. Bryan Berry, *The Impact of Urban Renewal on Small Business: The Hyde Park-Kenwood Case* (Chicago: Center for Urban Studies, 1968).

83. Edward H. Berman, *The Influence of the Carnegie, Ford, and Rockefeller Foundations on American Foreign Policy: The Ideology of Philanthropy* (Albany: State University of New York Press, 1983).

84. John Evans, "U of C Opens 3 Year Drive for 32 Million: Trustees Pledge First 4 Million of Goal." *Chicago Daily Tribune*, June 3, 1955, 3.

85. Midway Trust Documents, Folders 13–14, Box 173, KAP, UCSC. See also Board of Trustees Minutes, September 30, 1957, pp. 227–31, UCSC.

86. Board of Trustees Minutes, September 30, 1957, pp. 244–45.

87. Julian Levi to Lawrence Kimpton, May 1, 1956, Folder 3, Box 231, KAP, UCSC.

88. Memo from W. B. Harrell to Lawrence Kimpton, August 10, 1955, "Confidential," Folder 12 IIT 1955–65, Box 36, KAP, UCSC. The university began implementing this strategy later the same fall. Memo from Lawrence Kimpton to Julian Levi, October 31, 1955, Folder 3, Box 231, KAP, UCSC.

89. Memo from W. B. Harrell to Lawrence Kimpton, August 10, 1955, "Confidential," Folder 12 IIT 1955–65, Box 36, President's Papers, 1952–1961, UCSC. Trustee Harold Swift expressed interest in following IIT's lead in the 1940s, quoted in Hirsch, *Making the Second Ghetto*, 135.

90. Beadle, *Where Has All the Ivy Gone?* Despite their frequent invocation in speeches and publications, I have yet to find a single specific parcel or building labeled as a "threat property" in the course of my research in administrative communications. There are only properties that the University of Chicago wants.

91. In many cases, Blakiston would track the building through the newspapers until, if it were unable to sell, an ad would appear in the Chicago *Defender*, at which point he and Levi would prompt the university to act. Don Blakiston to W. B. Harrell, September 4, 1956, Folder 3, Box 231, KAP, UCSC. Don Blakiston to W. B. Harrell, August 28, 1956, Folder 3, Box 231, KAP, UCSC.

92. Alison Dunham et al., "Report of the Faculty Committee on Rental Policies," Folder 1, Box 272, BAP, UCSC. U.S. Census of Housing data for 1960 from Minnesota Population Center, National Historical Geographic Information System, Minneapolis, University of Minnesota, 2004 (http://www.nhgis.org).

93. See, for example, Levi to Morton Bodfish, August 19, 1953, Folder 5, Box 230, KAP, UCSC. Bodfish was the president of the First Federal Savings and Loan Association of Chicago. Levi to Mendel Flanders, August 19, 1953, Folder 5, Box 230, KAP, UCSC. Levi also suggested to Kimpton and trustees local banks that could be taken over or have their management replaced using the influence of trustees to bring their activities in line with university goals. Kimpton to Edward Eagle Brown, November 18, 1954, Folder 1, Box 231, KAP, UCSC.

94. Levi to Kimpton, Kirkpatrick, Harrell, July 7, 1959, Folder 1, Box 233, KAP, UCSC.

95. Julian Levi to Gardner Stern, August 15, 1955, Folder 13, Box 231, KAP, UCSC.

96. Memo from Levi to Kimpton, June 9, 1955, Folder 1, Box 231, KAP, UCSC.

97. J. R. McNeill, "Gigantic Follies? Human Exploration and the Space Age in Long-Term Historical Perspective," in *Remembering the Space Age: Proceedings of the 50th Anniversary Conference* (Washington, DC: GPO, 2009), 6.

98. John D. Morris, "Johnson Outlines Broad Agenda for Senate Inquiry on Missiles: Hearing to Open Monday to Stress Need of Speed—Dr. Keller to Testify First—House Unit Now Touring Bases," *New York Times* (1923–Current file), November 23, 1957, 7.

99. This term was coined by Arkansas Senator J. William Fulbright. Stuart Leslie, *The Cold War and American Science* (New York: Columbia University Press, 1994), 2.

100. Where previous scholarship has characterized this program as a federal offer of incentives and subsidies for universities to support urban renewal efforts, I argue that these provisions were created by university interests to serve their desires for expansion and to create political leverage for their projects. Margaret Pugh O'Mara, *Cities of Knowledge: Cold War Science and the Search for the Next Silicon Valley* (Princeton, NJ: Princeton University Press, 2005), 78.

101. Letter from Kimpton to Carroll Newsom, Clark Kerr, Nathan Pusey, Ethan Sheply, January 7, 1959; "Enactment in 1959 of Section 112 of Housing Act," n.d.; and Memo from Levi to J. I. Kirkpatrick, June 4, 1959, all in Folder 1, Box 233, KAP, UCSC.

102. United States Congress, "Housing Act of 1959: Hearings Before the Subcommittee on Housing, United States Congress, Eighty-Sixth Congress, First Session, on Various Bills to Amend the Federal Housing Laws" (Washington, DC: GPO, 1959), 245.

103. United States Congress, "Housing Act of 1959: Hearings Before the Committee on Banking and Currency, United States Senate, Eighty-Sixth Congress, First Session, on Various Bills to Amend the Federal Housing Laws" (Washington, DC: GPO, 1959), 520–21.

104. *New York Times*, October 1, 1961, E7. "Colleges Clear Out Slums to Extend City Campuses," *New York Times*, January 13, 1965. In his new introduction to *The Limits to Capital*, David Harvey locates universities and education within the neoliberal prescriptions for continuing prosperity in the last quarter-century. Christopher Newfield documents efforts to repeal the democratizing postwar promise of public higher education. Harvey, *The Limits to Capital*, rev. ed. (New York: Verso, 2007). Newfield, *Unmaking the Public University: The Forty-Year Assault on the Middle Class* (Cambridge, MA: Harvard University Press, 2008).

105. Julian Levi, *The Neighborhood Program of the University of Chicago* (Chicago: University of Chicago, 1961).

106. See *Compiled Statutes of the United States,* v. 73, P.L. 86–372, September 23, 1959. Amanda Seligman discusses Sears, Roebuck & Company's urban renewal activities on the west side at greater length in her book on Chicago. Seligman, *Block by Block: Neighborhoods and Public Policy on Chicago's West Side* (Chicago: University of Chicago Press, 2005), 82. Notes from the University of Chicago Trustees Committee on Budget meeting, October 19, 1959, Folder 1, Box 233, KAP, UCSC.

107. The amount of $7 million inflates to $56 million in 2016 dollars. CPI Inflation Calculator, http://data.bls.gov/cgi-bin/cpicalc.pl (accessed April 27, 2016).

108. Julian Levi interview, p. 26, UCSC.

109. Census Tracts 628–633 for Woodlawn, Volume I Census Tracts, Part 26, Chicago, Tables P-1 and H-5. U.S. Bureau of the Census, *U.S. Censuses of Population and Housing: 1960* (Washington, DC: GPO, 1962). PDFs available at https://www.census.gov/prod/www/decennial.html (accessed February 22, 2017).

110. Memo from Levi to Kimpton, November 3, 1954, Folder 1, Box 231, KAP, UCSC.

111. For recent work on the grandest agenda for urban renewal, see Samuel Zipp, *Manhattan Projects: The Rise and Fall of Urban Renewal in Cold War New York* (New York: Oxford University Press, 2010). For more on the decline of urban renewal, see Christopher Klemek, *The Transatlantic Collapse of Urban Renewal: Postwar Urbanism from New York to Berlin* (Chicago: University of Chicago Press, 2011).

112. Bauer had written an influential book on social housing in Europe, directed the U.S. Housing Authority, and served on the faculty at both MIT and Berkeley, where her husband, William Wurster, was the dean. Catherine Bauer, *Modern Housing* (New York: Houghton Mifflin, 1934). Catherine Bauer Wurster, "The Dreary Deadlock of Public Housing," *Architectural Forum* (May 1957), 140–42, 219–21.

113. Levi had helped fund an existing organization, the United Woodlawn Conference, which "discourages raids from Alinsky, et al." Levi to Kimpton, April 7, 1955, Folder 1, Box 231, KAP, UCSC. Sanford Horwitt, *Let Them Call Me Rebel: Saul Alinsky, His Life and Legacy.* (New York: Alfred A. Knopf, 1989), 375–80.

114. Horwitt, *Let Them Call Me Rebel*, 375–80. Rossi and Dentler, *Politics of Urban Renewal*, 232–34. Hirsch, *Making the Second Ghetto*, 207.

115. John Hall Fish, *Black Power/White Control: The Struggle of the Woodlawn Organization in Chicago* (Princeton, NJ: Princeton University Press, 1973).

116. Saul Alinsky, *Rules for Radicals: A Practical Primer for Realistic Radicals* (New York: Random House, 1971), 116.

117. Von Hoffman subsequently became a journalist for the *Chicago Daily News, Washington Post,* and *New York Observer,* as well as author of several books.

118. Fish, *Black Power/White Control*, 31.

119. Jane Jacobs, "Chicago's Woodlawn—Renewal by Whom?" *Architectural Forum* (May 1962): 124.

120. Fish, *Black Power/White Control*, 18.

121. Horwitt, *Let Them Call Me Rebel*, 399–401, 414–20. Abernathy would later live in West Side tenements with Martin Luther King Jr. to demonstrate the effects of racial segregation in the North.

122. Horwitt, *Let Them Call Me Rebel*, 416–17. For discussion of Dawson's role as a machine politician, see Wilson, *Negro Politics*, and Christopher Manning, *William L. Dawson.*

123. Horwitt, *Let Them Call Me Rebel*, 364–65, 393–95, 430–31.

124. Editorials in the *Chicago Maroon*, the campus newspaper, were regularly in favor of redevelopment, for example.

125. Kimpton resigned in 1960 to become a vice president at Standard Oil of Indiana. He had maintained a long relationship with the Rockefeller family, which continued to support the University of Chicago.

126. "UC Admits Housing Segregation," *Chicago Maroon*, January 17, 1962.

127. "CORE, UC Hassle: Students 'Sleep-In,'" *Chicago Maroon*, January 24, 1962. "Realty Sit-Downers Arrested," *Chicago Maroon*, January 25, 1962. As the *Maroon* reported, two protesters were nonuniversity CORE members, two were students from the University of Wisconsin, and the remainder were University of Chicago students.

128. Editorial, *Chicago Tribune*, January 26, 1962. Editorial, *Chicago Maroon*, January 16, 1962.

129. Editorial, "Seat of the Intellect," *Chicago Tribune*, January 26, 1962, 14.

130. Editorial, *Chicago Daily Defender*, January 29, 1962, 11.

131. In the history department, for example, one graduate student and his wife were arrested for participating in the protest, while another graduate student wrote George Beadle a supportive letter describing the university's "limited segregation policy" as "wholly justified." Exhibit U, Letter from Kenneth T. Jackson to Beadle, January 20, 1962, "Diary of the Sit-Ins," Folder 1, Box 272, BAP, UCSC.

132. "4 Comment on Segregation," *Chicago Maroon*, January 29, 1962.

133. "U of C Sit-Ins Suspended in CORE Group: Beadle Urges Sounder Understanding," *Chicago Daily Tribune,* February 6, 1962.

134. "Diary of the Sit-Ins," Folder 1, Box 272, BAP, UCSC. Alison Dunham et al., "Report of the Faculty Committee on Rental Policies," Folder 1, Box 272, BAP, UCSC.

135. Memo from Ely Aaron to George Beadle, March 26, 1962, Folder 8, Box 22, Commission on Human Relations 1956–62, BAP, UCSC.

136. Memo from William Harrell to Ray Brown, May 18, 1962, Folder 8, Box 22, BAP, UCSC.

137. Michael Pakenham, "All City Bond Issues Lose; Conti Wins: Voters Rise Up Against Mayor's Plan," *Chicago Tribune*, April 11, 1962, 1.

138. LaDale Winling, "Students and the Second Ghetto: Federal Legislation, Urban Politics, and Campus Planning at the University of Chicago," *Journal of Planning History* 10, no. 1 (2011): 74–75.

139. Memo from J. Levi to Urban Renewal Agency Commissioners, July 18, 1963, Folder 2, "South East Chicago Commission South Campus Plan," Box 310, BAP, UCSC.

140. "Quadrangles Enrollment." Folder 1, Box 238, KAP, UCSC.

141. "University of Chicago Sets Record $160 Million Drive," *Wall Street Journal*, October 21, 1965, 14.

142. Richard F. O'Brien, "The Campaign for Chicago: A Manual," Folder 4, Box 72, BAP, UCSC. "The University of Chicago Campaign for Chicago—Summary of Goals and Progress, July 1, 1965 through May 31, 1966," Folder 4, "Reports, Campaign Planning Committee," Box 270, BAP, UCSC.

143. Program for Cornerstone Laying of the Joseph Regenstein Library, November 15, 1968, Folder "Library, Joseph Regenstein, Cornerstone Laying, 1965–1968," Box 233, Levi Administration Papers (LAP), UCSC.

144. The staunch Republican further indicated that she would never offer philanthropic support for undergraduate students after seeing the protests of young activists at the Democratic National Convention earlier that August. Letter from Michael Claffey to file, August 28, 1968, Folder 8, Box 233, LAP, UCSC.

Chapter 4

1. Mark Kitchell, Susan Griffin, Veronica Selver, and Stephen Most, 1990, *Berkeley in the Sixties* [United States]: Kitchell Films in association with POV Theatrical Films. For a detailed timeline of the semester's activities, see Michael V. Miller and Susan Gilmore,

eds., *Revolution at Berkeley: The Crisis in American Education* (New York: Dial Press, 1965), or the concise online adaptation at http://www.lib.berkeley.edu/MRC/FSM /fsmchronology1.html.

2. Total enrollment at the Berkeley campus grew from 11,824 in 1930 to 22,346 in 1950. From documents in the Marilynn S. Johnson, *The Second Gold Rush: Oakland and the East Bay in World War II* (Berkeley: University of California Press, 1993). Donna Murch, *Living for the City: Migration, Education, and the Rise of the Black Panther Party in Oakland, California* (Chapel Hill: University of North Carolina Press, 2010), 15–16.

3. From 1940 to 1990, the metropolitan population of the American West grew more than fivefold, while the rest of the metropolitan United States grew just over twofold. Carl Abbott, *The Metropolitan Frontier: Cities in the Modern American West* (Tuscon: University of Arizona Press, 1993), xix.

4. An excellent critical introduction to the region is Martin Kenney, ed., *Understanding Silicon Valley: Anatomy of an Entrepreneurial Region* (Palo Alto, CA: Stanford University Press, 2000). The leading historical account of this transformation, featuring Stanford University, is Margaret Pugh O'Mara's *Cities of Knowledge: Cold War Science and the Search for the Next Silicon Valley* (Princeton, NJ: Princeton University Press, 2005).

5. James Clayton, "Defense Spending: Key to California's Growth," *Western Political Quarterly* 15 (June 1962): 280, 286.

6. In 1940, Berkeley had 85,547 residents and in 1950, 113,805 residents, a 33 percent increase. Sixteenth Census of the United States (Washington, DC: GPO, 1942). Seventeenth Census of the United States (Washington, DC: GPO, 1952). PDFs available at https://www.census.gov/prod/www/decennial.html (accessed February 22, 2017).

7. Table 32, United States Department of Commerce, Bureau of the Census, *Sixteenth Decennial Census of the United States*, vol. 2, "Characteristics of the Population, Part 1, Reports by States, California" (Washington, DC: GPO, 1942). https://www.census .gov/prod/www/decennial.html (accessed February 22, 2017).

8. League of Women Voters of Berkeley, Albany, and Emeryville, Records, 1911–ongoing, Carton 6, Folder 37, Planning, Fair Housing, Berkeley, 1944 Report, Bancroft Library, University of California, Berkeley. Cited in Patricia Eget, "Envisioning Progressive Communities: Race, Gender, and the Politics of Liberalism, Berkeley, California and Montclair, New Jersey, 1920–1970" (PhD dissertation, Rutgers University, 2011). See Home Owners' Loan Corporation security map and area descriptions for Oakland and Berkeley, which recommend limited investment in these neighborhoods. Home Owners' Loan Corporation City Survey Files, Entry 39, Folder "Oakland-Berkeley, California Master File," Box 145, RG 195 National Archives and Records Administration II, College Park, MD.

9. In 1940, statistics showed 85,547 population; 28,210 occupied units; and 3.03 persons per occupied unit. In 1950, these statistics were 113,805 population; 37,460 occupied units; and 3.11 persons per occupied unit. United States Department of Commerce, Bureau of the Census, *Sixteenth Decennial Census,* 1940 Census Reports with Statistics for Census Tracts, Tables B-1, B-6 (Washington, DC: GPO, 1940). PDFs available at https://www.census.gov/prod/www/decennial.html (accessed February 22, 2017).

10. Part of this preference may be explained by a 1923 fire resulting in total loss of buildings in the neighborhood north of campus, a discontinuity in the built environment that pushed students to other areas around campus.

11. Jack Kerouac, *The Dharma Bums* (New York: Viking, 1956).

12. Berkeley City Planning Commission, *Preliminary Master Plan for Berkeley,* 1953, 16. Institute of Government Studies, University of California, Berkeley.

13. While anti-Communism was fairly widespread, it became a particularly popular cudgel among postwar developers, who sought to promote an unregulated housing and real-estate market to exploit. Kevin Starr, *Embattled Dreams: California in War and Peace, 1940–1950* (New York: Oxford University Press, 2003), 281–307.

14. On Nixon and California politicians, see Starr, *Embattled Dreams,* 285–86. Rick Perlstein, *Nixonland: The Rise of a President and the Fracturing of America* (New York: Simon & Schuster, 2008), 29–36.

15. David Gardner, *The California Oath Controversy* (Berkeley: University of California Press, 1967), 14. On HUAC, see Gardner, 32, and John Gladchuk, *Hollywood and Anticommunism: HUAC and the Evolution of the Red Menace, 1935–1950* (New York: Routledge, 2006).

16. Letter to Lawrence M. Giannini from Edward H. Heller, May 1, 1950, Bancroft MSS C-B 881, Folder 1950, Box 180, Loyalty Oath via the California Loyalty Oath Digital Collection. http://bancroft.berkeley.edu/collections/loyaltyoath/ (accessed February 22, 2017).

17. The measure built on older political controls like Rule 17, a regulation adopted in 1934 prohibiting all forms of explicitly political activity on university grounds. Gardner, *California Oath Controversy,* 15.

18. Gardner, *California Oath Controversy,* 14, 18–22.

19. Carl E. Schorske, "Intellectual Life, Civil Libertarian Issues, and the Student Movement at the University of California, Berkeley, 1960–1969," oral history, interviewer Ann Lage, 1996 and 1997, p. 32, Regional Oral History Office, Bancroft Library, University of California, Berkeley (ROHO).

20. For description of the development of another such campus district, see Blake Gumprecht, *The American College Town* (Amherst: University of Massachusetts Press, 2008), 108–44. Austin's campus district, the Drag on Guadalupe, was the site of development of the Austin counterculture and radical movement for some of the same reasons. I argue that the design and development of these areas at the intersection of public and private investment, densely populated by commercial, religious, cultural, and political institutions, are essential to the emergence of a vibrant social scene and political culture. Douglas Rossinow, *The Politics of Authenticity: Liberalism, Christianity, and the New Left in America* (New York: Columbia University Press, 1998).

21. Roger Geiger, *Research and Relevant Knowledge: American Research Universities Since World War II* (New York: Oxford University Press, 1993), 73–81.

22. James Corley, "Serving the University in Sacramento: Oral History Transcript," interviewer Verne Stadtman, 1969, xv, ROHO.

23. Gerald Adams, "T. J. Kent, 81, a Man Who Helped Create the City," *SF Gate*, May 3, 1998, http://www.sfgate.com/bayarea/article/T-J-Kent-81-a-man-who-helped -create-The-City-3092286.php (accessed February 11, 2015).

24. T. J. Kent, "Berkeley's First Liberal Democratic Regime: 1961–1970," in Harriet Nathan and Stanley Scott, *Experiment and Change in Berkeley: Essays on City Politics, 1950–1975* (Berkeley: Institute of Governmental Studies, 1978).

25. Paddy Riley, "Clark Kerr: From the Industrial to the Knowledge Economy," in *American Capitalism: Social Thought and Political Economy in the Twentieth Century*, edited by Nelson Lichtenstein (Philadelphia: University of Pennsylvania Press, 2006), 71–87.

26. One history of the 1960s suggests another Cold War leader for comparison, calling Kerr "the Robert McNamara of higher education, a skillful manager of complex systems." William O'Neill, *Coming Apart: An Informal History of America in the 1960s* (New York: Times Books, 1971).

27. The previous effort was the 1951 document "Planning the Physical Development of the Berkeley Campus," which contains an early version of Berkeley's growth policy. University of California, Berkeley, "Long Range Development Plan," June 1962, College of Environmental Design Library, University of California, Berkeley (CEDL).

28. "Proposed Statement of Educational Policy and Program for the Berkeley Campus of the University of California," 1957, University of California Archives, Bancroft Library (UABL).

29. The Regents subsequently delineated the boundaries of the traditional campus but dramatically exceeded the 25 percent coverage ratio on university land outside this tightly defined area. University of California, Berkeley, "Long Range Development Plan," June 1962, p. 25, CEDL.

30. State assemblyman Sheridan Hegland, formerly a community college instructor, successfully ushered it through the legislature to passage. Illustrating his commitment to higher education, Hegland later arranged for the establishment of the San Diego campus of the University of California, located in La Jolla within his own district. "1957 Legislative Measures List," March 8, 1957. *Journal of the Assembly of the Legislature of California*. See also note from June 17, 1957 memo: "Regents Requested Legislation," CU-5 Series 2 1957: 341. UABL.

31. See, for example, the oral history of UC property manager Robert Underhill, "University Lands, Finances, and Investments," ROHO. The Board of Regents records from this period are littered with condemnation actions. See, for example, Board of Regents Committee on Finance meeting, August 24, 1956; November 16, 1956; and March 13, 1959. UABL.

32. Ed Salzman, "City Gains Seen in UC Expansion Plan," *Berkeley Daily Gazette*. March 8, 1957, 1. This statement of the economic relationship is supported by a report sponsored by the Bureau of Public Administration (predecessor to the Institute for Government Studies), James Harvey, "The University and the City." Report by Bureau of Public Administration, University of California, 1958. Institute for Government Studies, UCB.

33. Salzman. "City Gains Seen."

34. City planning commissioners expressed hope that the city plan and the campus plan could be brought into agreement, but, as one commissioner pointed out, the city was a powerless player since the university had special status that eliminated the need to seek local approval for construction and demolition. Salzman. "City Gains Seen."

35. James Sparrow, *Warfare State: World War II Americans and the Age of Big Government* (New York: Oxford University Press, 2011).

36. For an industry-oriented examination of this phenomenon, see Barry Bluestone, *The Deindustrialization of America: Plant Closings, Community Abandonment, and the Dismantling of Basic Industry* (New York: Basic, 1982).

37. Contra Costa County land increased 250 percent in value from 1935 to 1960 and Santa Clara County land, 350 percent, while land value for the whole state increased 120 percent. Dept. of Finance, Economic Development Agency of the State of California. *California Statistical Abstract, 1962*. Table Q-14, p. 187.

38. "Brown OKs Master Plan for Schools," *Los Angeles Times*, April 27, 1960, 10.

39. For a close, thorough reading of Kerr's thinking, see Ethan Schrum, "Administering American Modernity: The Instrumental University in the Postwar United States" (PhD dissertation, University of Pennsylvania, 2009), 188–261. For a key work illuminating a transitional point in his thinking about industrialism, see Riley, "Clark Kerr," 71–87.

40. Clark Kerr, *The Uses of the University*, 4th ed. (Cambridge, MA: Harvard University Press, 1963; reprint, 1995).

41. Schrum, "Administering American Modernity," 145.

42. UC sociologists Burton Clark and Martin Trow became disciplinary leaders studying the sociology and organizational behavior of students and higher education. See Burton Clark, *Educating the Expert Society* (San Francisco: Chandler, 1962). Burton Clark and Martin Trow, "Determinants of College Student Subculture," in *College Peer Groups: Problems and Prospects for Research*, edited by Theodore Newcomb and Everett Wilson (Chicago: Aldine, 1960).

43. W. J. Rorabaugh, *Berkeley at War: The 1960s* (New York: Oxford University Press, 1989), 50.

44. Kerr, *Uses of the University,* 6. Glenn Seaborg and Ray Colvig, *Chancellor at Berkeley* (Berkeley, CA: Institute for Government Studies Press, 1994).

45. Office of the Architects and Engineers, University of California, "Planning the Physical Development of the Berkeley Campus," December 1951, CEDL. Le Corbusier, *Towards a New Architecture*, trans. Fredrick Etchells (London: J. Rodker, 1931). See especially Le Corbusier's Ville Contemporaine from 1922 and Plan Voisin from 1925.

46. Le Corbusier was one of the leading practitioners of the rationalist discourse. See Le Corbusier, *Towards A New Architecture*. For more context on the modern movement, see Eric Mumford, *The CIAM Discourse on Modernism, 1928–1960* (Cambridge, MA: MIT Press, 2000). Mauro Guillen, *The Taylorized Beauty of the Mechanical: Scientific Management and the Rise of Modern Architecture* (Princeton, NJ: Princeton University Press, 2006).

47. The firm's principal, John Carl Warnecke, earned renown as the designer of the eternal flame marking President John F. Kennedy's grave in Arlington National Cemetery.

48. Excerpt of meeting of Board of Regents Committee on Finance, July 19, 1957, Folder 27, "Residence Halls at UC—Need, Financing . . . etc. 1957," Box 30, Office of the Chancellor Records CU-149, UABL.

49. Excerpts of meetings of Board of Regents Committee on Finance, March 29, 1956, and July 19, 1957, Folder 7, "Land Acquisition Plans Vol II," Box 17; and Folder 27, "Residence Halls at UC—Need, Financing . . . etc. 1957," Box 30, Office of the Chancellor Records CU-149, UABL. The Regents advanced $4.4 million from overhead from federal contracts during dormitory construction, then loaned $1.8 million from the same overhead fund, with repayment amortized over forty years. These sums were for the university overall, with $960,000 earmarked for Berkeley residence halls. Notes from Regents Committee on Finance, March 17, 1961, "Financing of Residence Hall Program," Folder "Financing of Residence Halls 1961," Box 29, Office of the Chancellor Records CU-149, UABL. The university diverted overhead funds, which were split with the state, for capital projects on other occasions as well, such as for the Lawrence Hall of Science. Seaborg and Colvig, *Chancellor at Berkeley*, 25–26.

50. The organization first went by the name "Slate," as in a "slate of candidates." Members later adopted the name "SLATE," though it is not an acronym. See http://www.jofreeman.com/sixtiesprotest/slate.htm (accessed October 5, 2016).

51. Among the key issues prompting the formation of SLATE was outlawing discrimination among fraternities and sororities. SLATE began to distribute the *Cal Reporter* on campus as an alternative to the main student newspaper, the administration-friendly *Daily Cal*, in order to politicize the student body and begin engaging off-campus issues. Rorabaugh, *Berkeley at War*, 15. In the 1960s, the *Daily Cal* staff became more critical of the administration, but in the 1950s, the editorial leadership was on friendly terms with UCB administrators, and both were critical of SLATE and the *Cal Reporter*. University of California Digital Library, "The Free Speech Movement," http://texts .cdlib.org/view?docId=kt687004sg&chunk.id=d0e1180&doc.view=entire_text (accessed July 7, 2015).

52. Marv Sternberg, "Student Welfare," and "About SLATE," Fall 1959, Folder 5, *Cal Reporters*, Box 23, Office of the Chancellor Records CU-149, UABL. Seaborg and Colvig, *Chancellor at Berkeley*, 193–95.

53. Phil Roos, "The Student and His Education," and Sternberg, "Student Welfare," Folder 5, *Cal Reporters*, Box 23, Office of the Chancellor Records CU-149, UABL.

54. Kerr suggested MIT in Cambridge, Massachusetts, as an ideal example of a university thus situated. Kerr, *Uses of the University*, 67.

55. O'Mara, *Cities of Knowledge*.

56. Clarence Ting, "Dormitories at UC Berkeley," *Kroeber Anthropological Society Papers* 80 (January 1996): 108–36.

57. Ibid., 108.

58. Sim Van der Ryn, *Dorms at Berkeley: An Environmental Analysis* (Berkeley, CA: Center for Planning and Development Research, 1967). Stewart Brand, *How Buildings Learn* (New York: Penguin, 1993).

59. Martin Trow, "Reflections on the Residence Hall Program," talk given at Residence Hall Workshop, October 29, 1961, University of California, Berkeley, Box 29, Office of the Chancellor Records CU-149, UABL.

60. Richard Fariña, *Been Down So Long It Looks Like Up to Me* (New York: Penguin, 1966), 17.

61. Hayden lived in South Quadrangle his first year at Michigan. Tom Hayden, *Reunion: A Memoir* (New York: Random House, 1988), 27.

62. James Miller, *Democracy Is in the Streets: From Port Huron to the Siege of Chicago* (Cambridge, MA: Harvard University Press, 1994).

63. *Urban Renewal in Berkeley: Recommendations for Local Action—A Joint Report to the City Manager* (Berkeley, CA: City of Berkeley, 1957), CEDL.

64. Ibid.

65. *The Problem of Blight in Berkeley: A Neighborhood Analysis for Urban Renewal* (Berkeley, CA: City of Berkeley, 1958), CEDL.

66. Riches Research, Inc., Economic Analysis South Campus Area, January 1964, IGS UCB.

67. Memo from Strong to E. W. Jennings, June 1, 1962, Folder 37, Box 88, Urban Renewal, Office of the Chancellor Records CU-149, UABL.

68. Initially, the city plan merely reinforced the city's traditional land use choices, but after the 1940s, zoning largely restricted the spread of commercial land use from Telegraph Avenue.

69. Seaborg and Colvig, *Chancellor at Berkeley*, 171–80.

70. The student union was financed in part by a federal loan from the same Housing and Home Finance Agency program that financed the residence halls after the legislation was expanded to include other types of student facilities. November 1960 Report, Office of Vice President for Business, "Summary of Federal Loans," Folder "Financing of Residence Halls," Box 29, Office of the Chancellor Records CU-149, UABL.

71. Seaborg and Colvig, *Chancellor at Berkeley*, 172–79.

72. Max Heirich and Sam Kaplan, "Yesterday's Discord," in *The Berkeley Student Revolt: Facts and Interpretations.*, edited by Seymour Martin Lipset and Sheldon S. Woldin (Garden City, NY: Anchor Books, 1965), 26. Doug McAdam, *Freedom Summer* (New York: Oxford University Press, 1988). Robert Cohen, *Freedom's Orator: Mario Savio and the Radical Legacy of the 1960s* (New York: Oxford University Press, 2009), 49–97.

73. The original "Hyde Park" speakers' corner is in London's Hyde Park.

74. Jo Freeman, *At Berkeley in the Sixties: The Education of an Activist, 1961–1965* (Bloomington: Indiana University Press, 2002), 11. In March 1962 the UCB administration suggested moving the Hyde Park location to a sunken plaza behind the student union and about two hundred meters from the intersection of Bancroft and Telegraph. However, students rejected this option because it was a low-traffic area outside the popular path between Telegraph and Sather Gate. Heirich and Kaplan, "Yesterday's Discord," 26.

75. An examination of the practice earlier in the year prompted the legal staff to clarify what activities would be allowed and was the basis for imposition of the new policy in September 1964. Alex C. Sherriffs, "The University of California and the Free Speech Movement: Perspectives from a Faculty Member and Administrator," interviewer

James H. Rowland, in 1978 *Governmental History Documentation Project, Godwin Knight/ Edmund Brown, Sr., Era*, Appendices 3 and 4, ROHO.

76. Weinberg had briefly pursued graduate studies at UCB but was not affiliated with the university any longer. Martin Roysher, "Recollections of the FSM," in Robert Cohen and Reginald Zelnik, *The Free Speech Movement: Reflections on Berkeley in the 1960s* (Berkeley: University of California Press, 2002). 140–156.

77. Mark Kitchell, Susan Griffin, Veronica Selver, and Stephen Most, *Berkeley in the Sixties.*

78. Office of the Dean of Students, "Mailing List for Off-Campus Groups, Fall 1964," Box 57, Office of the Chancellor Records CU-149, UABL.

79. Robert Self frames the area's importance more broadly, as part of a political reaction to racial and economic reorganization in the East Bay. Robert Self, *American Babylon: Race and the Struggle for Postwar Oakland* (Princeton, NJ: Princeton University Press, 2003), 223.

80. Savio lived at 2536 College Avenue.

81. Freeman, *At Berkeley in the Sixties*, 187.

82. Ibid., 177.

83. Rorabaugh, *Berkeley at War*, 30–31.

84. Ibid., 32–33.

85. Sherriffs claimed "Savio would come in to see a philosopher, John Searle, and he would say, 'What do I say now, John?'" Sherriffs interview, 85, ROHO.

86. Rorabaugh, *Berkeley at War*, 36.

87. Roger Heyns, "Berkeley Chancellor, 1965–1971: The University in a Turbulent Society," oral history, interviewer Harriet Nathan, 1986, p. 82, ROHO. Memo, August 29, 1969, Folder 5 "Rent Strike 1969–1972," Box 6, President's Papers CU-2, UABL.

88. For analysis of this regional transformation and a comparison to the Boston region, see John H. Mollenkopf, *The Contested City* (Princeton, NJ: Princeton University Press, 1983).

89. City of Berkeley, *South Campus Urban Renewal Plan and Related Documents*, March 3, 1966, CEDL. Clark Kerr, first as chancellor, then as president, had been involved in the University of Chicago–led coalition to develop urban renewal strategies and legislation, but had never been a forceful advocate in the effort. When the city of Berkeley developed its first urban renewal plan, set for the South Campus neighborhood, the university remained publicly aloof from the effort, even while members of the faculty provided research, planning, and design expertise to the initiative.

90. See Chapter 3 for an explanation of the Section 112 credits program.

91. However, additional university expenditures for land acquisition were anticipated to increase the federal match and the amount of transferable credits, raising them from $330,000 into the millions. Mike Culbert, "Figures Called 'Phony,'" *Berkeley Gazette*, March 22, 1966.

92. Mike Culbert, "Telegraph Avenue in Spotlight," *Berkeley Gazette.* March 15, 1966.

93. David Harvey, *The Condition of Postmodernity: An Enquiry into the Origins of Cultural Change* (Cambridge, MA: Blackwell, 1989).

94. Jane Jacobs, *The Death and Life of Great American Cities* (New York: Vintage, 1961). Martin Anderson, *The Federal Bulldozer: A Critical Appraisal of Urban Renewal, 1942–1962* (Cambridge, MA: MIT Press, 1964). Herbert Gans, *The Urban Villagers: Group and Class in the Life of Italian-Americans* (New York: Free Press, 1962). Robert Venturi, *Complexity and Contradiction in Architecture* (New York: Museum of Modern Art Press, 1966).

95. I group freeway revolts and urban riots here, but categorize them both as forms of opposition to the state-led physical reorganization of the metropolitan order. Thomas Sugrue, *The Origins of the Urban Crisis: Race and Inequality in Postwar Detroit*, 2nd ed. (Princeton, NJ: Princeton University Press, 2003). Samuel Zipp, *Manhattan Projects: The Rise and Fall of Urban Renewal in Cold War New York* (New York: Oxford University Press, 2010). For a transnational examination of this phenomenon, see Christopher Klemek, *The Transatlantic Collapse of Urban Renewal: Postwar Urbanism from New York to Berlin* (Chicago: University of Chicago Press, 2011).

96. On countercultural opposition to centralized management, see Theodore Roszak, *The Making of a Counter Culture: On the Technocratic Society and Its Youthful Opposition* (Garden City, NY: Doubleday, 1969).

97. For a broader exploration of this phenomenon, see Rebecca Klatsch, *A Generation Divided: New Left, New Right, and the 1960s* (Berkeley: University of California Press, 1999).

98. Mike Culbert, "2nd Hearing Set for Tonight on Urban Renewal," *Berkeley Gazette*, March 21, 1966.

99. Mike Culbert, "South Campus Urban Renewal Plan—A Thorn in Berkeley's Rosy Future?" *Berkeley Gazette*, March 10, 1966, and "Merchants 'Favor But Oppose' Plan," *Berkeley Gazette*, March 11, 1966.

100. Mike Culbert, "New Fury Unleashed on Renewal," *Berkeley Gazette*, March 22, 1966, and "South Campus Urban Renewal Project—How the People Affected Feel About It," *Berkeley Gazette*, March 23, 1966. "South Campus Urban Renewal Project: Why It Failed," memo to University of California Regents, n.d., Folder 37 Urban Renewal, Box 88, Office of the Chancellor Records CU-149, UABL.

101. Mike Culbert. "Renewal Official Denies 'Phony Figure' Charge," *Berkeley Gazette*, March 28, 1966. There was, in fact, another plan for Oceanview, which several years later went down to defeat.

102. Lari Blumenfeld, "Not Harassing Beatniks, Says Chief; 'Radicals' Plaguing Us," *Berkeley Daily Gazette*, June 15, 1966, 1.

103. DeBonis was a staunch conservative and longtime opponent of regulation and liberal-led government action. The Berkeley City Council was a nine-member body, with eight council members elected on a citywide, at-large basis to four-year terms, half in one set of odd years, half and the four-year mayor in the next odd year; however, this geographic diffusion did not preclude the development of particular constituencies and bases of support. Mayor Wallace Johnson later claimed to have been leading a common-sense effort against the plan for several years. Wallace Johnson, *Responsible Individualism: Perspectives on a Political Philosophy for Our Time* (New York: Devin-Adair, 1967), 205. Klatsch, *A Generation Divided*, 153–58.

104. The university officially supported renewal with a policy statement in 1962. Memo from R. Heyns to Urban Renewal Agency, March 3, 1966, Folder 37, Box 88, Office of the Chancellor Records CU-149, UABL.

105. "South Campus Urban Renewal Project: What Can the University Do Now?" n.d., Folder 37 Urban Renewal, Box 88, Office of the Chancellor Records CU-149, UABL.

106. Self, *American Babylon*, 135–76.

107. John Griffith and Dallas Holmes. "BART and the Victoria Line: A Comparison of New Commuter Transport in California and London," *California Law Review* 55, no. 3, article 6 (August 1967): 780–812.

108. Ronald Reagan, "The Morality Gap at Berkeley," speech at Cow Palace, May 12, 1966, in Ronald Reagan, *The Creative Society: Some Comments on Problems Facing America* (New York: Devin-Adair, 1968), 125–29.

109. Arleigh Williams, "Dean of Students Arleigh Williams: The Free Speech Movement and the Six Years' War, 1964–1970," oral history, interviewer Germaine LaBerge, 1988 and 1989, ROHO.

110. Grace Hechinger, "Clark Kerr, Leading Public Educator and Former Head of California's Universities, Dies at 92," *New York Times*, December 2, 2003.

111. Stanley Glick, "The People's Park" (PhD dissertation, State University of New York at Stony Brook, 1984), 32–33.

112. Ibid.

113. The *Berkeley Barb* was an underground newspaper published by Max Scherr, part of an alternative media sphere in the Bay Area that included *Ramparts* magazine and City Lights Publishers, among a host of other leading publications.

114. Rorabaugh, *Berkeley at War*, 156–57.

115. Sim Van der Ryn, "Building a People's Park," 59–60, publisher unknown, quoted in Glick, "The People's Park," 54. His use of the phrase "ticky-tacky" illustrates the fusion of culture and politics that New Left activists in the Bay Area developed in their movement and coalition activities in the period. The term is an allusion to the 1962 song "Little Boxes" by Malvina Reynolds about stucco-covered suburban houses in the Bay Area hills. By the late 1960s, the song and phrase were employed regularly to decry various types of change in the built environment, from suburban greenfield construction, to downtown redevelopment, to almost any building or landscape that used synthetic materials and nontraditional design.

116. Pete Seeger later adopted and performed the song, making it internationally famous.

117. Mark Kitchell, Susan Griffin, Veronica Selver, and Stephen Most, *Berkeley in the Sixties*.

118. Rorabaugh, *Berkeley at War*, 156.

119. Glick, "People's Park," 95, 98.

120. "Protest: The Street People." *Time* v. 93, May 23, 1969.

121. Steven Roberts, "Berkeley Students and 'Street People' Form Tenants Union to Withhold Rents," *New York Times*, October 26, 1969, 72.

122. Joel Rubenzahl, "Berkeley Politics, 1968–1974: A Left Perspective," in Nathan and Scott, eds., *Experiment and Change in Berkeley*, 333–35.

123. Lawrence Davies. "Berkeley Eyes Tenants' Strike," *New York Times*. February 8, 1970, 54. Philip Hager, "Berkeley Tenants Form Union, Plan Rent Strike," *Los Angeles Times*, October 12, 1969, AA. Five hundred households withheld rent, a small but notable share of the city's more than 23,000 rental units. Rubenzahl, "Berkeley Politics," 335.

124. Local activists organized the Palo Alto Tenants Union and made a legal strike against the city's zoning regime, which privileged families over mixed households and detached single-family residences over density. Their legal challenges reached federal courts before their final loss, part of a spate of tenant-initiated court actions in university communities. *Palo Alto Tenants Union v. Morgan*, 487 F.2d 883 (1973).

125. Throughout the postwar period, liberal Democrats had built a political organization incorporating the black East Bay Democratic organization, white working-class flatlanders, and foothills professionals, until liberals took majority control of the city council during the 1960s. The coalition's greatest triumph was the housing nondiscrimination ordinance passed through Berkeley's city council in 1963, repealed by citywide ballot initiative. Subsequently, Berkeley and Oakland state assemblyman Byron Rumford, head of the black East Bay Democratic organization, passed a statewide nondiscrimination bill through the legislature. "Legislator for Fair Employment, Fair Housing, and Public Health: William Byron Rumford," in Nathan and Scott, eds., *Experiment and Change in Berkeley*.

126. Two scholars of Black Power in the Bay Area discuss these alliances and the political culture of the East Bay in Self, *American Babylon*, 223, and Donna Murch, *Living for the City,* 197–207.

127. The franchise was restricted to those twenty-one years of age and older in federal elections until ratification of the 26th Amendment in 1971. In California, state and local elections were restricted to those twenty-one and older. Donald Hopkins, "Development of Black Political Organization in Berkeley Since 1960," Nathan and Scott, eds., *Experiment and Change,* 105–36.

128. Dellums was also an alumnus of UCB, earning a master's degree there in 1962. Earl Caldwell, "Black Insurgent Who Won Berkeley Race Is an Outspoken Radical," *New York Times*, June 14, 1970, 46. Self, *American Babylon*, 295–97. Ilona Hancock, "'New Politics' in Berkeley: A Personal View," in Nathan and Scott, eds., *Experiment and Change in Berkeley*, 390.

129. Jack Slater, "The Guard Changes in Berkeley," *Ebony* 26 (October 1, 1971): 74–82.

130. Hancock, "New Politics," 390. All of these elections up to 1971 were conducted without the vote of eighteen- to twenty-one-year-olds, with the exception of the 1970 Ron Dellums general election for U.S. Congress, pursuant to 1970 amendments to the Voting Rights Act (later overturned). After ratification of the 26th Amendment in May 1971, eighteen-year-olds could vote in state and local elections, invigorating radicals in local politics nationwide. However, in Berkeley, undergraduates were a small part of the population in 1970, and graduate students had already been showing a significant presence in local politics.

131. An alternative strain of urban planning surfaced in the 1970s, emerging from both public policy professionals and, in this case, from grassroots political coalitions. Norman Krumholz, working in Cleveland, termed one version "equity planning," in

which cities, dealing with scarce and shrinking resources, devoted those resources to "expand choices for those who had few" and to "serve populations most in need." Pierre Clavel developed the framework of "progressive politics," including planning, which he characterized as promoting public ownership of resources; working in opposition to concentrated power; and emphasizing the needs of the people who already resided in a locality. Krumholz, *Making Equity Planning Work: Leadership in Public Policy* (Philadelphia: Temple University Press, 1990), xvii. Pierre Clavel, *The Progressive City: Planning and Participation, 1969–1984* (New Brunswick, NJ: Rutgers University Press, 1986), 188–90.

132. The baby boom's increased demand for student housing was amplified by the inflationary pressure on rents created by the student loan program in the 1965 Higher Education Act.

133. Clavel, *Progressive City*, 116–21. On the legacy of progressive planning in Berkeley, see Stephen E. Barton, "The City's Wealth and the City's Limits: Progressive Housing Policy in Berkeley, California, 1976–2011," *Journal of Planning History* 11, no. 2 (May 2012): 160–78.

134. Berkeley Department of Community Development, *Rent Control in the City of Berkeley, 1978–1994: A Background Report* (Berkeley, CA: Department of Community Development, 1998), Local History Room, Berkeley Public Library.

135. In the fall of 1972, council members introduced competing but weaker proposals, which coalition members felt would undercut their efforts. Martha Nicoloff, "Comments on Housing in Berkeley," December 1971, *Berkeley Neighborhood Preservation Ordinance: Documenting a Community in Action*, p. 41, Local History Room, Berkeley Public Library.

136. Berkeley Republicans, whose numbers and influence had been on the wane, ran no candidates in the 1973 municipal election and instead supported moderate Democrats in opposition to the leftist coalition. Kent, "Berkeley's First Liberal Democratic Regime," 102–3.

137. Keith Harmon, "BART Rolls into City—with a Hitch," *Berkeley Daily Gazette*, January 30, 1973, 1–2. The eventual costs only came to $12 million. Wallace Johnson, "Twelve Years as the Nation in Microcosm," in Nathan and Scott, eds., *Experiment and Change in Berkeley*, 179–230. In 2016 dollars, the amount becomes $64.4 million. CPI Inflation Calculator, http://data.bls.gov/cgi-bin/cpicalc.pl. (accessed April 1, 2016).

138. Editorial, "For Johnson Station Here," *Berkeley Daily Gazette*, January 30, 1973.

139. Harmon, "BART Rolls into City," 1.

Chapter 5

1. Massachusetts Institute of Technology, Infinite History website, "Hypothetical Risk: Cambridge City Council's Hearings on Recombinant DNA Research," https://infinitehistory.mit.edu/video/hypothetical-risk-cambridge-city-councils-hearings-recombinant-dna-research-1976 (accessed May 3, 2016).

2. Peter S. Britell, "Al Velucci," *Harvard Crimson*, March 14, 1961, http://www.thecrimson.com/article/1961/3/14/al-vellucci-pal-vellucci-does-not/ (accessed May 3, 2016).

3. Metropolitan and policy historians have voluminously documented this topic: Bruce Schulman, *From Cotton Belt to Sunbelt: Federal Policy, Economic Development, and*

the Transformation of the South (New York: Oxford University Press, 1991); Thomas Sugrue, *The Origins of the Urban Crisis: Race and Inequality in Postwar Detroit* (Princeton, NJ: Princeton University Press, 1996); Jefferson Cowie, *Capital Moves: RCA's Seventy-Year Quest for Cheap Labor* (Ithaca, NY: Cornell University Press, 1999); Robert Self, *American Babylon: Race and the Struggle for Postwar Oakland* (Princeton, NJ: Princeton University Press, 2003); Andrew Highsmith, *Demolition Means Progress: Flint, Michigan, and the Fate of the American Metropolis* (Chicago: University of Chicago Press, 2015).

4. Radcliffe began issuing joint diplomas with Harvard in 1963 and merged in a process continuing between 1977 and 1999. Owing to its increasing affiliation with and eventual absorption by Harvard in this era, I do not scrutinize Radcliffe as an independent, autonomous body from Harvard.

5. Richard Chacon, "Menino Softens Stance on Harvard, Cites Panel Planned on Development," *Boston Globe*, June 19, 1997, B8.

6. *Report of the President and the Chancellor Issue 1972–1973*, Massachusetts Institute of Technology, Office of the President, Reports to the President, http://dome.mit.edu /handle/1721.3/59054 (accessed May 10, 2016).

7. Frederick Rudolph, *The American College and University: A History* (New York: Random House, 1962), 6–8.

8. Susan Maycock, *East Cambridge* (Cambridge, MA: Cambridge Historical Commission, 1965).

9. By 1930, approximately three-quarters of Cambridge residents were either a first- or a second-generation immigrant to the United States, with 44,616 native white residents of foreign-born parents; 32,330 foreign-born whites; and a handful of immigrants from other parts of the world. *Fifteenth Decennial Census of the United States*, 1930, vol. 3, Population, Part 1. PDFs available at https://www.census.gov/prod/www/decennial .html (accessed February 22, 2017).

10. Cambridge Historical Society, "Industry in Cambridge," http://www .cambridgehistory.org/discover/industry/index.html (accessed April 1, 2016).

11. G. W. Bromley and Co., *Atlas of the City of Cambridge, Massachusetts* (Philadelphia, 1930), MIT Library. This number more than triples the professional workforce in Cambridge of 5,295. 1930 Census of Population, Occupations by States, vol. 4, Table 3. PDFs available at https://www.census.gov/prod/www/decennial.html (accessed February 22, 2017).

12. Regionally, we can see manufacturing jobs shifting away from the Northeast and Midwest and toward the West and South. Manufacturing employment dropped from about 10.2 million in 1950 to 9.5 million in 1981. Data from the U.S. Department of Labor, Bureau of Labor Statistics, *Employment and Earnings* reports, cited in Bernard L. Weinstein, Harold T. Gross, and John Rees, *Regional Growth and Decline in the United States*, 2nd ed. (New York: Praeger, 1985), 2–16.

13. 1980 U.S. Census, vol. 1, Characteristics of the Population, Chapter C, General Social and Economic Characteristics, Part 15, Illinois, Section 1, Table 122. PDFs available at https://www.census.gov/prod/www/decennial.html (accessed February 22, 2017).

14. The 1980 population was 77,216; in 1990, the population was 71,035. *1980 Census of Population and Housing*, vol. 16, Census Tracts Indiana, Table 1. *1990 Census of*

Population, Social and Economic Characteristics, vol. 16, Indiana, Table 1. PDFs available at https://www.census.gov/prod/www/decennial.html (accessed February 22, 2017).

15. "Lever Bros. Offices Here," *New York Times.* December 5, 1949, 34.

16. Citizens Advisory Committee for Cambridge, "How to Make Cambridge a Better City," vertical files. Francis L. Loeb Library, Harvard University.

17. "Rogers Block Families Shun Public Housing," *Cambridge Chronicle*, August 8, 1957, 1.

18. "Cambridge Declares War on Urban Blight and Slums," *Cambridge Chronicle*, November 28, 1957, 1.

19. Ibid.

20. "Rogers Block Families Shun Public Housing."

21. For a broader examination of changes in metropolitan Boston, including the development of Route 128 and suburban communities, see Lily Geismer, *Don't Blame Us: Suburban Liberals and the Transformation of the Democratic Party* (Princeton, NJ: Princeton University Press, 2015).

22. NASA was the successor to the National Advisory Committee for Aeronautics.

23. Howard W. Johnson, *Holding the Center: Memoirs of a Life in Higher Education* (Cambridge, MA: MIT Press, 1999), 139.

24. Kevin Lynch, Donald Appleyard, and Harry Ellenzweig, "Kendall Square Opportunities," Folder MIT—Opportunities in Kendall Square, 1965, Box 105, AC205, MIT Archives.

25. See correspondence for Kendall Square, Box 105, AC205, MIT Archives.

26. "Considerations in the Future Development of Simplex and Related MIT Properties," January 1970, Box 3, AC205, MIT Archives.

27. "Final O.K. for NASA Site," *Boston Globe*, October 10, 1965, 2

28. Garret Fitzpatrick, "Duck Pin, We Have a Problem," *MIT Technology Review*, August 21, 2012, http://www.technologyreview.com/article/428696/duck-pin-we-have-a-problem/ (accessed May 3, 2016).

29. Robert McDonald, "Hard Times for Planners in East Cambridge," *Harvard Crimson*, June 14, 1973.

30. Oscar Hernandes and Zachary Robinson, "Neighborhood Bully: Harvard, the Community, and Urban Development," in *How Harvard Rules: Reason in the Service of Empire*, edited by John Trumpbauer (Boston: South End, 1999), 181–98.

31. Maurice Isserman and Michael Kazin, "The Failure and Success of the New Radicalism," in *The Rise and Fall of the New Deal Order, 1930–1980*, edited by Steve Fraser and Gary Gerstle (Princeton, NJ: Princeton University Press, 1989). Suleiman Osman, "The Decade of the Neighborhood," in Bruce Schulman and Julian Zelizer, *Rightward Bound: Making America Conservative in the 1970s* (Cambridge, MA: Harvard University Press, 2008). See also, for example, Tamar Carroll, *Mobilizing New York: AIDS, Antipoverty, and Feminist Activism* (Chapel Hill: University of North Carolina Press, 2015).

32. Hernandez and Robinson, "Neighborhood Bully," 189–90.

33. Rudolph Brown, "Tenants Uniting in Cambridge," *Boston Globe*, June 2, 1969, 2.

34. Hernandez and Robinson, "Neighborhood Bully," 186–87.

35. Ibid., 189.

36. Britell, "Al Vellucci."

37. Evan Johnson, "Duehay Dedicates Life to Cambridge," *Harvard Crimson*, June 6, 2005, http://www.thecrimson.com/article/2005/6/6/duehay-dedicates-life-to-cambridge-in/?page=single. Robert McDonald, "Politics Badger the Schools of Cambridge," *Harvard Crimson*, September 18, 1972, http://www.thecrimson.com/article/1972/9/18/politics-badger-the-schools-of-cambridge/?page=single (accessed April 1, 2016).

38. Hilary Moss, Yinan Zhang, and Andy Anderson, "Assessing the Impact of the Inner Belt: MIT, Highways, and Housing in Cambridge, Massachusetts," *Journal of Urban History* 40, no. 6 (November 2014): 1054–78. Patti Saris, "Barbara Ackermann: Not Your Typical Boss," *Harvard Crimson*, December 15, 1972, http://www.thecrimson.com/article/1972/12/15/barbara-ackermann-not-your-typical-boss/?page=single (accessed May 3, 2016).

39. Saris, "Barbara Ackermann."

40. William Galeota, "City's Second Housing Convention Will Ask Lower Cambridge Rents," *Harvard Crimson*, December 2, 1968, http://www.thecrimson.com/article/1968/12/2/citys-second-housing-convention-will-ask/ (accessed May 3, 2016).

41. Cambridge median contract rent (listed rent exclusive of utilities) was $119. Boston median contract rent was $98, and the Standard Metropolitan Statistical Area (SMSA) median contract rent was $106. Cambridge had the highest median contract rent in the SMSA among municipalities with more rental units than owner-occupied units. U.S. Census of Population and Housing, 1970, Report 29, Table H-1. PDFs available at https://www.census.gov/prod/www/decennial.html (accessed February 22, 2017).

42. William Galeota, "Rent Control Showdown: Brass Tacks," *Harvard Crimson*, August 1, 1969, http://www.thecrimson.com/article/1969/8/1/rent-control-showdown-pbtbhe-fight-over/?page=single (accessed May 3, 2016).

43. Joyce Heard, "Landlords' Request Fails to Prevent Rent Control," *Harvard Crimson*, October 22, 1970, http://www.thecrimson.com/article/1970/10/22/landlords-request-fails-to-prevent-rent/ (accessed May 5, 2016).

44. Galeota, "Rent Control Showdown."

45. See Lawrence Eichel, Kenneth Jost, Robert Luskin, and Richard Neustadt, *The Harvard Strike* (Boston: Houghton Mifflin, 1970).

46. John Kifner, "Kennedy Museum Blocked by Combination of Forces," *New York Times*, February 12, 1975, 40.

47. John Kifner, "Cambridge Loses Kennedy Museum," *New York Times*, February 7, 1975, 1.

48. Ronald Formisano, *Boston Against Busing: Race, Class, and Ethnicity in the 1960s and 1970s* (Chapel Hill: University of North Carolina Press, 1991).

49. James Q. Wilson, "Urban Renewal Does Not Always Renew," Harvard University Francis Loeb Library. Martin Anderson, *The Federal Bulldozer: A Critical Appraisal of Urban Renewal, 1942–1962* (Cambridge, MA: MIT Press, 1964).

50. Christopher Klemek, *The Transatlantic Collapse of Urban Renewal: Postwar Urbanism from New York to Berlin* (Chicago: University of Chicago Press, 2011), 175.

51. Thomas O'Connor, *Building a Better Boston: Politics and Urban Renewal, 1950–1970* (Boston: Northeastern University Press, 1995).

52. Ben Wisner, "Advocacy and Geography: The Case of Boston's Urban Planning Aid," *Antipode* 2 (August 1970): 25–29.

53. Robert McDonald, "Hard Times for Planners in East Cambridge," *Harvard Crimson*, June 14, 1973, http://www.thecrimson.com/article/1973/6/14/hard-times-for-planners-in-east/?page=single (accessed May 3, 2016).

54. Anne Kirchheimer, "We're Not in Business 'To Be Popular,' Cambridge Development Director Says," *Boston Globe*, May 13, 1973, 13.

55. "Stop Kendall Square Project!" Folder "Propaganda 1970–1973," Box 103, AC205, MIT Archives.

56. Letter from Cambridge Civic Association to MIT, n.d., Folder P78-04 Kendall Square, Box 176, AC205, MIT Archives.

57. J. C. Kim, "Citizens Sound Off on Kendall Development," *Boston Herald-American*, May 30, 1974.

58. Memo from O. Robert Simha, "Re: Kendall Square Urban Renewal Hearings 10-7, 10-9, October 29, 1974," P73-07 City Council 1974, 1975, AC205, MIT Archives.

59. "MIT Moves on Kendall Square," Folder "Propaganda 1970–1973," Box 103, AC205, MIT Archives.

60. Draft memo, Donna Berman to O. Robert Simha et al., September 3, 1975, Folder 3, Box 32, AC205, MIT Archives.

61. "US Gives Boost to Kendall Sq. Project," *Boston Globe*, January 3, 1976, 19

62. In 1974, $37 million in payroll went to Cambridge residents, of $81 million in local expenditures. "The University and the City . . . Facts About Harvard and MIT in Cambridge," Folder 4, Box 32, AC205, MIT Archives.

63. Siddhartha Mukherjee, *Emperor of All Maladies: A Biography of Cancer* (New York: Scribner, 2010).

64. John Durant, "Please Refrain from Using the Alphabet," in *Becoming MIT: Moments of Decision*, edited by David Kaiser (Cambridge, MA: MIT Press, 2010), 146–48.

65. "Cambridge Council Bids Harvard Delay Its Gene Research," *New York Times,* July 8, 1976, 12.

66. Durant, "Please Refrain from Using the Alphabet," 154.

67. "Cambridge Council Allows Harvard DNA Research," *New York Times*, February 8, 1977, 16.

68. Durant, "Please Refrain from Using the Alphabet," 156.

69. Sheldon Krimsky, *Genetic Alchemy: The Social History of the Recombinant DNA Controversy* (Cambridge, MA: MIT Press, 1985), 294–307.

70. Henry Etzkowitz, *MIT and the Rise of Entrepreneurial Science* (New York: Routledge, 2002).

71. Ibid., 117. Harbridge House, Inc., *Government Patent Policy Study: Final Report* prepared for the Federal Council for Science and Technology, Committee on Government Patent Policy, (Washington, DC: GPO, 1968).

72. The Society of University Patent Administrators later changed its name to the Association of University Technology Managers.

73. Etzkowitz, *MIT and the Rise of Entrepreneurial Science*, 118. Richard D. Lyons, "Improving the Mousetraps at the U.S. Patent Office," *New York Times*, January 13, 1980, E24.

74. MIT lobbied Massachusetts senator Edward Kennedy, the chair of the Judiciary Committee, which had jurisdiction, but was unable to persuade him to prioritize the issue. Etzkowitz, *MIT and the Rise of Entrepreneurial Science*, 119.

75. David Mowery et al., *Ivory Tower and Industrial Innovation: University-Industry Technology Before and After the Bayh-Dole Act in the United States* (Stanford, CA: Stanford Business Books, 2004), 89.

76. Paul Barrett, "Harvard Fears Congress May Not Pass Patent Bill," *Harvard Crimson*, October 7, 1980, http://www.thecrimson.com/article/1980/10/7/harvard-fears -congress-may-not-pass/ (accessed March 25, 2015).

77. Ashley Stevens, "The Enactment of Bayh-Dole," *Journal of Technology Transfer* 29 (2004): 93–99. Gene Quinn, "Exclusive Interview: Senator Birch Bayh on Bayh-Dole at 30," *IP Watchdog*, November 7, 2010, http://www.ipwatchdog.com/2010/11/07/exclusive -interview-senator-birch-bayh-on-bayh-dole/id=13198 (accessed May 5, 2016).

78. See Elizabeth Popp Berman, *Creating the Market University: How Academic Science Became an Economic Engine* (Princeton, NJ: Princeton University Press, 2015). Mowery et al., *Ivory Tower and Industrial Innovation*.

79. Mowery et al., *Ivory Tower and Industrial Innovation*, 133.

80. In 2004, MIT was the third highest recipient overall, with $922,000,000 in industry funding; in 2008, it was the eleventh highest recipient overall. INDEXP in Statistics Access for Technology Transfer (STATT) Database, Association of University Technology Managers. Data in possession of the author.

81. The endowment grew from $442 million in 1955 to $1 billion in 1964. Morton Keller and Phyllis Keller, *Making Harvard Modern: The Rise of America's University* (New York: Oxford University Press, 2001), 182. $442M in 1955 inflates to $511M in 1964 dollars; the endowment had nearly doubled in nine years through donation and investment, even after inflation. CPI Inflation Calculator, http://data.bls.gov/cgi-bin/cpicalc .pl (accessed May 5, 2016).

82. Keller and Keller, *Making Harvard Modern*, 366–68. Harvard University, Report of the President of Harvard College and reports of departments. 1970–1971, President's Report, 12 (seq. 13460), Harvard University Archives,http://nrs.harvard.edu/urn -3:hul.arch:15008?n=13460 (accessed October 14, 2014).

83. Thomas W. Janes, "Harvard Learns a Lesson About Portfolio Management," *New York Times,* July 30, 1978, F3.

84. Ibid.

85. Richard Eder, "Harvard's Drive for $250 Million Aims at Maintaining Standards," *New York Times*, December 3, 1979, 1.

86. For recent histories on the rise of conservative politics and especially economic policy, see Kimberly Phillips-Fein, *Invisible Hands: The Making of the Conservative Movement from the New Deal to Reagan* (New York: W. W. Norton, 2009). Schulman and Zelizer, eds., *Rightward Bound*. Angus Burgin, *The Great Persuasion: Reinventing Free Markets Since the Great Depression* (Cambridge, MA: Harvard University Press, 2014).

87. "$356 Million Is Raised in Harvard Fund Drive," *New York Times*, January 13, 1985, 21.

88. Ibid.

89. Kendall Square had been separated into four parcels. Initially, the CRA contracted with Boston Properties to develop parcels 3 and 4.

90. David Sanger, "Software Shifts: As Industry Tightens, Jobs 'Hide' In Unexpected Places," *New York Times*, October 13, 1985, C33.

91. For analyses of these changes more broadly and the dismantling of the New Deal coalition, see Gerstle and Fraser, eds., *The Rise and Fall of the New Deal Order*. Bruce Schulman, *The Seventies: The Great Shift in American Culture, Society, and Politics* (Cambridge, MA: Da Capo, 2001). Jefferson Cowie, *Stayin' Alive: The 1970s and the Last Days of the Working Class* (New York: New Press, 2010). For an account of this transformation across metropolitan Boston, see Geismer, *Don't Blame Us*.

92. Jane Jacobs, *The Death and Life of Great American Cities* (New York: Random House, 1961).

93. Richard Florida, "The Rise of the Creative Class: Why Cities Without Gays and Rock Bands Are Losing the Economic Development Race," *Washington Monthly*, May 2002, http://www.washingtonmonthly.com/features/2001/0205.florida.html.

94. Richard Florida, *The Rise of the Creative Class: And How It's Transforming Work, Leisure, Community and Everyday Life* (New York: Basic, 2002). Florida, *Cities and the Creative Class* (New York: Routledge, 2004).

95. Cambridge Redevelopment Authority, *Forty-Third Annual Report of the Executive Director*, December 31, 1999, Cambridge Redevelopment Authority Archives, Cambridge, MA.

96. "Battle Goes On as Rent Control Is Defeated in Massachusetts," *New York Times*, November 22, 1994, A18.

97. Harvard University Planning Office, "A Long Range Plan for Harvard University and Radcliffe College in Cambridge and Allston," Cambridge, MA, 1975.

98. Sara Rimer, "Some Seeing Crimson at Harvard 'Land Grab,'" *New York Times*, June 17, 1997, http://www.nytimes.com/1997/06/17/us/some-seeing-crimson-at-harvard -land-grab.html?pagewanted=print (accessed May 1, 2016).

99. Tina Cassidy, "Pressured to Compensate, University Says It Does Plenty," *Boston Globe*, June 12, 1997, B1.

100. Tina Cassidy and Don Aucoin, "Harvard Reveals Secret Purchases of 52 Acres Worth $88M in Allston," *Boston Globe*, June 10, 1997, A1.

101. Eileen McNamara, "A Hard Lesson, Harvard-Style," *Boston Globe*, June 11, 1997, B1.

102. Tina Cassidy and Don Aucoin, "Harvard Says Its Purchases Violated Trust— Menino Demands Scholarships in Return for Allston Land Buys," *Boston Globe*, June 11, 1997, A1.

103. *Harvard University Fact Book 1998–1999* (Cambridge, MA: Office of Budgets, Financial Planning and Institutional Research, 2007), http://oir.harvard.edu/fact-book (accessed May 2, 2016).

104. James Bandler, "Harvard Ponders a River Crossing: Some Graduate Facilities May Relocate to Allston," *Boston Globe*, August 22, 1999, B1.

105. Richard Chacon, "Menino Softens Stance on Harvard Cites Panel Planned on Development," *Boston Globe*, June 19, 1997, B8.

106. Cassidy and Aucoin, "Harvard Reveals Secret Purchases," and "Harvard Says Its Purchases Violated Trust."

107. Bandler, "Harvard Ponders a River Crossing."

108. Patrick Healy, "Harvard Poised to Put Its Stamp on Boston," *Boston Globe,* July 1, 2001, A1.

109. Amendment 3, Cambridge Redevelopment Authority, "Kendall Square Urban Renewal Area Plan," October 1977, Cambridge Redevelopment Authority Archives, Cambridge, MA.

110. Stewart Brand, *How Buildings Learn: And What Happens to Them After They're Built* (New York: Penguin, 1994), 24–28.

111. For accounts of Gehry's methods, see Mark Rappolt and Robert Violette, eds., *Gehry Draws* (Cambridge, MA: MIT Press, 2004), or the film documentary, *Sketches of Frank Gehry*, directed by Sydney Pollack (Sony Pictures Home Entertainment, 2006). Kristina Luce, in "Revolutions in Parallel: The Rise and Fall of Drawing in Architectural Design" (PhD dissertation, University of Michigan, 2009), situates Gehry's work in the history of the profession.

112. David Maurer, "Gehry Project Near Completion at MIT," *Architectural Record* 191, no. 11 (November 2003): 30. Ted Smalley Bowen, "MIT's Stata Center Opens, Raising Issues About Cost Control," *Architectural Record* 192, no. 6 (June 2004): 50.

113. After three years of occupancy, MIT sued Gehry's firm, Gehry Partners, and the contractor, Skanska, alleging that each entity had not exercised due care in design and construction, leading to building leaks, masonry cracking, and drainage problems. Sam Lubell, "Gehry, Skanska Point Fingers over MIT Lawsuit," *Architectural Record* 195, no. 12 (December 2007): 27.

114. Katie Zezima, "Harvard Outlines Plans to Expand Campus Across the Charles River," *New York Times*, January 12, 2007, A18.

115. Joseph B. Martin, "Summers's Bold Vision for Life Sciences," *Boston Globe*, February 24, 2006.

116. Donovan Slack, "Harvard Unveils Its Vision of Campus Across Charles; A Public Square Seen for Allston," *Boston Globe*, January 12, 2007, A1.

117. Zezima, "Harvard Outlines Plans." "Harvard's 50 Year Plan," *Harvard Magazine*, March–April 2007, http://harvardmagazine.com/2007/03/harvards-50-year-plan-html (accessed March 31, 2015).

118. Harvard announced in 2004 that if the families of Harvard students made less than $40,000 per year, there would be no expected family contribution. This initiative at Harvard grew more generous and spread to a wide variety of institutions around the country. Karen W. Arenson, "Harvard Says Poor Parents Won't Have to Pay," *New York Times*, February 29, 2004, N14.

119. "Endowment Value Declines 29.5% as Investment Return Is Negative 27.3%," *Harvard Magazine*, September 10, 2009, http://harvardmagazine.com/2009/09/sharp-endowment-decline-reported (accessed May 1, 2016).

120. Bernard Condon and Nathan Vardi, "Harvard: The Inside Story of Its Finance Meltdown," *Forbes*, February 26, 2009, http://www.forbes.com/forbes/2009/0316/080_harvard_finance_meltdown.html (accessed March 31, 2015).

121. Maggie Lloyd and Vinayak Ranade, "Economic Crisis Hits MIT, Necessitates Budget Cuts Throughout the Institute," *The Tech*, February 2, 2010, http://tech.mit.edu/V129/N64/budgetcuts.html (accessed May 1, 2016).

122. University of Chicago Annual Report 2016, "The Endowment," Figure 2, Endowment Market Value Through June 30, 2013, https://annualreport.uchicago.edu/page/endowment. National Center for Education Statistics, "Digest of Education Statistics," Table 372, Endowment Funds of the 120 Colleges and Universities with the Largest Endowments, by Rank Order: 2008 and 2009, http://nces.ed.gov/programs/digest/d10/tables/dt10_372.asp (accessed May 1, 2016).

Epilogue

1. Richard A. Greenwald, *The Triangle Fire, the Protocols of Peace, and Industrial Democracy in Progressive Era New York* (Philadelphia: Temple University Press, 2005). Numerous workers on the tenth floor escaped to the roof of the New York University building next door. Higher education was immediately a literal salvation for endangered workers, while it later became a more general savior for cities and economies in crisis.

2. Hilary Ballon, "Robert Moses and Urban Renewal," in *Robert Moses and the Modern City: The Transformation of New York*, edited by Hilary Ballon and Kenneth T. Jackson (New York: W. W. Norton, 2007), 95–115.

3. See, for example, Robert Fishman, *Bourgeois Utopias: The Rise and Fall of Suburbia* (New York: Basic, 1985); Andres Duany, Elizabeth Plater-Zyberk, and Jeff Speck, *Suburban Nation: The Rise of Sprawl and the Decline of the American Dream* (New York: North Point, 2000); and Robert Bruegmann, *Sprawl: A Compact History* (Chicago: University of Chicago Press, 2005).

Index

Acknowledgments

I owe thanks to many individuals and institutions for supporting me and this project in its many stages. At Western Michigan University, Kristen Szylvian and Michael Chiarappa were encouraging mentors to a promising but very rough undergraduate student, and the late Nora Faires joined them in support of my graduate career. Joshua Cochran and Cori Derifield were colleagues who continue to live the dream we all shared. At the University of Michigan, Robert Fishman was committed and generous as he illustrated what a scholarly life could be. I return to his advice and adept storytelling again and again. Kristina Luce and Stephanie Pilat were both wonderful senior colleagues, fellow architectural historians who provided models for a scholar of the built environment. Will Glover and Lydia Soo both demonstrated how to teach in a way that would inspire students. Thanks also go to Claire Zimmerman and Lan Deng. In the History Department at Michigan, I found a collegial group of scholars with shared interests who remain valued colleagues. Tamar Carroll, Nathan Connolly, Lily Geismer, Andrew Highsmith, Clay Howard, and Drew Meyers provided insightful comments on papers and scholarship and perceptive views on the urban and political scene, and pursued fascinating research projects, many of which are now books that will help shape the profession for a generation. They set a high standard to reach. Matt Lassiter led this group, and his effect on metropolitan history through his scholarship and mentoring has been profound.

Many nonhistorians also helped make my life what it is and, thus, made this book possible. Brandon Zwagerman, Julia Lipman, Heidi Sulzdorf-Liszkiewicz, Murph Murphy, Dave Askins, and Scott Trudeau were highlights of the Ann Arbor planning, blogging, house show, and teeter-totter scene. Kevin Alschuler, Carl Anderson, Pam Besteman, Annie Hiniker, Mike Perry, Bryan Tryon, and Andrew Whelan formed a sculling community that gave me routine and direction that still guides my daily practice. I think of those mornings on the water and at the diner fondly.

At conferences and colloquia, I benefited from the comments, questions, and collaborative efforts of Michael Carriere, J. Mark Souther, Ethan Schrum, Robin Bachin, Blake Gumprecht, Amy Howard, Carla Yanni, James Connolly, and Bruce Geelhoed. The Urban History Group at the Newberry Library in Chicago was a home away from home, and special thanks are due to David Spatz and Margaret Lee. The American history seminar at Johns Hopkins University included an intense session of questioning, and presenting to the Urban History Seminar at the Chicago History Museum was a joy for which I owe Michael Ebner a debt of gratitude.

Special thanks go to librarians and archivists at the Map Library at the University of Michigan; Jen Green in the Spatial and Numerical Data lab at Michigan; John Straw at the Ball State University Archives; staff at the University of Texas archives, the Lyndon Johnson Presidential Library, and the Austin History Center; archivists at the University of Chicago Special Collections and the University of Illinois Chicago Special Collections; the University of California's Bancroft Library and university archives; and the MIT archives. They all made this possible. Their work preserving and providing access to our shared past is essential to maintaining, reproducing, and improving our society; university archives are among the best at fulfilling this mission.

This research found support from a wide variety of sources, including research funds from the University of Michigan's Rackham School, the Center for Middletown Studies at Ball State University, the Lyndon Baines Johnson Presidential Library Foundation, the National Building Museum, and the Virginia Tech Department of History and College of Liberal Arts and Human Sciences. Precious time in the archives would not have been possible without it.

Along the way, I have been fortunate to teach at several institutions that gave me exposure to a wide variety of departments, scholarly models, and cultures. My gratitude goes out to Ted Karamanski and Patricia Mooney-Melvin, who supported me in teaching public history at Loyola University Chicago. While there, I got to know a group of scholars with interests in Chicago, including Lew Erenberg, Elizabeth Fraterrigo, Tim Gilfoyle, Susan Hirsch, Christopher Manning, and Harold Platt. I never wrote with as much joy, hope, or vigor as when I was teaching at Loyola. I spent a year in Philadelphia teaching at Temple University, which may have been the happiest of my life. Seth Bruggeman was an excellent, creative, and irreverent mentor and colleague, and the public history program is in capable hands between him and Hilary Iris Lowe. Beth Bailey and Bryant Simon, especially, were admirable colleagues, willing to talk over coffee or visit one of my classes. During the last five years in the Department of History at Virginia Tech and in Blacksburg, I have made good friendships, received critical and meaningful comment from colleagues, mentored students at multiple levels, and participated in the full life of a department. It has been quite a professional home. Thanks go to my writing partners Danna Agmon, Carmen Gitre, Elizabeth Mazzolini, and Matt Wisnioski, as well as to chair Mark Barrow for so much support, and to all the participants of The Historians Writing Group who commented on my drafts. Virginia Tech also supported a mentee relationship with David Freund, who was a vigorous intellectual model in the course of writing this book and gave valuable comment.

My editor, Robert Lockhart at the University of Pennsylvania Press, has been an enthusiastic and patient advocate for this book. I first got in touch when Robert Fishman suggested I should talk to the best editor in the country. Thanks go to my copy editor, Kate Epstein and copyeditors at the University of Pennsylvania Press; to the two anonymous readers who gave comments for Penn; and to Tim Gilfoyle, Tim Mennel, and the anonymous readers at the University of Chicago Press.

In this process, my family has been an enduring source of strength. My parents, Jan and Larry Winling, have helped shape me in ways that I am only now fully realizing as I raise my own son. My brother and sister, Kerry and Jill, are full of love and support. My second family, John and Cecil Bosher, Hal and Virginia and Sylvie and Lise Bosher and Peter McIntyre, have been key to my survival in the latter years of this work. The late, great cat, Samuel S. Samuelson, was an unending source of entertainment and comfort all our days together. My son, Ernest, came along just as I was rising to the professional ranks and now gives my work and life direction and joy as I try to provide for his future. I hope someday to be able to explain this work to him and that he will understand why I so often had to rush in the morning to have time to read, research, and write, or had to get a sitter to tend to some professional obligation. I did it for you, buddy.

Finally, no one has been more important to this project or to my adult life than my late wife, Kathryn Bosher. From the day we met until the day she died, Kate was my alpha and omega. As a scholar, a colleague, an athlete, a spouse, a parent, a cook, and a friend, she set a standard that I aspire to still. I am certain this book would be better had I been able to discuss it with her more and to draw from her strength and erudition. I hope it is worthy nonetheless.